DIETRICH BONHOEFFER

Reality and Resistance

LARRY L. RASMUSSEN

WJK WESTMINSTER
JOHN KNOX PRESS
LOUISVILLE · KENTUCKY

Cover design by designpointinc.com

Published by Westminster John Knox Press
Louisville, Kentucky

This book is printed on acid-free paper that meets the American National Standards Institute Z39.48 standard. ∞

PRINTED IN THE UNITED STATES OF AMERICA

05 06 07 08 09 10 11 12 13 14 — 10 9 8 7 6 5 4 3 2 1

Library of Congress Cataloging-in-Publication Data is on file at the Library of Congress, Washington, D.C.

ISBN 0-664-23011-3

To Nyla

When Christ calls a man, he bids him come and die.

The Cost of Discipleship

CONTENTS

INTRODUCTION TO THE 2005 EDITION

April 9, 2005, marked the sixtieth anniversary of the death of Dietrich Bonhoeffer for his part in the attempted overthrow of the Nazi regime. February 4, 2006, marks the one-hundredth anniversary of his birth in Breslau, Germany. Few pastors and theologians of such youth have captured the interest and attention of the church worldwide as he. (Bonhoeffer, like Martin Luther King Jr., was thirty-nine years and four months old when his life, like King's, was cut short by the very violence he abhorred.)

What explains the interest and attention? Why the continued outpouring of texts—his own and those about him—as well as documentaries, made-for-TV movies, musical compositions (including an opera), conferences, and commemorative worship services? Whence "the Bonhoeffer phenomenon"?[1]

Certainly part of the reason is the integrity of a life of faith and its lure. Bonhoeffer's words and actions were of a piece: his understanding about what it means to be a disciple was matched by his deeds.

Yet there is more. This twentieth-century Christian leads into the twenty-first century because he is both rooted and postmodern, both grounded and capable of living with fragments, both theologically traditional and theologically innovative, both church-centered and worldly, both sensuously bound to earth and deeply pious. The variety of Bonhoeffer's keen sensibilities, and how they belong and hold together, intrigues us.

---

[1] The title of a volume by Stephen R. Haynes: *The Bonhoeffer Phenomenon: Portraits of a Protestant Saint* (Minneapolis: Augsburg Fortress Press, 2004).

But what about that most intriguing journey of all, from a commited Christian pacifism to Christian participation in tyrannicide and a coup d'état? What explains Bonhoeffer's twisting path of resistance in the Church Struggle and in the military-political conspiracy? Does his journey, varied in form and perhaps contradictory and ethically problematic, also belong and hold together?

These questions gave rise to this book. At the time it was initially published—1972—it was the only book-length treatment of Bonhoeffer's resistance and its theological-ethical grounding. Oddly, it still is! "Oddly" because the intervening decades have uncovered in great detail the inner workings of the Hitler regime and the varied forms of resistance to it—in the churches, in some university circles, among socialists, and in the ranks of the German military forces and civil service. "Oddly" as well because we now have the von Dohnanyi papers and their detailed account of the resistance circle of which Bonhoeffer himself was a part. And "oddly," not least, because we have a wealth of Bonhoeffer studies that inevitably touch on his role and understanding as a figure of resistance—hardly a surprise, since Bonhoeffer's journey of resistance has intrigued students of his life from the beginning.

Nonetheless, this remains the fullest treatment of this subject, albeit now supported in ways I could not have known of in 1972. I am delighted that Westminster John Knox Press has seen fit to republish it in time for the centennial of Bonhoeffer's birth and in light of ongoing interest in his life and pilgrimage.

The text here remains the same as the original, as does the dedication to Nyla, with whom I now enjoy the years of retirement. The exclusively masculine language of these pages is, to be sure, an embarrassment. But I let it stand, as a sober and needed reminder about insensitivity and myopia.

LARRY RASMUSSEN
APRIL 2005

KEY

1. The Writings of Dietrich Bonhoeffer.

   AB   *Act and Being*
   CC   *Christ the Center.*
   CD   *The Cost of Discipleship.* Second edition.
   CS   *The Communion of Saints.*
   E   *Ethics.* Sixth edition.
   GS   *Gesammelte Schriften.* Four volumes. Second edition.
   LPP *Letters and Papers from Prison.* Revised and enlarged edition.
   NRS *No Rusty Swords.*

2. Secondary Sources.

   Biographie   *Dietrich Bonhoeffer: Eine Biographie.* Third edition.
   Biography   *Dietrich Bonhoeffer: Man of Vision, Man of Courage.*
   I Knew DB   *I Knew Dietrich Bonhoeffer: Reminiscences by His Friends.*

3. Terms.

   Abwehr   The Military Counter-Espionage Service.
   Kirchenkampf The German Church Struggle.

9

4. Other.

Initial entries will be made in full; abbreviations will be used thereafter. All biblical quotations are taken from the Revised Standard Version of the Holy Bible.
Unless otherwise indicated, all translations from German sources have been made by the author.

PREFACE

"How did it come about that Dietrich Bonhoeffer took that great decision to be actively involved in preparing the events which had their explosive effect on 20 July 1944?"[1] asks Visser 't Hooft.[2] This book wrestles with that question, provided it be understood as a far-ranging inquiry. How is it that this man, neither born nor educated for conspiracy, nevertheless moved through many forms and stages of passive and active resistance, including conspiracy, until he was hanged for his participation in the plot to end the reign of Adolf Hitler? How is it that he, so self-consciously an admirer of Martin Luther, departed from almost all his Lutheran colleagues in sounding pacifist themes and carrying out conspiratorial deeds? Where, if anywhere, does the intense experience of the prewar and war years come to expression in Bonhoeffer's writings, writings that evidence so little explicit treatment of resistance? Where do the threads run between Bonhoeffer's resistance activity, on the one hand, and his theological reflection and ethical decisions, on the other? And is understanding Bonhoeffer the gentle resister crucial for understanding Bonhoeffer the pathfinding theologian?

More questions might be raised. Many will be in the course of this study. But they all hold this in common; they emerge from the simultaneous resistance activity, theological reflection, and ethical decisions that marked the

[1] The day of Count Stauffenberg's attempt on Hitler's life.
[2] Willem A. Visser 't Hooft, "An Act of Penitence," *I Knew Dietrich Bonhoeffer: Reminiscences by His Friends,* eds. Ronald Gregor Smith and Wolf-Dieter Zimmermann (New York: Harper, 1966), p. 193.

11

course and style of Dietrich Bonhoeffer's life in the 1930s and 1940s. This book attempts to discern and sort out these intriguing and complex relationships in Bonhoeffer's life and thought during this period and to assess them from the perspectives of Christian ethics. How indeed did it come about that Dietrich Bonhoeffer took that great decision to be actively involved in preparing the events that had their explosive effect on July 20, 1944? Where was this decision grounded, as well as innumerable others leading to both public protest and clandestine deeds? How did these compare with those of his colleagues? And how do they now measure up to the critiques of those who have the good fortune to assess *post facto*?

The path traversed to answer these and other questions will be: first, to explicate the theological and ethical bases of Bonhoeffer's resistance activity, noting the intimate linkages to resistance in the course of exposition; then to investigate particular polar points in Bonhoeffer's opposition to Nazism, such as his pacifism and his approval of tyrannicide; and finally to review the highlights critically.

This approach does neglect the biography of resistance, although that is inserted wherever it is needed to illumine the systematic exposition. Less attention to the biographical and historical setting is explained only by the fact that the indispensable biography has already been written, and that in a superbly masterful way.[3] By contrast, an analytical study of Bonhoeffer's resistance does not exist.

Yet the *Sitz-im-Leben* has by no means been omitted, and hopefully the historicity of the entire enterprise will be graphic enough that the reader may feel the burdened ethos of decision-making in those extraordinary days of wrath—and of grace.

I doubt anyone has written a book alone. If he has, he is to be pitied. The pleasures of writing this one have been multiple because the persons contributing have been many. The project began as a dissertation in Union Theological Seminary, New York, under the guidance of John Bennett, Reginald Fuller, and Roger Shinn. I owe a special debt to Shinn, who both directed the thesis work and served as editor for the revised text, and to James Gustafson and Paul Ramsey for their meticulous readings of the drafts. My thanks to all these men runs between the lines of every page, as it does to Paul Wee, whose interest and helpful criticism were so sustained he deserves to be listed as a virtual co-author. The reader will also note a lengthy list of men and women

[3] Eberhard Bethge, *Dietrich Bonhoeffer: Man of Vision, Man of Courage* (New York: Harper, 1970).

who shared their time, experiences, and unpublished materials with me in interviews. Being named in footnotes is far too little tribute, and the least I can do is acknowledge a pleasant collective debt to them here. It goes without saying, however, that none of these contributors is held responsible for any errors in presentation or analysis in this work. Many typists have worked on the drafts at some point or another. They would all receive more acknowledgment than this had they not already typed more pages than allowed! The Ford Foundation and a Humanities Faculty Development Award at St. Olaf College aided the cause by providing funds for preparing the final drafts; a Fulbright Fellowship and a Rockefeller Doctoral Fellowship permitted the necessary year of research in Germany. My thanks for these sources is understood.

Most "Preface's" conclude with praise to the author's spouse. For good reason! And this one is certainly no exception. The dedication of this book to my wife is intended as a little song of her husband's adoration.

LARRY RASMUSSEN

June, 1971

Part I
THEOLOGY, ETHICS, AND RESISTANCE

1
Reality, Christology, and the Structure of Ethics

The Claim

The thesis of this study is that Dietrich Bonhoeffer's resistance activity was his Christology enacted with utter seriousness. Bonhoeffer's resistance was the existential playing out of christological themes. Changes and shifts in his Christology were at the same time changes and shifts in the character of his resistance. In the other direction, changes in his resistance activity had an impact upon his Christology. What is before us then, is the interaction of Bonhoeffer's Christology, ethics, and resistance.

The priority must be given to Christology as the point of departure. This sudden press toward the vital center of Bonhoeffer's theology may strike the reader as a rather abrupt beginning. Yet it is nonetheless necessary, for Bonhoeffer thought as a theologian, and the heart of his theology was Christology. So while these first pages will explore the lofty terrain of systematic theology and ethical method and will be shorn of all but a few references to resistance, we are not off course in seeking the animating core of Bonhoeffer's thought and action at the very commencement of our inquiry.

Reality, Theologia Crucis, *and "The Man for Others"*

In 1933 Bonhoeffer delivered his lectures on Christology. He spoke unabashedly of Jesus Christ as the center of man, nature, and history. "The one who is present in Word, sacrament and community is in the centre of human

15

existence, history and nature. It is part of the structure of his person that he stands in the centre." [1]

Though such a statement is ambiguous, there can be no doubt that Bonhoeffer conceptualizes reality christologically. Reality has a christocratic structure.[2] This central conviction in Bonhoeffer's theology leads him to make the pretentious claim that "Christology is *the* science." [3]

The christocratic character of reality is articulated most extensively in *Ethics*, where Bonhoeffer states vividly that Christ's taking up the world into himself in the Incarnation established an "ontological coherence" [4] of God's reality with the reality of the world.

. . . In Jesus Christ the reality of God entered into the reality of the world. The place where the answer is given, both to the question concerning the reality of God and to the question concerning the reality of the world, is designated solely and alone by the name Jesus Christ. God and the world are comprised in this name. In Him all things consist (Col. 1:17). Henceforward one can speak neither of God nor of the world without speaking of Jesus Christ. All concepts of reality which do not take account of Him are abstractions.[5]

. . . Whoever sees Jesus Christ does indeed see God and the world in one. He can no longer see God without the world or the world without God.[6]

The ontological coherence of God's reality and the world's means that Bonhoeffer's vision is a Christo-universal one; his is a christocratic understanding of all reality.

Bonhoeffer's cosmic Christ is, at the same time, unmistakably the Christ of the Lutheran "theology of the cross" [*theologia crucis*]. Bonhoeffer's is "condescension" or "kenotic" Christology—the whole fullness of God is found precisely in the earthly, human life of Jesus; infinitude is "emptied" into finitude. But Bonhoeffer says it better, and in the very lectures that view all reality in Christ.

[1] Dietrich Bonhoeffer, *Christ the Center,* ed. Eberhard Bethge, trans. John Bowden (New York: Harper, 1966), p. 62.

[2] "Reality" is already a major theme in Bonhoeffer's earlier writings. See Dietrich Bonhoeffer, *Act and Being,* trans. Bernard Noble (New York: Harper, 1961). The direction of thought given in this book holds for all Bonhoeffer's theology and ethics: "From God to reality, not from reality to God, goes the path of theology" (p. 89).

[3] *CC*, p. 28. Emphasis in the original. One should note that "science" in German (*Wissenschaft*) has a broader meaning than in English. It means a rigorous systematic search for knowledge in any area, the arts and humanities included.

[4] The term is borrowed from Eberhard Bethge, "The Challenge of Dietrich Bonhoeffer's Life and Theology," *The Chicago Theological Seminary Register*, February, 1961, p. 30.

[5] Dietrich Bonhoeffer, *Ethics,* ed. Eberhard Bethge, trans. Neville Horton Smith, 6th ed. (New York: Macmillan, 1965), p. 194.

[6] *Ibid.,* p. 70.

16

. . . We have the Exalted One only as the Crucified, the Sinless One only as the one laden with guilt, the Risen One only as the Humiliated One. Were this not so, the *pro nobis* would be done away with, there would be no faith. Even the resurrection is not a penetration of the incognito. Even the resurrection is ambiguous. It is only believed in where the stumbling block of Jesus has not been removed. Only the disciples who followed Jesus saw the resurrection. Only blind faith sees here.[7]

"The Risen One as the Humiliated One" is Bonhoeffer's Christ. Jesus is the beggar among beggars, the one laden with guilt who bears it to the end, the powerless one, the despised and forsaken one, the suffering one, the crucified one.

Whether one hears Bonhoeffer in the thirties or forties the echoes of the *theologia crucis* are resonant. Examples are frequent and clear in his sermons. A 1932 text reads: "The wonderful but, to many people, horrifying theme of the Bible is that the single visible sign of God in the world is the cross"; [8] "God's way in the world leads to the cross and through the cross to life." [9] A 1934 sermon records thoughts nearly identical to those of *Letters and Papers from Prison,* written ten years later: [10]

Our God is a suffering God. Suffering forms man into the image of God. The suffering man is in the likeness of God. . . . Whenever a man in the position of weakness—physical or social or moral or religious weakness—is aware of his existence with God and his likeness to God, he shares God's life.[11]

A 1935 manuscript shows the existential force with which Bonhoeffer could preach the Christology of condescension.

. . . Should your poverty lead you into temptation—Christ was poorer. Should your godless surroundings lead you into temptation—Christ stood deeper in these surroundings. Should the will of the flesh lead you into temptation—Christ suffered the agony of the flesh even more. Should loneliness lead you to vexation—Christ was lonelier. Should you become grieved about disbelief—Christ was even more

---

[7] *CC*, p. 116.

[8] Dietrich Bonhoeffer, "Abend-Predigt zum Volkstrauertag," *Gesammelte Schriften,* ed. Eberhard Bethge, 2nd ed. (Munich: Char. Kaiser Verlag, 1965), IV, 38.

[9] *Ibid.,* p. 42.

[10] Cf. the letters of July 16 and 18, 1944. "The Bible directs man to God's powerlessness and suffering; only a suffering God can help . . . Christ helps us, not by virtue of his omnipotence, but by virtue of his weakness and suffering." "To be a Christian . . . is to be a man—not a type of man, but the man that Christ creates in us. It is not the religious act that makes the Christian but participation in the sufferings of God in the secular life." Dietrich Bonhoeffer, *Letters and Papers from Prison,* ed. Eberhard Bethge, trans. Reginald Fuller and revised by Frank Clark and others; revised and enlarged ed. (New York: Macmillan, 1967), pp. 188, 190 respectively.

[11] "Zwei Abend-Predigten in der deutschen reformierten St.-Pauls-Kirche," *GS* IV, 182. The English is Bonhoeffer's.

grieved. Should you despair over the remoteness of God—Christ died with the despairing cry of this remoteness. He was tempted as we; he can indeed have compassion.[12]

Wherever the reader leafs through Bonhoeffer's writings, the themes of the *theologia crucis* appear: the centrality of the cross, the way of suffering, God's power in weakness, the full "emptying" of God and identification of Jesus with man, his sacrifice on man's behalf. Jesus Christ is the center of human existence, history, and nature; but "the single visible sign of God in the world is the cross." "To be a Christian is . . . to be a man"; but what makes a Christian a Christian and a man a man is "participation in *the sufferings of God* in the secular life." [13] In Jesus Christ, the Lord of the Cosmos, all created things have their origin, goal, and essence; through the command of the cosmic Christ all creation is set free to fulfill its own laws; that is, to be genuinely worldly.[14] However, it is the *cross* of atonement that sets men free for life before God in the midst of the godless world: "[The cross] sets men free for life in genuine worldliness." [15]

This is not to say there are not changes and developments in Bonhoeffer's Christology. It was not given all at once. It is only to claim that the Christology that takes on theocratic breadth in Bonhoeffer's writings never loses its character as kenotic Christology.

Who is this Christ? Can more be said?

Letters and Papers from Prison calls him "the man for others." [16] This piece of nonreligious interpretation is pregnant with the theological base and the ethical outcome of Bonhoeffer's resistance. The christological title itself arises from Bonhoeffer's understanding of the essence of Christ's person. This is transparent in the 1933 lectures where the *pro nobis* of Christ is grounded ontologically. There is no more important tenet in Bonhoeffer's Christology.

. . . Christ is Christ not as Christ in himself, but in his relation to me. His being Christ is his being *pro me*. This being *pro me* is in turn not meant to be understood as an effect which emanates from him, or as an accident; it is meant to be understood as the essence, as the being of the person himself. This personal nucleus itself is the *pro me*. That Christ is *pro me* is not an historical or an ontical statement, but an ontological one. That is, Christ can never be thought of in his being in himself, but only in his relationship to me. That in turn means that Christ can only be conceived of existentially, viz. in the community. . . . It is not only useless to meditate on a Christ in himself, but even godless.[17]

[12] "Predigt-Entwurf ueber den Hohenpriester," *GS* IV, 217.

[13] Repeated from note 10. Emphasis mine.

[14] *E*, p. 298.   [15] *Ibid.*, p. 297.   [16] "Outline for a Book," *LPP*, p. 202.

[17] *CC*, pp. 47-48.

. . . He is the center in three ways; in being-there for men, in being-there for history and in being-there for nature.[18]

. . . the form of humiliation is the form of the *Christus pro nobis.* In this form Christ means and wills to be for us in freedom.[19]

Being-for-others has an ontological ground for Bonhoeffer. It is the essence of being Christ. To conceive of Christ in any other way is literally *"godless."*

Bonhoeffer's anthropology is based in his Christology. Because the essence of Christ is his *pro nobis Sein* and because he is true man, the essence of the human self is a *fuer-andere Dasein,* being-there-for-others. The ontological structure of man is thus located in the self-other relationship, just as the ontological structure of Christ is located in Christ's being-for man, nature, and history. Man is only man in the Thou-I, I-Thou relationship, just as Christ is only Christ in his *pro nobis Sein.*

Bonhoeffer appreciated Luther's portrayal of the heart-turned-in-upon-itself (*cor curvum in se*) and understood this egocentricity as the enemy and obstructor of true selfhood.[20] It is rather the self turned toward others which finds fulfillment. Turned in upon itself, the self is bound; it must be a self in mutuality with others if it is to touch the transcendent ground of its own essence. Reality itself is so shaped that personal relatedness in human sociality is the only way man comes to "being." For this reason, *The Communion of Saints* names the I-Thou relationship the basic social category.[21] The person-in-community is the only person possible.

When Bonhoeffer portrays man as a *socius* and locates transcendence firmly in the self-other relationship, much is at stake. For it denotes that the relation of the I to the Thou is all-important to whether or not the self will find its true ground of being. This is the meaning intended by the sentence, "the question of transcendence is the question of existence and the question of existence is the question of transcendence." [22]

This is not all. Bonhoeffer goes so far as to say "the Thou of the other man is the divine Thou. So the way to the other man is also the way to the divine Thou, a way of recognition or rejection." [23] Or, "the character of a Thou is in fact the form in which the divine is experienced." [24] Bonhoeffer here is taking with radical seriousness the Lutheran formula "the finite bears the infinite" [*finitum capax infiniti*]. Thus it is anything but out of character that his favorite quotation from F. C. Oetinger is: "Corporeality is the end of God's path." [25] Bonhoeffer is declaring that because Christ is in, with, and under

---

[18] *Ibid.,* p. 62.   [19] *Ibid.,* p. 114.   [20] *Ibid.,* p. 31.

[21] Dietrich Bonhoeffer, *The Communion of Saints,* trans. Ronald Gregor Smith (New York: Harper, 1963), pp. 33-37.

[22] *CC,* p. 31.   [23] *CS,* p. 37.   [24] *Ibid.,* p. 36.

[25] Cited in Eberhard Bethge, *Dietrich Bonhoeffer: Eine Biographie,* 3rd ed. (Munich: Chr. Kaiser Verlag, 1967), p. 174.

human sociality, a man only finds self-fulfillment, indeed self-formation, in being with and for others; and being with and for others is the way in which a man is formed in Christ.

There is something dramatic here for ethics, something that Benjamin Reist claims is both the contribution and promise of Bonhoeffer, namely, his "ethical intensification of *all* theological concepts,"[26] resulting in "an ethical theology."[27] If, as Bonhoeffer asserts, experiencing transcendence *and* realizing selfhood both turn upon my being with and for my neighbor, then the question of the neighbor and his claim becomes one with the question of the self finding its true ground in God. The question of authentic selfhood turns on the question of love for neighbor, the encounter with the other man and being for him in that encounter. For this reason Bonhoeffer labels transcendence "moral" rather than "epistemological";[28] it is inextricably bound to the claims essential to self-formation and fulfillment.

The enigmatic discussion about responsibility in Bonhoeffer's earliest writing now makes sense. He asserts that the Christian concept of the person can only be grasped by someone engaged in responsibility,[29] responsibility meaning response to the presence and claim of the other. "The I arises only with the Thou; responsibility follows on the claim."[30] Reality itself is so ordered.

. . . Reality is "experienced" in the contingent fact of the claim of "others." Only what comes from "outside" can show man the way to his reality, his existence. In "sustaining" the "claim of my neighbor" I exist in reality, I act ethically; that is the sense of an ethics not of timeless truths but of the "present."[31]

A long-standing theme, now quoted from one of the last entries in *Letters and Papers from Prison,* provides a nice summation of Bonhoeffer's theological anthropology:

. . . The transcendental is not infinite and unattainable tasks, but the neighbor who is within reach in any given situation. God in human form . . . "the man for others," and therefore the Crucified, the man who lives out of the transcendent.[32]

For Bonhoeffer, then, the essence of Christ's being and man's is being-for-others. The same is true of the Church.

[26] Benjamin A. Reist, *The Promise of Bonhoeffer* (Philadelphia: Lippincott, 1969), pp. 118-19. Emphasis in the original.

[27] *Ibid.,* p. 118.

[28] *CS,* p. 33. It is hardly a surprise that the theologian who at the outset says transcendence is a "moral" matter should regard writing an ethic as the culmination of his undertakings. ("15 December 1943," *LPP,* p. 90.)

[29] *CS,* p. 33. [30] *Ibid.,* p. 36. [31] *AB,* p. 86. [32] "Outline for a Book," *LPP,* p. 202.

... The only way in which the Church can defend her own territory is by fighting not for it but for the salvation of the world.[33]
... The Church is the Church only when it is there for others.[34]

Bonhoeffer's sharpest indictment of the Confessing Church in the experience of resistance came at this point.

... Generally in the Confessing Church: standing up for the Church's "cause," but little personal faith in Christ. . . . The decisive factor: the Church on the defensive. No taking risks for others.[35]

Our concern, however, is Christology. Yet it is important for later discussion to note the unity of Bonhoeffer's Christology, anthropology, and ecclesiology. The unity is the being-there-for-others; this is grounded in reality itself.
On this theme the Christology of *Letters and Papers from Prison* is identical with the 1933 lectures. Among Bonhoeffer's last pieces, an outline for a future book includes:

... Encounter with Jesus Christ. The experience that a transformation of all human life is given in the fact that "Jesus is there only for others." His "being there for others" is the experience of transcendence. It is only this "being there for others," maintained till death, that is the ground of his omnipotence, omniscience, and omnipresence. Faith is participation in this being of Jesus (incarnation, cross, and resurrection). Our relation to God is not a "religious" relationship to the highest, most powerful, and best Being imaginable—that is not authentic transcendence— but our relation to God is a new life in "existence for others," through participation in the being of Jesus.[36]

If the question is, who is the Christ of Bonhoeffer's kenosis Christology and his Christo-universal vision, the answer is, he is "the man for others" whose very essence is being-there for man, nature, and history.
A summary of the findings on Bonhoeffer's Christology is in order. His is consistently a Christology of the *theologia crucis,* yet it is also markedly expanded beyond the Lutheran heritage of *theologia crucis* because Bonhoeffer's

---

[33] *E*, p. 202.
[34] "Outline for a Book," *LPP*, p. 203. Trans. corrected as suggested by John Godsey, "Reading Bonhoeffer in English Translation," *Union Seminary Quarterly Review*, Fall, 1967, p. 89.
Those who see little ecclesiology in the Bonhoeffer of the prison letters have not properly explored the parallel of Jesus as "the man for others" and the Church as Church only in existing for others. They have not noted the ontological dimensions of being-for-others in Bonhoeffer's thought. They have detached ecclesiology from Christology, something Bonhoeffer never does. Hanfried Mueller does this in *Von der Kirche zur Welt* (Hamburg: Herbert Reich Evag. Verlag GmbH., 1961), pp. 264 ff.
[35] "Outline for a Book," *LPP*, pp. 201-2.
[36] *Ibid.*, p. 202.

vision is that of the *Christus Pantocrator.* Bonhoeffer thus develops a theology of the cross with a christocratic understanding of all reality.

If a claim might be risked, it is that Bonhoeffer's resistance cannot be understood apart from major themes in his condescension Christology and its reading of reality.

But Bonhoeffer's "reading of reality" has only been little more than mentioned to this point. Its meaning *for ethics* has not been developed. So before turning to resistance we must ask: given Bonhoeffer's christocentric reading of reality, what becomes his mode of decision-making? What is the structure of the ethical method rooted in this cosmic Christology of "Being-for" man, nature, and history?

The ontological coherence of God's reality and the world's in Christ leads Bonhoeffer to discuss moral action in two ways that in the end are the same: "conformation to Christ" (*Gleichgestaltung*)[37] and action "in accordance with reality" or "with due regard for reality" (*Wirklichkeitsgemaessheit*).[38] That they are the same for Bonhoeffer is stated as such: "Our conclusion . . . must be that action which is in accordance with Christ is action which is in accordance with reality."[39] The discussion of any and all facets of Christian ethics, then, rests upon the prior assumption of this ontological coherence in Christ.

Heinrich Ott, in his analysis of Bonhoeffer's method of decision-making, is correct when he writes: "Bonhoeffer's ethic as a whole is the attempt to make these thoughts about conformation to Christ into *the* principle of the Christian ethic and to work out the whole ethic from this standpoint."[40]

[37] Dietrich Bonhoeffer, *Ethik,* ed. Eberhard Bethge (Munich: Chr. Kaiser Verlag, 1963), p. 85. The reader should note that the richness of the German *Gestalt* and *Gestaltung* or *Gleichgestaltung* is not immediately obvious from the English "form" and "formation" or "conformation." The connotations in German are those of dynamism and alteration in the process of an organism's growth, while yet remaining the same organism.

[38] *Ibid.,* p. 241. [39] *E,* p. 229.

[40] Heinrich Ott, *Wirklichkeit und Glaube* (Zurich: Vandenhoeck und Ruprecht, 1966), pp. 241-42. Emphasis mine. The emphasis is warranted by the preceding sentence in which Ott calls conformation to Christ the *"oberstes materielles Prinzip dieser Ethik."*

It is my judgment that Ott is correct if "conformation" is understood broadly enough. As an *explicit* theme in Bonhoeffer it forms the conclusion of *The Cost of Discipleship* and a large section of *Ethics* entitled "Ethics as Formation." If this were all that could properly be called "conformation" in Bonhoeffer, Ott's claim (and this book's) could not stand since Bonhoeffer also wrote sections of *Ethics* from other starting points: the breadth of the Lordship of Christ, the penultimate and the ultimate, and responsibility in light of the Incarnation. But in all these in *Ethics* and in earlier and later writings the *Gestalt Christi* is central, and ethics is the ethics of the fitting response to the living Lord. This is Bonhoeffer's ethics throughout his wide-ranging actions. It is in this sense that "conformation" is properly used to designate Bonhoeffer's ethics even beyond his own use of that term. Ott, however, short-cuts somewhat the complexity and richness of ethics as formation by dealing almost exclusively with *Ethics* and *Letters and Papers from Prison.* To omit especially *The Cost of Discipleship* simplifies matters considerably, but it does injustice to Bonhoeffer's theme of conformation as radical discipleship.

It follows that Bonhoeffer's methodological procedure can be constructed along the following lines: the Christian, in a setting of resistance or any other, answers the question "What am I to do?" by first answering the question "How is Christ taking form in the world?" (Or, as the question is put in *Letters and Papers from Prison*, "Who is Christ for us today," the question Bonhoeffer says is bothering him incessantly.)[41] The methodology could as easily be stated in the following manner. The first question is, "What is the real?" The second is, "What action on my part would be in accord with reality?"

With this methodology moral action is action that conforms to Christ's form in the world (that accords with reality); immoral action is action that deviates from Christ's form in the world (from reality). Since the primary difference between moral and immoral action corresponds, therefore, directly to the degree of con-*form*-ity or non-con-*form*-ity to the *form* that Christ takes in the world, the ethical system itself warrants Bonhoeffer's title "Ethics as Formation."

The striking advantage of this method consists in its potential applicability for both the Christian and the non-Christian, a consideration that in my judgment cannot be separated from Bonhoeffer's resistance work with non-Christians. In the above sets of methodological questions, the first set is for the Christian (viz., "How is Christ taking form in the world?" and "How can I conform to Christ's form in the world?"); the second set is for the non-Christian (viz., "What is the real?" and "How can I conform to reality?"). Yet they are identical because of Bonhoeffer's identification of the world-in-Christ with reality. The assumption is that because the coherence of God's reality and the world's reality in Christ is ontological, the form of Christ in the world, the real, is ultimately open to apprehension and acknowledgment by every man.[42] The ontological-cosmological reality of the world is already endowed with a universal christological character ("the reality of God in the world") that only awaits the proper stimulus in order to become realized. This bringing to realization of the world's essential character is, for Bonhoeffer, the heart of the ethical life.

The christocratic structure of reality means, then, that ethical inquiry is inquiry about the coming to expression in this world of "the cosmic reality given in Christ."

In Christ we are offered the possibility of partaking in the reality of God and in the reality of the world, but not in the one without the other. The reality of God discloses itself only by setting me entirely in the reality of the world, and when I

---

[41] "30 April 1944," *LPP*, p. 139.

[42] There is a major difficulty that arises on the issue of epistemology, however. This is handled in a section on critique, pp. 169-71.

encounter the reality of the world it is always already sustained, accepted and reconciled in the reality of God. This is the inner meaning of the revelation of God in the man Jesus Christ. Christian ethics enquires about the realization in our world of the divine and cosmic reality which is given in Christ.[43]

Contextuality: *The* Gestalt Christi *in Time and Space*

What more can be said of Bonhoeffer's ethic of reality and its realization? His is clearly a contextual ethic. Reality is indeed one. But it has a history. Christ is the same yesterday, today, and forever. Yet the ways in which he wins *Gestalt* vary with time and place. "Who is Christ for us *today?*"[44] Ethics as a "matter of history" and "a child of the earth"[45] is a theme recurrent in Bonhoeffer's writings from the first to the last.

The historicity of reality, or the polyphonic character of Christ's *Gestalt* through time and space, means a contextual ethic for Bonhoeffer. It is contextual because the manifestations of Christ's form in the world are always revealed and apprehended within the context of the concrete, ever-changing dynamic of the historical process. Thus, "who Christ is for us today" may not be who Christ was for us yesterday. "What can and must be said is not what is good once and for all, but the ways in which Christ takes form among us here and now."[46]

To discern the form of Christ "today," to "realize" reality here and now, requires considerable. Immersion in the life of the community of saints, the Body of Christ, and theological insight are the indispensable starting points.[47] But they alone will not suffice. Uncovering the "conforming" action among the various alternatives (i.e., discovering Christ's concrete command) also requires an empirical knowledge of the situation in which the Christian is deciding and acting. Without this knowledge, the Church's proclamation of the command to do what conforms to Christ is simply without authority. Authority demands credibility, and credibility demands a well-informed knowledge of the ever-changing context of decision.

Bonhoeffer's ecumenical address of July, 1932, serves as a nice case in point. It includes the striking formulation: "What the sacrament is for the preaching of the Gospel, the knowledge of firm reality is for the preaching of the command. *Reality is the sacrament of command.*"[48] Bonhoeffer explains.

---

[43] *E*, p. 195. [44] "30 April 1944." *LPP*, p. 139. Emphasis mine.
[45] Dietrich Bonhoeffer, "Grundfragen einer christlichen Ethik," *Gesammelte Schriften,* ed. Eberhard Bethge; 2nd ed. (Munich: Chr. Kaiser Verlag, 1960), III, 48. This was written in 1929. Similar thoughts can be found in portions of *Ethics* written in 1942-43. Much changes in Bonhoeffer's conception of ethics between these dates, but he never tires of campaigning against ethics as ahistorical principles—or any other mode of saying "what is good for once and for all."
[46] *E*, p. 85. [47] *Ibid.*, pp. 39, 84.
[48] Dietrich Bonhoeffer, "Zur theologischen Begruendung der Weltbundarbeit," *Gesammelte Schriften,* ed. Eberhard Bethge, 2nd ed. (Munich: Chr. Kaiser Verlag, 1965), I, 147. The

. . . The word of the church to the world must . . . encounter the world in all its present reality from the deepest knowledge of the world, if it is to be authoritative. Out of this knowledge the church must here and now be able to speak the Word of God, the word of authority in the most concrete way. Therefore, the church must not preach timeless principles however valid, but only commands which are valid today. To us God is "always" *God "today."* [49]

The example is timely.

. . . In the event of taking a stand on war the church cannot just say, "there should really be no war, but there are necessary wars" and leave the application of this principle to each individual; it should be able to say quite definitely: "Engage in this war" or "Do not engage in this war." [50]

For Bonhoeffer the conclusion of the matter is this.

. . . But if the church really has a command of God, it must proclaim it in the most definite form possible, from the fullest knowledge of the matter, and it must utter a summons to obedience. A command must be definite, otherwise it is not a command. God's command now requires something quite definite from us. And the church should proclaim this to the community.[51]
. . . Today God's command for us is the order of *international peace.*[52]

Bonhoeffer's ethic is therefore contextual in a double sense. On the one hand, the Christian should make his decisions in a particular *theological* context, namely within a Christo-universal understanding of the world, a world reconciled in Christ, the ontological center of existence. On the other hand, the Christian's decisions are also made in a particular *historical* context, the knowledge of which is indispensable for discerning Christ's peculiar *Gestalt* in this time and place, for uncovering the concrete command of God that will bring reality to expression here and now.

Although it is the theological context which maintains prior importance

---

emphasis is Bonhoeffer's. Here the error in *No Rusty Swords,* p. 164, is serious. The translation there reads "for the preaching of the sacrament" instead of "for the preaching of the command" (*Gebot*). It should not be overlooked that "reality" here is not the same as the expansive christocratic expression in *Ethics.* The reference above is to empirical data.

[49] Dietrich Bonhoeffer, *No Rusty Swords,* ed. Edwin Robertson, trans. John Bowden (New York: Harper, 1965), pp. 161-62. Emphasis in the original. Trans. corrected. *No Rusty Swords* should be used sparingly for Bonhoeffer research. In addition to inexact and sometimes erroneous translations, it contains introductions to the materials which are rather sensationalist and occasionally inaccurate.

[50] *GS,* I, 146.   [51] *NRS,* p. 163. Trans. corrected.

[52] *Ibid.,* p. 167. Trans. corrected. Emphasis in the original.

throughout Bonhoeffer's ethical deliberations, the historical context nevertheless takes on increasing significance as his involvement in the resistance deepens, as we shall see. Here the salient point is that ethics is always contextual in a double sense, theological and historical.

A "Filled" Ethic: The Move away from Atomism

A logical question of any contextual ethic is whether it is atomistic. Is the "here and now" so separated, methodologically, from the "there and then" and each present situation so unique that every ethical decision must be considered a case unto itself? In an atomistic contextual ethic, each case must be methodologically approached as *sui generis*.

In his 1929 lecture, "What is a Christian Ethic?" Bonhoeffer clearly exemplifies methodological atomism.

. . . From all this it now follows that the content of ethical problems can never be discussed in a Christian light; the possibility of erecting generally valid principles simply does not exist, because each moment, lived in God's sight, can bring an unexpected decision. Thus only one thing can be repeated again and again, also in our time: in ethical decisions a man must consider his action *sub specie aeternitatis* and then, no matter how it proceeds, it will proceed rightly. . . . The decision which is really required must be made freely in the concrete situation.[53]

It is significant that this passage was written before Bonhoeffer drew the *Gestalt Christi* into his ethics. After he does so his ethics continues to carry its contextualism, but it loses the atomism in increasing measure. Although the emphasis on the uniqueness of each ethical context, and therefore each ethical decision, is not denied in the years following, the terms depicting the *sui generis* character of such decisions are replaced by categories of a more general nature. This move from the unique to the universal, the particular to the general, represents Bonhoeffer's growing insight into the structured ontological unity of the form of the world and the form of Christ. Reality is seen to be christocratic, shaped by the form of Christ. Thus the totality of "natural life is formed life"[54] bearing universal rights, duties, and relationships.[55] Natural life is formed life because:

. . . Christ Himself entered into the natural life, and it is only through the incarnation of Christ that the natural life becomes the penultimate which is directed

---

[53] What is a Christian Ethic?" *NRS*, pp. 45-46. Translation corrected. The original text is printed in *GS* III, 55-56.

[54] *E*, p. 149.

[55] The content of these is found in part in Bonhoeffer's discussion of "The Natural," pp. 149 ff. and "The Four Mandates," pp. 207 ff. and pp. 287 ff. in *Ethics*.

toward the ultimate. Only through the incarnation of Christ do we have the right to call others to the natural life and to live the natural life ourselves.[56]

With this christological "discovery" and treatment of the natural, Bonhoeffer's contextual ethic becomes what might be termed a "filled" contextual ethic because Christ has taken form in the world. Christ is the same yesterday, today, and tomorrow, and so there is coherency and continuity in his form in the world and in his winning *Gestalt* among men. Methodologically, Bonhoeffer's remains a christocentric contextual ethic of reality and its realization. But it begins to lose its atomistic character through the drawing out of Christ's centeredness amidst the many arenas of conformation. And as the resultant elaboration of universal laws, rights, duties, and relationships takes shape, Bonhoeffer's method of deciding, though still done contextually, involves more and more neo-casuistic reasoning.[57]

Before continuing to survey Bonhoeffer's ethic from a structural perspective, it should be interjected that a number of possible bases for decision-making are already excluded by 1932, the year the *Kirchenkampf* began. The following appears in the extant student manuscripts from Bonhoeffer's seminar, "Is there a Christian Ethic?"

The possibility of judging whether our action is good lies alone in Christ, the present and future One. All other "secure" possibilities, which appear to give continuity to the action, are to be rejected: 1. the orders of creation; 2. conscience; 3. a Christian principle of love; 4. the situation itself; 5. laying claim to the forgiveness of sins; 6. the Law, even in the form of the Sermon on the Mount.[58]

Thus even in the early thirties Bonhoeffer rejected every basis for Christian moral judgment except a lively christocentric one. In the Germany of these years, this indeed seemed a master stroke.[59]

---

[56] *E*, p. 145.

[57] For example, see the discussions of various rights in the section "The Natural" in *Ethics*, pp. 143 ff.

[58] *Biographie*, p. 1075. Dr. Bethge's redaction of the recurring themes in the student manuscripts appears as Appendix C.

[59] When others were talking of "the orders of creation" (*Schoepfungsordnungen*) as a basis for social ethics, Bonhoeffer was using "orders of preservation" (*Erhaltungsordnungen*). (See the address "Dein Reich Komme" written in 1932, printed in *GS* III, 270 ff.) He feared that the employment of "orders of creation" would be used for the purpose of undergirding Nazi racism. When the term, "orders of preservation," was also used by conservative Lutherans in 1933 Bonhoeffer dropped it once and for all. Positive statements about the state now disappear even though Bonhoeffer still held to a rather traditional "two kingdoms" doctrine in the mid-1930s. But even this was formulated in such a way as to demand churchly resistance. (See Dietrich Bonhoeffer, "Die Kirche vor der Judenfrage," an address given in April, 1933, printed in *Gesammelte Schriften*, ed. Eberhard Bethge, 2nd ed. [Munich: Chr. Kaiser Verlag, 1965], II, 44-53.) Nor could the "two kingdoms" doctrine with its separation of spheres be retained in the face of Bonhoeffer's insistent Christocentricity. Thus he undertook a major revision because his theological heritage "assumed there are realities which lie outside the

The conclusion of *The Cost of Discipleship* carries on and clarifies what this Christocentricity means for ethics.

> To be conformed to the image of Christ is not an ideal to be striven after. It is not as though we had to imitate him as well as we could. We cannot transform ourselves into his image; it is rather the form of Christ which seeks to be formed in us (Gal. 4:19), and to be manifested in us. . . . We must be assimilated to the form of Christ in its entirety, the form of Christ incarnate, crucified and glorified.[60]

This language is striking in its virtual identity with the section "Ethics as Formation" written in the fall of 1940.[61] Yet the conclusion of *The Cost of Discipleship* bears a marked difference from the beginning of *Ethics,* a difference of momentous importance for Bonhoeffer's ethics. It is the expanded arena of conformation. The expansion is in fact the key to the move from the ethics of *The Cost of Discipleship* to those of *Letters and Papers from Prison.* Its theological expression is recorded in these words: "The more exclusively we acknowledge and confess Christ the Lord, the more fully the wide range of His dominion will be disclosed to us." [62]

In both books (*The Cost of Discipleship* and *Ethics*), the ethics of formation sounds a clear tone. But ethics as formation in *The Cost of Discipleship* is strictly a churchly ethic. It is what disciples do regardless of the world's response. In *Ethics* it is clearly an ethic of the Christian in the world. Here realism, pragmatism, and the careful calculation of consequences enter, though they are clearly secondary to Bonhoeffer's altered theological view of the world. The "wide range of His dominion" has been uncovered in *Ethics.* "Exclusiveness of Christ's lordship—that is the message of *The Cost of Discipleship;* the wide range of his lordship—that is the new emphasis of *Ethics.*" [63]

In short the *Gestalt Christi* has taken on theocratic breadth. And with the elaboration of the Incarnation and Lordship of Christ the formal structure of Bonhoeffer's ethics has moved from a contextual ethic that was wholly atomistic to an ethic that speaks of universal rights, duties, and relationships that

---

reality in Christ" (*E,* p. 196). The point is simply that Bonhoeffer's early insistence upon an exclusively christocentric basis for moral judgment lies at the bottom of these developments, developments extremely important for his resistance activity, as we shall see. The nature and extent of the resistance activity made possible on the basis of this christocentric theology and ethic become even more intense and demanding through Bonhoeffer's turn to the radical Jesus of the Sermon on the Mount. (See especially *The Cost of Discipleship* and excerpts from "Christ and Peace" in the *Biography,* pp. 158-59.)

[60] Dietrich Bonhoeffer, *The Cost of Discipleship,* trans. Reginald Fuller, 2nd ed. (New York: Macmillan, 1963), p. 341.

[61] *E,* pp. 64-119. *Ethics* should be read as the transition piece from *The Cost of Discipleship* to *Letters and Papers from Prison.*

[62] *Ibid.,* p. 58. It is far more than coincidence that Bonhoeffer's move from churchly to military/political resistance parallels this change. This must be taken up elsewhere, however.

[63] *Biography,* p. 622.

may indeed alter through time but that carry continuity because of the coherent form of Christ.

The mandates illustrate the foregoing and also play a structural role in Bonhoeffer's mode of doing ethics. To them we now turn.

The Media of Conformation: The Mandates

In the section on formation in *Ethics* we first meet Bonhoeffer's conceptualization of the mandates. They constitute his attempt, in the face of some uncertainty and reconsideration,[64] to treat the overarching christological unity in a concrete, even empirical fashion, as well as a theological one. The mandates are an attempt to portray the media of conformation.

Discussion of the mandates will also provide the opportunity to discern what Bonhoeffer means by the "ethical." We shall see that he does not mark the same borders drawn by most theologians and philosophers.

The mandates are solely dependent upon the one command of God in Jesus Christ,[65] but no *single* mandate embodies this one command or is superior to any other mandate. Rather they are conjoined in such a manner that only by cooperation, coordination, *and opposition* to one another do they properly function in fulfillment of the one command.[66] Mutual complementarity and mutual limitation, checking and balancing, are important aspects of their function as the media of God's commands.

. . . The supremacy of the command of God is shown precisely by the fact that it juxtaposes and coordinates these authorities in a relation of mutual opposition and complementarity and that it is only in this multiplicity of concrete correlations and limitations that the command of God takes effect as the command which is manifest in Jesus Christ.[67]

[64] Bonhoeffer was experimenting in any case. One time he names four (*E*, p. 207). Another time he substitutes one for another (*E*, p. 286). Still another time he wonders where "friendship" belongs and if culture and education should not be added to marriage and family, work, state, and church (the letter of 23 January 1944, in *LPP*, p. 104).

[65] *E*, p. 288. [66] *Ibid.*, p. 291.

[67] *Ibid.*, p. 279. Trans. corrected. Bonhoeffer's conception of the mandates as mutually complementing and limiting one another is grounds for opposition to the Hitler state. Bonhoeffer regarded the totalitarian claims by one of the mandates, the state, as a flagrant violation of the command of God and cause for resistance. This emerges in an interesting way in a 1941 book review in which Bonhoeffer writes that the struggle against totalitarianism by Germans arises out of the arbitrary dissolution of genuine God-ordered and God-circumscribed bonds, i.e. out of flagrant violation of the mandates. (See "Gedanken zu William Paton: *The Church and the New Order*," *GS* I, 356-60.) The book review was actually Bonhoeffer's medium for carrying out a resistance assignment. Bonhoeffer met Visser 't Hooft in Geneva for the purpose of contact with the Allies about resistance plans, and Visser 't Hooft sent the information to circles in Great Britain and the United States, together with a cover letter disclosing the true significance of the "book review." (See Willem Visser 't Hooft, "Begegnung mit Dietrich Bonhoeffer," *Das Zeugnis eines Boten: Zum Gedaechtnis von Dietrich Bonhoeffer* [Geneva: Oekumenische Kommission fuer

The mandates are definite, circumscribed historical forms of the *Gestalt Christi*. In fulfilling one's duties within the mandates (as for example a husband, father, breadwinner, citizen, and churchman) the person conforms to Christ, does God's will, whether he is cognizant of it or not. Here "the flood of life flows freely" in accord with God's intents for man.[68]

Bonhoeffer regards this normal discharge of responsibilities as *pre-ethical*.[69] For him, the rather self-evident nature of duties in marriage and family, state, church, and work is certainly a matter of morals, but not ethics. The ethical arises only when the normal moral course is called into question.

There are, of course, undoubtedly occasions and situations in which the moral course is not self-evident, either because it is not, in fact, followed or because it has become questionable from the point of view of its content. It is at such times that the ethical becomes a theme.[70]

Earlier Bonhoeffer concludes that the ethical is "tied to a definite time and . . . place."[71] The ethical as a theme arises, and can only find its adequate resolution, when the normal processes of life are interrupted and the assumed values seriously called into question; it arises when the question of "who Christ is for us today" demands and alteration of the attitudes and actions which had previously been accepted as normative.

Bonhoeffer found himself in just such a time; thus, his attention to the ethical as a matter of "big guns" in extraordinary times is crucial.[72] But to restate the point here is to say the following.

The mandates are historical forms of the *Gestalt Christi* which embody and

---

die Pastoration der Kriegsgefangenen, 1945].) What is of interest here for the above discussion is how Bonhoeffer's efforts to portray the forms of the *Gestalt Christi* in the mandates work their way into his resistance mission and how the violation of the mandates is grounds for resistance to the totalitarian state. The sections on the mandates were in fact written between resistance assignments.

[68] *E*, p. 283.   [69] *Ibid.*   [70] *Ibid.*, p. 267.   [71] *Ibid.*, p. 264.

[72] Bonhoeffer's own delimitation of the ethical pushes him to undertake systematic ethical reflection in the most turbulent of times. As will be shown later, he is very careful not to make the extraordinary the normative. But there is a special attention given to breaking points, to the emerging, to the extremes, to the new, to the *Grenzfall*, as ethically significant. It is interesting that Bonhoeffer wrote ethics in virtual isolation in the German church during the Third Reich. This is not due, he says, to lack of concrete ethical problems—on the contrary! It is due to the chaotic character of the times with its consequent ethical confusion. Yet Bonhoeffer's own understanding is one that views such times as the most significant ethically (*E*, p. 64). Compare this with one of the few others doing ethics out of the Third Reich experience, Helmut Thielicke: "The problems [in ethics] do not arise with the ordinary cases, but with the borderline cases, those involving transitions or complications. It is the abnormal rather than the normal case which brings us up against the real problems. Hence the real test, even in respect of foundational principles, is whether an ethics has been proved in the crucible of the borderline situation and emerged with even deeper insights." (Helmut Thielicke, *Theological Ethics*, trans. John Doberstein, [Philadelphia: Fortress Press, 1966], I, 578.)

direct the normal processes of life. The ethical as a theme arises when "who Christ is for us today" becomes questionable at the point of our behavioral response to his changing forms among men. Such times are usually those when the relatively normal flow of history is interrupted by those extraordinary events that challenge the basic values understood from the mandates themselves. The ethical arises in these exceptional times and can only be answered with an eye to them. New courses of action then become possible, based upon redirection from the concrete command of God-in-Christ.

Personal-Relational: Koinonia *Ethics*

One more item about Bonhoeffer's ethics should be noted before turning to the interplay of his christological ethics and his resistance.

Bonhoeffer's ethic is clearly personalist-relational. While this is readily seen as an implication of Bonhoeffer's anthropology,[73] special attention is warranted by his own emphasis.

The central justification for the designation, "personalist-relational," is simply that it is the person of Christ who wins *Gestalt* in the world of men. It is the living Christ who is encountered again and again at every juncture of personal and social life, who is present at the heart of every concrete human relationship; and it is this Christ who, through dynamic encounter within the ambiguities of historical existence, provides the source and direction for the ethical life. He is the giver of forms, to use Bonhoeffer's language. In the compelling meeting with him, most often through other persons, one taps the source for the direction of action.[74] Ethics, then, is done in communion with Christ and one's fellowman; it is *koinonia* ethics, a social event of the fitting response to the Living Lord.

---

[73] See pp. 19-21.

[74] Edward LeRoy Long, Jr. describes the relational motif in ethics as that in which "the direction of action is shaped by the sense of excitement or gratitude which arises from a live, dynamic, and compelling encounter with the source of moral guidance." Edward LeRoy Long, Jr., *A Survey of Christian Ethics* (New York: Oxford University Press, 1967), p. 117. This is precise for Bonhoeffer (and I have borrowed the language above), as is Long's judgment that Bonhoeffer, among others, felt this approach superior to analytical and prescriptive ones. (*Ibid.*, p. 119.)

2
Christological Ethics and Resistance

Resistance and Christological Expansion

The task now is to relate Bonhoeffer's Christology and ethics to his resistance. Whereas the *theologia crucis* threads an even line throughout Bonhoeffer's writings, the vision of *Christus Pantocrator* does not. This vision first crystallizes in *Ethics*, even though the foundational tenets were present in the Christology lectures of 1933. What was then latent becomes activated as Bonhoeffer's resistance deepens in the 1940s. The kenotic Christology takes on theocratic breadth in the course of resistance work.

A major essay on Christology and resistance[1] documents the expanding horizons. It does so in biographical/theological fashion. That is, Bonhoeffer reveals that precisely the experience of resistance shifts the christological horizons even though his fundamental theological assertion—Christ the center of man, nature, and history—was present all the while.

The experience of resistance in the thirties was one in which men and women of liberal humanist persuasion came to the Confessing Church at the very time she made the severely exclusive christological claims epitomized in the Barmen Declaration. This was the first time the Church had been of serious concern for many of them. The phenomenon of broad humanist values, now under fire from the Nazis, finding their refuge and center in Jesus Christ,

---

[1] The term "resistance" is used very broadly here, referring to all forms of active opposition to Nazism. Later its meaning will become more exact.

is the wholly unexpected event [2] with which Bonhoeffer wrestles in this essay. The date is important—1939/1940. It means this was written not long after Bonhoeffer had trumpeted the exclusivist claims of *The Cost of Discipleship* with its mood of "the world for Christ." That exclusivism remains strong here —indeed, the language is still that of *The Cost of Discipleship*—but the experience of resistance breaks Bonhoeffer's propensity to locate Christ's forming men solely in the Church. The experience of resistance even brings with it the speculation that there seems to be a "general unconscious knowledge" [3] in the world which draws men to Christ.

In this transitional document [4] the cross remains central. What is "new," although anticipated in the Christology lectures, is the developing Christo-universalism. It is remarkable to note the perceptible line from Bonhoeffer's experience of resistance to this critical expansion within his Christology.

Bonhoeffer describes the Nazi rule, the resultant experience of those who opposed it, and the discovery of the breadth of the Church's responsibility.

It was not metaphysical speculation, it was not a theologumenon of the *logos spermatikos,* but it was the concrete suffering of injustice, of the organized lie, of hostility to mankind and of violence, it was the persecution of lawfulness, truth, humanity and freedom which impelled the men who held these values dear to seek the protection of Jesus Christ and therefore to become subject to His claim, and it was through this that the Church of Jesus Christ learnt of the wide extent of her responsibility.[5]

"Under the pressure of anti-Christian forces" [6] clear decisions had to be made for or against Christ. Thus the saying, "He that is not with me is against me," [7] became the living experience of those Christians who did not join the heresy of the "German Christians" (*Deutsche Christen*) or the equally dangerous band of "neutrals." [8]

The firing of the metal and the loosening of the dross in the *Kirchenkampf* now attracted "men who came from very far away," [9] men to whom the Church could not refuse fellowship and protection. "Injured justice, oppressed

---

[2] *E*, p. 55. "We will begin this section ['The Church and The World'] by referring to one of our most astonishing experiences during the years when everything Christian was sorely oppressed."

[3] *Ibid.,* p. 56.

[4] Transitional from the exclusiveness of Christ's claims in *The Cost of Discipleship* to the inclusiveness of his reign in *Ethics* and *Letters and Papers from Prison.*

[5] *E*, pp. 58-59.   [6] *Ibid.,* p. 58.   [7] Matthew 12:30.

[8] *E*, p. 58. The "Deutsche Christen" were the adherents of a "Germany theology" that subscribed to many basic Nazi tenets. They actively supported Hitler. The "neutrals" joined neither the "Deutsche Christian" nor the Confessing Church and sought political neutrality over against the State. Bonhoeffer says their indecision showed their "true hostility to Christ." (*Ibid.*)

[9] *Ibid.*

truth, vilified humanity and violated freedom all sought for her [the Church], or rather for her master, Jesus Christ." [10] Rather unexpectedly the Church came up against Mark 9:40: "He that is not against us is for us."

This unexpected alliance between the defenders of the broadly based values of the Enlightenment and the small party of the Confessing Christians came out of the mutual opposition to Nazism although, on the face of it, they opposed it from quite different sources. Bonhoeffer began to realize, however, the sources were all drawn from Jesus Christ. In his view, those holding Enlightenment values, which were so often used polemically against Christianity, now sensed the origin of these values in Jesus Christ.

Nor was the grounding of general humanist themes in Christ any less a surprise to the Church than it was to the children of the Enlightenment. "Christian thought acquired . . . an entirely unexpected new wide field of activity" [11] as "reason, justice, culture, humanity and all the kindred concepts" [12] returned to their origin in Jesus Christ. Bonhoeffer's own Christology had asserted as much. But it remained for the experience of Nazism and of opposition to Hitler's mad *Weltanschauung* to awaken these earlier themes from their academic slumbers.

We will begin this section by referring to one of our most astonishing experiences during the years when everything Christian was sorely oppressed. The deification of the irrational, of blood and instinct, of the beast of prey in man could be countered with an appeal to reason; arbitrary action could be countered with the written law; barbarity with the appeal to culture and humanity; the violent maltreatment of persons with the appeal to freedom, tolerance and the rights of man; the subordination of science, art and the rest to political purposes with the appeal to the autonomy of the various different fields of human activity. In each case this was sufficient to awaken the consciousness of a kind of alliance and comradeship between the defenders of these endangered values and the Christians. Reason, culture, humanity, tolerance and self-determination, all these concepts which until very recently had served as battle slogans against the Church, against Christianity, against Jesus Christ Himself, had now, suddenly and surprisingly, come very near indeed to the Christian standpoint.[13]

The alliance of a general humanism and a sharp Christocentrism was indeed a surprise, no less so because this was not the Christ of the Middle Ages whose name was, in part, the designation of society-wide institutional power. Nor was this the Christ of the Post-Apostolic Church who was the embodiment of the true aspirations of the classical heritage.[14] Rather, the Christ of the *Kirchenkampf* was the Christ of the *theologia crucis*.

[10] *Ibid.*   [11] *Ibid.,* p. 55.   [12] *Ibid.,* p. 56.   [13] *Ibid.,* p. 55.   [14] *Ibid.,* p. 59.

. . . the crucified Christ has become the refuge and the justification, the protection and the claim for the higher values and their defenders that have fallen victim to suffering. It is with the Christ who is persecuted and who suffers in His Church that justice, truth, humanity and freedom now seek refuge; it is with the Christ who found no shelter in the world, the Christ who was cast out from the world, the Christ of the crib and of the cross, under whose protection they now seek sanctuary, and who thereby for the first time displays the full extent of His power. The cross of Christ makes both sayings true: "He that is not with me is against me" and "He that is not against us is for us." [15]

This Jesus gives his support to all those who suffer for any just cause, whether that cause involves confession of his name or not, says Bonhoeffer.[16] The joining with others persecuted for any just cause was the experience "in which the power of Jesus Christ became manifest in fields of life where it had previously remained unknown."[17] Indeed, "we in our time[18] must say . . . that before a man can know and find Christ he must first become righteous like those who strive and who suffer for the sake of justice, truth and humanity."[19]

A band of men had appeared, men who were the catalyst for the expansion of Bonhoeffer's condescension Christology so as to reach out and take in the wide range of the Exalted Lord's dominion. It is no surprise, then, that this essay on the experience of resistance to Nazism by this band of men is the very document that records the major shift in Bonhoeffer's Christology.

These two sayings [Mark 9:40 and Matthew 12:30] necessarily belong together as the two claims of Jesus Christ, the claim to exclusiveness and the claim to totality. The greater the exclusiveness, the greater the freedom. But in isolation the claim to exclusiveness leads to fanaticism and slavery; and in isolation the claim to totality leads to secularization and self-abandonment of the Church. The more exclusively we acknowledge and confess Christ as our Lord, the more fully the wide range of His dominion will be disclosed to us.[20]

The last phrase points the direction Bonhoeffer now moves. The very theological borders of *The Cost of Discipleship* have been burst by the experience of resistance, and Bonhoeffer turns to draw upon his own earlier christological themes in order to give expression to this experience.

The development can be summarily formulated this way: if *The Cost of Discipleship* is a commentary on Matthew 12:30, "He that is not with me is against me," then *Ethics* and *Letters and Papers from Prison* become a com-

---

[15] *Ibid.* The sayings are Matthew 12:30 and Mark 9:40, respectively.
[16] *Ibid.*, p. 60. [17] *Ibid.*
[18] One of the "times which are out of joint . . . when lawlessness and wickedness triumph in complete unrestraint." (*E*, p. 61.)
[19] *E*, p. 61. [20] *Ibid.*, p. 58.

mentary on Mark 9:40, "He that is not against us is for us." And this earliest section of *Ethics* charts the movement in Bonhoeffer's Christology by expounding the two verses side by side.

It would be incorrect to see a full break between *The Cost of Discipleship* and *Ethics,* despite a very definite and decisive shift. *The Cost of Discipleship* also interprets Matthew 5:10 [21] in a "secular" sense: "Jesus gives his blessings not merely to suffering incurred directly for the confession of his name, but to suffering in any just cause." [22] Too, a foretaste of Bonhoeffer's discussion of the ultimate and the penultimate can be found in the mention of "the first step" that places a man in a situation where faith is possible. [23] Yet these are minor themes at most and are placed within such stringent church/world boundaries as to make *The Cost of Discipleship* clearly a "two-kingdoms" document. The Bonhoeffer of *Ethics* could never have written: "Like a sealed train travelling through foreign territory, the Church goes on its way through the world." [24] With the "wide range of His dominion" having been "disclosed to us," the "world" in *Ethics* is not "foreign territory" but the *only* place Christ is Christ. "Christ died for the world, and it is only in the midst of the world that Christ is Christ." [25]

Is it too much to make a major claim based on this early testimony in *Ethics?* The experience of resistance is the catalyst that works to bring to expression the theocratic breadth latent in Bonhoeffer's consistent Christology of condescension.

The Gestalt Christi *and Resistance*

Questions and Claims. What are the themes of resistance that emanate from this theology "where the crucified Lord is the triumphant center and the triumphant one is the Crucified"? [26] If Christology is indeed at the center of Bonhoeffer's thinking, where is the key here to his move from passive to active resistance? If his opposition to Nazism is christologically grounded, is this to be found in his writings? If the *Gestalt Christi* is at the core of Bonhoeffer's dogmatics, does his ethic of resistance take form from this *Gestalt?* In the other direction, where, if anywhere, does the involvement in resistance influence Bonhoeffer's Christology?

The years between the Christology lectures of 1933 and the outline for a book

[21] "Blessed are those who are persecuted for righteousness' sake, for theirs is the kingdom of heaven."

[22] *CD*, p. 127.   [23] *Ibid.,* p. 67.   [24] *Ibid.,* p. 313.

[25] *E*, p. 206. This sentence is from the section of *Ethics* which is Bonhoeffer's own implicit critique of *The Cost of Discipleship*—"Thinking in Terms of Two Spheres" (pp. 196-207).

[26] Eberhard Bethge, "Bonhoeffer's Christology and His 'Religionless Christianity,' " *Union Seminary Quarterly Review*, Fall, 1967, p. 75.

in 1944 were the years of passive and active resistance. As we shall see, the controlling motif of being-there-for-others did not fade but developed and grew forceful, especially under the rubrics of responsibility, deputyship, acceptance of guilt, and freedom. The development is one of ethical intensification; that is, Christian action and its ground are Bonhoeffer's preoccupations throughout. This direction can be documented in the fully existential matters comprising his resistance activity. Whether it was deputyship as intervening on behalf of Jews,[27] or the deed of free responsibility as the rationale for consenting to plans for assassination, or the acceptance of guilt as the hinge of his move from passive to active resistance, the lines lead back to the *Gestalt Christi,* to the Christ whose very being is being-there-for-others.

At least this is the argument of this section. We shall substantiate it by first turning to the section of *Ethics* in which Bonhoeffer describes the structure of responsible life.[28] This will be used as a convenient framework for tracing theological themes important to resistance. Where the themes then lead can best be followed after the initial exposition.

Responsibility and Deputyship. With the term "responsibility," Bonhoeffer designates the basic answering (*Verantwortung*) of the person to life. That is, Bonhoeffer is not speaking first of all about specific responses to particular persons in given situations. He is speaking of a fundamental response of one's own life to life itself. He means a basic posture, an overarching life-orientation that affects all actions, all responsibilities. In Bonhoeffer's case, this means a man's response to "the reality which is given us in Jesus Christ." [29] Or, in more noticeably ethical terms, Bonhoeffer defines responsibility as "the total and realistic response of man to the claim of God and of our neighbor." [30] The holistic element is clear.

[27] Bonhoeffer used Proverbs 31:8 over and again for calling the Confessing Church and others to exercise deputyship for the Jews. A Finkenwalde lecture makes clear how serious active intercession was for Bonhoeffer. Whether the Church is the Church of Christ depends upon its being for the Jews. "The service of the church has to be given to those who suffer violence and injustice. The Old Testament still demands right-dealing of the state, the New Testament no longer does so. Without asking about justice or injustice, the church takes to itself all the sufferers, *all* the forsaken of every party and of every status. 'Open your mouth for the dumb' (Prov. 31:8). Here the decision will really be made whether we are still the church of the present Christ. The Jewish question." ("The Interpretation of the New Testament," *NRS,* p. 325.) The date is August, 1935. Emphasis Bonhoeffer's.

[28] *E,* pp. 224-62. Bonhoeffer describes this structure in terms of deputyship, correspondence with reality, conscience, and freedom. This will be roughly the outline followed above.

[29] *E,* p. 222. It is entirely in keeping with Bonhoeffer's highly personalized Christocentrism that the discussion of responsibility is prefaced by commentary on John 14:6 and 11:25: "I am the life."

[30] *E,* p. 245. The reader is reminded about the place of God's claim and the neighbor's in a person's achieving true selfhood. (See pp. 19-21 above.) The structure of the *responsive* life rather than *responsible* might have been a translation closer to Bonhoeffer's emphasis on human

Bonhoeffer does use "responsibility" in other ways, usually without acknowledging the changes of meaning. Yet these secondary definitions are always "sub-divisions" of responsibility as the basic answering to reality. One secondary usage refers to the objective duty or obligation inherent in concrete relationships. Another refers to the perception of responsibility, i.e., an understanding of God's claim and the neighbor's in the light of faith. "Free responsibility" is a further usage and one that occupies a special place in Bonhoeffer's ethic; its meaning and importance will be given separate attention shortly. In any event the inclusive meaning is the most basic one in Bonhoeffer's discussion of the structure of responsible life.[31]

Like all of Bonhoeffer's themes, responsibility has a christological foundation. It is grounded in Jesus Christ's being as being-for-others. "Responsibility . . . has its foundation in the responsibility of Jesus Christ for men, on the basis of our knowledge that the origin, essence and goal of all reality is the real, that is to say, God in Jesus Christ."[32]

The master mark of responsibility is deputyship.[33] Actually neither the overarching theme of responsibility nor its essential mark of deputyship is a new theme for Bonhoeffer in *Ethics*. His doctoral dissertation asserts that man is not man in and by himself but only in responsibility to and for another.[34] That same source is clear about the efficacy of Christ's deputyship—it restores communion between God and man.[35] What is highly significant in this early writing, however, is a double fact about deputyship for Bonhoeffer. The young Barthian sees such an abyss between God's action and man's behavior that vicarious action "is not a moral possibility or standard, but solely the reality of the divine love for the church; it is not a moral but a theological concept."[36] Second, deputyship is "in force only in Christ and his church."[37] Insofar as deputyship can be said to characterize any human action at all, it characterizes only the human community of the Church and cannot be regarded as a prop-

---

interaction and human response to the divine in I-Thou relations. However, *responsible* does carry the theme of accountability *for*, answering *for*, the emphasis on *claim*, which is strong in Bonhoeffer's thought.

[31] These uses are scattered throughout this section of *Ethics*, pp. 224-62. A systematic study of this section is made difficult by Bonhoeffer's unacknowledged changes in the meaning of responsibility.

[32] *E*, p. 235.

[33] The German (*Stellvertretung*) carries a load English often does not. This is all the more so for Bonhoeffer's use of *Stellvertretung*. Normal German usage may mean either acting for another or taking his place or both. "Deputyship" can mean this in English but the common connotation of a delegate or proxy action is short of a full substitution involving full responsibility. Bonhoeffer makes use of the strongest possible *German* overtones and intends this full substitution. When he speaks of "deputyship" the reader should understand *vicarious being and vicarious action*. The importance of exact meaning is underlined by the fact that Bonhoeffer uses *Stellvertretung* to describe the very essence of Christ's being, man's, and the Church's.

[34] *CS*, p. 32. [35] *Ibid.*, p. 114. [36] *Ibid.* [37] *Ibid.*

erty of the profane acts of secular men. Soon, however, the notion of deputy-ship takes on wider dimensions. This may have been latent earlier,[38] but it is stated clearly in a lecture at the Institute of Technology in Berlin in 1932. From Christ's sacrifice we recognize deputyship as the law of life for all men; it is the mark of what it means to become human. The one who is free to die, free to be a deputy unto death for his brother, is the one who is free to live.[39] Bonhoeffer sees not only the fulfillment of the individual, but of all forms of human community, including the nation, in the willingness to act vicariously for others.[40] He intimates that the East, exemplified in Ghandi and his move-ment, knows this better than the West.[41] In a 1931 letter Bonhoeffer had asked if, in the face of the death of Christendom, the gospel may not have been given to another people (Ghandi's India) and there preached with "wholly other words and deeds."[42] While this is not an explicit mention of deputyship, it is included in "gospel" for Bonhoeffer. Here he does not limit the gospel's expression to the Church; or at least he asks if the law of life—love and suffer-ing for others[43]—is not known elsewhere as well. Yet this remains speculation, and there is no doubt Bonhoeffer is almost wholly preoccupied with deputy-ship and responsibility as churchly themes at this time. Nevertheless, it should not escape our attention that by 1932 both themes have universal dimensions grounded in the being-for-all-men of Jesus. This is the conclusion of the lecture on "The Right of Self-Assertion."[44]

Only deputyship has been traced above, but responsibility is also stated as a universal.[45] (In any case it is clear that the discussion of deputyship assumes the notion of responsibility because of Bonhoeffer's anthropology.)[46]

In the notes from a 1932 seminar on "The Essence of the Church" Christ's deputyship is elaborated as the very foundation of the Church and determina-tive for her structure.[47] Deputyship resonates with equally strong tones in *The Cost of Discipleship*.

. . . All the foregoing may be summed up in the single phrase—Christ is "for us," not only in word and in his attitude towards us, but in his bodily life. He occupies in his body the place where we should be before God. He suffers and dies in our stead.[48]

---

[38] In *The Communion of Saints* vicarious action is also called a "life-principle." It is the life-principle of "the new mankind" (p. 107). But "the new mankind" is only realized in the Church for Bonhoeffer at this time, although it is clear that Jesus' vicarious being and action has made it possible for every person to join the new mankind.

[39] "Das Recht auf Selbstbehauptung," *GS* III, 269.

[40] *Ibid.*, pp. 268-69. [41] *Ibid.*, pp. 262-63. [42] "Briefwechsel mit Helmut Roessler," *GS* I, 61.

[43] "Das Recht auf Selbstbehauptung," *GS* III, 269.

[44] *Ibid.*, p. 265. [45] *Ibid.* [46] See pp. 19-21 above.

[47] "Das Wesen der Kirche," Appendix B in the *Biographie*, pp. 1062-63. [48] *CD*, p. 268.

Now deputyship is also a Christian's possibility and not only Christ's.

... But we do at least know that the man who suffers in the power of the body of Christ suffers in a respresentative capacity "for" the Church, the Body of Christ, being privileged to endure himself what others are spared. ... Such vicarious activity and passivity on the part of the members of the Body is the very life of Christ, who wills to be formed in his members (Gal. 4:19).[49]

Furthermore, this deputyship is an action for the sake of the world. The Church stands before God in the world as the representative of the world; the new mankind acts on behalf of the old mankind.[50] Yet being for the world in the world is at considerable distance from deputyship seen in the profane acts of secular men or deputyship viewed as permeating all worldly reality. Thus a new and decisive dimension is given deputyship in *Ethics,* despite the foretaste in *The Cost of Discipleship.* In *Ethics* deputyship is found throughout the full range of Christ's dominion. It is no longer a thoroughly ecclesiological term, although it remains a thoroughly christological one. Deputyship draws out its universal dimensions as Bonhoeffer's Christology draws out its theocratic breadth. Now it is seen in the behavior of *all* "responsible" men, whether Christian or not. The whole of life, rather than almost wholly the Church, is the locus for discovering and exercising deputyship.

In *Ethics* Bonhoeffer not only expands the locus of deputyship; he also elaborates it more and more as a matter of normal human conduct. In *The Communion of Saints* vicarious action, as we noted, is "not a moral possibility or standard, but solely the reality of the divine love for the church; it is not a moral but a theological concept ... in force only in Christ and his church." [51] In *Ethics* it remains "a theological concept" but it is *also* a moral one; and it is both a moral possibility *and* standard. Bonhoeffer has shifted the emphasis from the qualitative difference between Christ's deputyship and a man's doing good for his neighbor to the daily Christian *and* non-Christian life as a life that intimately partakes of Christ's deputyship at every turn and in a multitude of even unavoidable ways. Bonhoeffer, the young Lutheran *Barthian,* has *in ethics* become more and more Bonhoeffer, the young *Lutheran* Barthian, as the *Gestalt Christi* takes form in the "orders" (*Ordnungen*). *Finitum capax infiniti* is now as much a matter of ethics as it is of dogmatics.[52]

---

[49] *Ibid.,* pp. 273-74.   [50] *Ibid.,* p. 102.   [51] *CS,* p. 114.

[52] It is because of Bonhoeffer's Lutheran Christology that he writes about "the humanity of God" much earlier than Barth. Barth's lecture with that title was delivered in 1956. He marks it as a definite "change of direction" in "distinction from" but not in "opposition to" his earlier theology. (Karl Barth, *The Humanity of God,* trans. Thomas Wieser [Richmond: John Knox Press, 1960], p. 37.) By contrast Bonhoeffer in 1927 undertook a sociology of the Church because of "the social intention of all the basic Christian concepts." (*The Communion of Saints,* Preface.) The interest in the empirical by a Barthian of the late 1920s lies in one of

Life in the mandates exemplifies both the broadened applicability of the notion of deputyship for ethics and its permeation of all life. The mandates "are 'for' one another; otherwise they are not God's mandates." [53] And "the bearer of the mandate acts as a deputy in the place of Him who assigns him his commission." [54] They are orders "of the reality of Christ" [55] which possess a relative autonomy because of the liberation achieved by the vicarious action of Christ.[56] This "relative autonomy," grounded in Christ's deputyship, is neither a full autonomy of the orders (i.e., without basis in, and accountability to, God-in-Christ) nor heteronomy (i.e., dominion of the Church over the other orders of society, or vice versa). It is "Christonomy." [57] "The cross of atonement is . . . the setting free for life in genuine worldliness." [58] Christ has taken form in human sociality, and through his vicarious action the orders of that sociality are now freed to follow their own innate laws, freed to be "genuinely worldly" as intended from creation.[59]

This can be stated differently, perhaps thereby aiding clarification. Man is not born into an undifferentiated maze of atomized events and relations. Rather he is formed in the mandates; and this forming is one that, running its own natural course, pushes him in the direction of being-for-others. From birth to death he is in the midst of a corporate life filled with obligations, opportunities, relationships, and responsibilities which reflect the innate laws of the orders. These are laws subject to the dominion of Christ and laws that, when obeyed, realize reality, i.e., bring to expression the deputyship that is at the heart of the mandates. Moltmann's condensation is correct: derivative from Christ's deputyship, "vicarious action of men for one another is the resultant foundation of sociality in the mandates of marriage, labor, state, and church, of their personal relationships as well as their relation to things." [60]

Deputyship, then, is a possibility and a standard for all men, and it is a characteristic of normal human conduct as life is lived out in its divinely commissioned framework, the mandates. By meeting the built-in obligations as, for example, a husband, father, laborer, citizen, and churchman, a man exercises deputyship, a man conforms to Christ's form, whether cognizant of it or not. The christological and ecclesiological understanding of deputyship in Bonhoeffer's writings of the thirties becomes a christological and universal humanist one in the forties.

---

the many things Bonhoeffer learned from Luther's Christology—the orders contain Christ. We have seen, however, that *Ethics* did not follow immediately—although Bonhoeffer had already become preoccupied with ethics by 1932. (See "Briefe an Erwin Sutz," *GS* I, 33.)

[53] *E*, p. 291.   [54] *Ibid.*, p. 287.   [55] *Ibid.*, p. 288.   [56] *Ibid.*, p. 289.

[57] *Ibid.*, p. 299, note.   [58] *Ibid.*, p. 297.   [59] *Ibid.*, p. 298.

[60] Jürgen Moltmann, "The Lordship of Christ and Human Society," in Jürgen Moltmann and Jürgen Weissbach, *Two Studies in the Theology of Bonhoeffer*, trans. Reginald H. Fuller and Ilse Fuller (New York: Scribner's, 1967), p. 64.

Correspondence with Reality. The deputy's, i.e., the responsible man's, actions must correspond with reality if they are in fact to *be* responsible. The next section describing the structure of responsible life is thus entitled "Correspondence with Reality." [61]

Bonhoeffer consistently rules out two extremes as the normal and normative behavioral patterns of responsible men. In various places these extremes are termed "servility" and "revolt," [62] "compromise" (here meaning capitulation to evil) and "radicalism," [63] "sanction" and "destruction." [64] While the nuances of these and other pairs vary, all are used by Bonhoeffer to chart two unacceptable courses: that of noncritical acceptance of the given state of affairs on the one hand, and full-blown revolution or an apocalyptic anarchism on the other. The section on the structure of responsible life expresses it as follows.

. . . The origin of action which accords with reality is not the pseudo-Lutheran Christ who exists solely for the purpose of sanctioning the facts as they are, nor the Christ of radical enthusiasm whose function is to bless every revolution, but it is the incarnate God Jesus who has accepted man and who has loved, condemned and reconciled man and with him the world.[65]

The *Gestalt Christi* has formed and is forming the lives of men and societies. Yet the *full* realization of reality has not occurred. Thus the course of "servility," "compromise," "sanction" is ruled out as normative, for such a course would sanction the conformation of men to those principalities, powers, and conditions not in accord with Christ. But Christ *has* in fact taken form in the world. Thus, "revolt," "radicalism," and "enthusiasm" as a normative pattern is also excluded for responsible men.

A sober middle course is that of the responsible man. He does not know "absolute good" or have "ultimate knowledge of good and evil" as does ideological man; [66] he prefers the relatively better to the relatively worse, assesses in the light of the present possibilities, and follows through with an eye to the future. Sobriety, realism, and a measure of pragmatism belong to this course.[67] The tone is evident in this sentence: "One's task is not to turn the world upside-down, but to do what is necessary at the given place and with a due consideration of reality." [68]

[61] *E*, pp. 227-40.   [62] *Ibid.*, p. 228.   [63] *Ibid.*, p. 127.   [64] *Ibid.*, p. 133.
[65] *Ibid.*, p. 229.
[66] *Ibid.*, p. 234. Nazism is included in the ideologies about which Bonhoeffer writes so eloquently: "Ideologies vent their fury on man and then leave him as a bad dream leaves the waking dreamer. The memory of them is bitter. They have not made the man stronger or more mature; they have only made him poorer and more mistrustful. In the hour of this unhappy awakening, if God reveals Himself to men as the Creator before whom man can live only as the creature, that is grace and the blessing of poverty." (P. 216.)
[67] *Ibid.*, p. 233.   [68] *Ibid.*

Yet is this in fact a middle course that excludes all elements of extremism, of simple sanction and ripe revolution? More precisely the responsible man rules out the extremes *as normal and normative patterns and procedures.* They are not ruled out as *exceptional* instances of Christian behavior brought on by necessity.

The reason Bonhoeffer wants to hold to all possibilities is a christological one. He does not want to exclude on principle any behavior in the *vita christiana* that might be the appropriate moral expression of the great marks, even "extremes," of incarnation, crucifixion, and resurrection.

In Jesus Christ we have faith in the incarnate, crucified and risen God. In the incarnation we learn of the love of God for His creation; in the crucifixion we learn of the judgment of God upon all flesh; and in the resurrection we learn of God's will for a new world. There could be no greater error than to tear these three elements apart. . . .[69]

A Christian ethic must omit none of these grand strokes of Christ's life nor base itself upon a single one alone. It is rather the interplay of all three in the unity of *the* Life that is both the deepest source and highest standard of Christian existence. This means that an openness to virtually every possibility and an elasticity of behavior are integral to the Christian life.[70] Yet the coherency and consistency of the Christian's action are not lost in performing one action at one time and its opposite at another. The unity lies in conforming to the *Gestalt Christi* in the given time and place and finding the fitting response there (*sachgemaess*); that is, determining whether the conforming action is one of "incarnation" (affirmation and cooperation), "crucifixion" (judgment and rejection) or "resurrection" (bold creativity and newness). *Ethics* and *Letters and Papers from Prison* make clear that it is only by standing in the midst of the world, i.e., by "living unreservedly in life's duties, problems, successes and failures, experiences and perplexities," [71] and there taking one's orientation from "a live, dynamic and compelling encounter with the source of moral guidance" [72] that one learns these dialectics of "resistance and submission." [73]

---

[69] *Ibid.,* pp. 130-31.

[70] The images of polyphony and *cantus firmus* which so many find attractive in Bonhoeffer's picture of the Christian life also have christological referents. ("May not the attraction and importance of polyphony in music consist in its being a reflection of this Christological fact [the divine and human nature] and therefore of our *vita christiana?*") ("20 May 1944," *LPP,* pp. 150-51.) These images are used to portray the full range of human experience as belonging to the Christian life. Indeed, *to be Christian* the Christian life should know life in all its dimensions. The rudimentary reason is that incarnation, crucifixion, and resurrection are the very dynamics of reality; thus, he who would be a real man must "correspond to reality" in his very being. The polyphony of life is the shape of grace and the means to maturity.

[71] "21 July 1944," *LPP,* p. 193.   [72] Long, *A Survey of Christian Ethics,* p. 117.

[73] Dr. Bethge gave the German edition of *Letters and Papers from Prison* the title *Widerstand und Ergebung*—"Resistance and Submission." It carries both Bonhoeffer's picture of the Christian life and his own living of it; not least of all does it characterize the movement in Bonhoeffer's

The whole must be held to even though the single deed mirrors but a part.

> . . . A Christian ethic constructed solely on the basis of the incarnation would lead directly to the compromise solution. An ethic which was based solely on the cross or the resurrection of Jesus would fall victim to radicalism and enthusiasm. Only in the unity is the conflict resolved.[74]

This unity, calling for polyphony in the Christian life, forbids making radicalism or compromise into *norms* while yet not excluding radical or compromising deeds as possibilities—and occasionally necessities. These extraordinary acts are usually *"Grenzfall"* cases and as such are of the utmost importance. (They most often arise in the time and place of the "ethical" in Bonhoeffer's sense.) But they are peripheral and uncharacteristic, despite the fact they may mirror the most vivid and moving pictures of incarnation, crucifixion, and resurrection in the common life of uncommon times.

Correspondence with reality as the foundation of the responsible life is thus not a separate middle course between polar extremist patterns. It is not the golden mean or any other middle way that eliminates *in principle* extreme courses of action on the right or the left. Rather, it is a diversity of deeds unified only in the Christ who is the coherence of the real. This diversity may include moments of virtually suspended extremism; but as a matter of course incarnation (affirmation of this world) will be counterpoint to crucifixion (judgment of this world) and resurrection (creativity for a new world). Each points to the other and back again, a diversity that has, in Christ, a unity in the far-ranging movements of grace.[75]

> . . . It is quite wrong to establish a separate theology of the incarnation, a theology of the cross, or a theology of the resurrection, each in opposition to the others, by a misconceived absolutization of one of these parts; it is equally wrong to apply the same procedure to a consideration of the Christian life.[76]

So whether correspondence with reality is viewed from the knowledge that the *Gestalt Christi* has formed reality to the point that "from its origin there is inherent in every thing its own law of being"[77] or whether correspondence

---

acts of active and passive resistance. The title was taken from a letter that is further documentation of the discussion above. "It is therefore impossible to define the boundary between resistance and submission on abstract principles; but both of them must exist, and both must be practised. Faith demands this elasticity of behavior. Only so can we stand our ground in each situation as it arises and turn it to gain." ("21 February 1944," *LPP*, p. 119.)

[74] *E*, p. 131.

[75] The notes for *Ethics* include the following: "High tensions in extremes, paradoxes as divine truth and reality, but not as psychical postures [*seelische Haltungen*]—steps of Christian living." (Dietrich Bonhoeffer, Microfilm No. 395, Frame No. 21. New York: Union Theological Seminary Library. Brackets added.) "Christ is not radical and yet radical. Pondered reality. Order and disorder. Life is both." (*Ibid.*, Frame No. 59.)

[76] *E*, p. 131. [77] *Ibid.*, p. 236.

with reality is viewed from knowledge of the contrapuntal dynamics of reality
—incarnation, crucifixion, resurrection—the outcome for the Christian life is
the same; namely, that the Christian life has a polyphonic tone; it moves
through a wide range of human experience draining the cups of joy and sor-
row; yet all the while it possesses, as a matter of normal course, a measured
character that shows in largely unreflected fulfilling of rather obvious duties;
it seeks extremist solutions only in time of necessity, never absolutizing extreme action as the standard profile of Christian conduct; nevertheless, it opens
itself and remains open to the fact that extremist deeds may be Christ's concrete command in the given situation and thus must be undertaken with full
resolution.

The decisive note here for later discussion is Bonhoeffer's designation of
extremist deeds as *exceptional* rather than *normal*, as *crucial* but *not normative*,
and thus not permitted except in matters of necessity.

The Deed of Free Responsibility. But Bonhoeffer's was not a normal time,
and his German Lutheran heritage was severely tried. When it became brittle
and finally splintered, Bonhoeffer, while yet working within this heritage,
sought its revision and repair.

In delineating the structure of responsible life Bonhoeffer interposes a crucial
element missing in that heritage and thus missing during the years of the Third
Reich, an omission with shuddering consequences. This was the deed of free
responsibility, the undertaking of a courageous venture that *simultaneously*
violates the laws of the civil order *and* conforms to the form of Christ in the
world (reality).

Here is Bonhoeffer's rationale for conspiracy. It is not coincidental that the
matter is taken up in a subsection on statecraft.[78] More specifically the discussion centers on breaking civil law,[79] under what conditions and toward what
end.

Bonhoeffer's remarks about law-breaking are not extensive, and they raise
more questions than they answer. But they bear directly upon his resistance
and should thus be before the reader.

In the course of historical life there comes a point where the exact observance
of a formal law of a state . . . suddenly finds itself in violent conflict with the in-
eluctable necessities of the lives of men; at this point responsible and pertinent action leaves behind it the domain of principle and convention, the domain of the
normal and regular, and is confronted by the extraordinary situation of ultimate

---

[78] *Ibid.,* pp. 235 ff.

[79] A slip of paper among Bonhoeffer's drafts for his *Ethics* includes this notation: "The
exaggeration of thinking in legal terms, as if the world could be saved through law. The
necessity of going beyond the law. The revolutionary." (Microfilm No. 395, Frame No. 66.)

necessities, a situation which no law can control. It was for this situation that Machiavelli in his political theory coined the term *necessità*. In the field of politics this means that the technique of statecraft has now been supplanted by the necessity of state. There can be no doubt that such necessities exist; to deny their existence is to abandon the attempt to act in accordance with reality. But it is equally certain that these necessities are a primary fact of life itself and cannot, therefore, be governed by any law or themselves constitute a law. They appeal directly to the free responsibility of the agent, a responsibility which is bound by no law. They create a situation which is extraordinary; they are by nature peripheral and abnormal events. They no longer leave a multiplicity of courses open to human reason but they confront it with the question of the *ultima ratio*. In the political field this *ultima ratio* is war, but it can also be deception and the breaking of treaties for the sake of one's own vital needs.[80]

Bonhoeffer knows about *necessità*. He wrote this section of *Ethics* between seditious assignments at the height of his conspiratorial activity. The passing mention of "deception . . . in the political field" is an understatement of the first order. It was his daily diet at the time he penned these words (1941-42).

Yet Bonhoeffer says little about measuring the arrival of *necessità*. Except for the mention of Machiavelli no political theories are brought forward which might prove helpful. The reader justifiably has the feeling that this is the reflection of one who is a relative novice to the strange and risky art of *ultima ratio* action and a stranger to those forces which suddenly compel him to make sense of what he "knows" he must do. He is not a professional revolutionary in any sense. Still he knows that an "extraordinary situation" is here and it calls for *ultima ratio* action *in order to* return to a course of events where just such action will no longer be necessary. Bonhoeffer is extremely guarded about justifying such desperate action and regards it in the final analysis as the venture of the individual in free responsibility, a venture that must be decided upon and undertaken by oneself, a venture in fact justifiable *not* by law, only by *necessità,* a venture that dare not become normative behavior, a venture finally delivered up to God alone for judgment. Such a venture becomes the last of the last resorts. It is undertaken only when all other "responsible" deeds have not accomplished the realization of reality. In its radicalism it exists not at the center of Christian life at all, but at the very farthest edges. Yet it is precisely there, at the point of most intense turbulence and uncertainty, when the boundary situation of life is thrust upon the individual with its demand for concrete positive response, that the radical venture must be carried out if the will of God is to be done.

The consideration of such extra-legal, *ultima ratio* action, belongs to the work of the "liberated conscience." That is, the deed of free responsibility may be

[80] *E*, pp. 238-39.

carried out in *good* conscience *if* "Jesus Christ has become my conscience."[81]

What does Bonhoeffer mean? For him the concept of conscience advances beyond, but does not negate, the conventional understanding (i.e., that faculty of accusation which creates guilt feelings in response to the transgression of laws and mores). But it is more; in its most basic sense conscience is the primal summons of a man to recover his lost unity and discover his authentic selfhood. In Jesus Christ this origin and goal of conscience is found[82] and a man's ego is liberated to be directed to the welfare of others.[83] The law itself no longer stands as a final boundary between a man and the good of his neighbor in those situations where obedience to law and deputyship conflict. Conscience as a faculty of accusation and an advocate of the law is still operative, to be sure; but it does not have the last word.

. . . The liberated conscience is still what it was as the natural conscience, namely the warner against transgression of the law of life. But the law is no longer the last thing; there is still Jesus Christ; and for that reason in the contest between conscience and concrete responsibility, the free decision must be given for Christ. This does not mean an everlasting conflict, but the winning of ultimate unity; for indeed the foundation, the essence and the goal of concrete responsibility is the same Jesus Christ who is the Lord of conscience. Thus responsibility is bound by conscience, but conscience is set free by responsibility.[84]

Law nevertheless remains a strong boundary, and "natural conscience" as its representative must not be ignored. Bonhoeffer is most tentative about the use of illegal, *ultima ratio* action, as is transparent in the following passage. On the other hand, the responsible man can perform this deed in good conscience ("liberated conscience"); therefore, he does not lack resolution in carrying through.

. . . The *ultima ratio* lies beyond the laws of reason, it is irrational action. The true order is completely reversed if the *ultima ratio* itself is converted into a rational law, if the peripheral case is treated as the normal, and if *necessità* is made a technique. Baldwin was right when he said that there was only one greater evil than violence and that this was violence as a principle, as a law and a standard. . . .

---

[81] *Ibid.*, p. 244.   [82] *Ibid.*

[83] *Ibid.* The reader is reminded of Bonhoeffer's anthropology.

[84] *E*, p. 247. The notes for *Ethics* include: "The conscience resting (tranquil) in Christ is not to be confused with the sleeping conscience!" (Microfilm No. 395, Frame No. 78.)

What Bonhoeffer means by "law" is frustratingly difficult to uncover. He uses it in many different contexts, sometimes meaning civil law, sometimes something he calls the "innate laws of creation," sometimes "the law of life," sometimes "law" as contrasted with "gospel," sometimes divine law exemplified in the Decalogue. At times the meaning is clear in the context, at times not. For our purposes here, however, the inexactitude is not too serious because the meaning is clear that the deed of free responsibility is an act violating civil law and occasionally divine law.

he did not wish to see the extraordinary and peripheral case confused with the normal case, with the law. He wished to preserve the relative order which is secured through the pertinent observance of law and convention, when to abandon this order for the sake of a peripheral event would mean chaos.

The extraordinary necessity appeals to the freedom of the men who are responsible. There is now no law behind which the responsible man can seek cover, and there is, therefore, also no law which can compel the responsible man to take any particular decision in the face of such necessities. In this situation there can only be a complete renunciation of every law, together with the knowledge that here one must make one's decision as a free venture, together also with the open admission that here the law is being infringed and violated and that necessity obeys no commandment. Precisely in this breaking of the law the validity of the law is acknowledged, and in this renunciation of all law, and in this alone, one's own decision and deed are entrusted unreservedly to the divine governance of history.[85]

Bonhoeffer's hesitation in approving the use of violence and his full rejection of transposing its use into a principle generate his conclusion that the man of free responsibility must stand under the accusation of him who acknowledges law as the ultimate authority. If the man of law incurs guilt by *not* venturing the necessary, but illegal deed, the man of free responsibility incurs guilt by breaking the law.[86] Law is therefore a strongly binding limit in Bonhoeffer's thought, but it is not the final one; it is the outer boundary in the normal course of events, but it is not the ultimate boundary for all events. Beyond lies the unique, the irrational, the extraordinary, the illegal, the precarious zone of the free man's responsibility facing the hazards of the *Grenzfall, necessità, ultima ratio,* the exceptional command of God. And beyond this there is no longer "ethics," but only (!) repentance, forgiveness, grace, justification, newness of life.[87]

In the section "State and Church" Bonhoeffer again underscores the private, individualistic and unprogrammatic nature of free responsibility. "Disobedience [to government] can never be anything but a concrete decision in a single particular case." [88]

---

[85] *E*, pp. 239-40.

[86] Dr. Bethge relates a discussion involving Bonhoeffer, and his brother-in-law, Hans von Dohnanyi. The latter asked Bonhoeffer about the word of Jesus to Peter that he who takes up the sword will die by the sword. Bonhoeffer replied that the word was valid for their circle as well, that they (the conspirators) fall under this judgment, too, but that just such men who take the reality of this word upon themselves are needed in tyrannical times. (*Biography*, p. 530.)

[87] Another of the slips of paper among Bonhoeffer's materials reads: "Recognition of the necessity of the situation—*necessità*—as the borderline case, *ultima ratio*—irrational, war, divine control of history. Violence as *ultima ratio* or as principle? The eternal law—which is last, an eternal law or the free responsibility before God? *An irresolvable dilemma!* Remains open! Also the doer of the deed must remain open for the indictment! Forgiveness! Grace! Justification!" (Microfilm No. 395, Frame No. 19. Emphasis in the original.) Here the dilemma is posed as one of adherence to eternal law or free responsibility. In *Ethics*, however, observance of state law and not only divine law is in irresolvable conflict with free responsibility.

[88] *E*, p. 343.

. . . Even in cases where the guilt of the government is extremely obvious, due consideration must still be given to the guilt which has given rise to this guilt. The refusal of obedience in the case of a particular historical and political decision of government must therefore, like this decision itself, be a venture undertaken on one's own responsibility. A historical decision cannot be entirely resolved into ethical terms; there remains a residuum, the venture of action. That is true both of the government and of its subjects.[89]

But the fact that Bonhoeffer stakes disobedience and resistance at the very edge of normal Christian existence does not cause him to shrink from such action as commanded of Christians. Its abnormal character does not make it any less the command of Christ. In fact the striking item in *Ethics* is precisely the disproportionate space given such themes as the deed of free responsibility and taking on the guilt of others.[90]

Freedom and Responsibility. From the discussion of the unlawful, responsible deed, Bonhoeffer moves *directly* to the subjects of acceptance of guilt and freedom. "From what has just been said it emerges that the structure of responsible action includes both readiness to accept guilt and freedom." [91]

The relation of responsibility to freedom is noteworthy for its subtle but substantial shift in the thirties and forties. The breaking of law is a convenient case in point.

Although Bonhoeffer, in *The Cost of Discipleship,* expounds Romans 13 in a way that matches any "two-kingdoms" call for submission to the governing powers,[92] state law cannot be considered a strong ethical boundary for Bon-

---

[89] *Ibid.,* pp. 343-44.

[90] The following outline is among Bonhoeffer's notes for *Ethics*: "The scope of responsibility: 1) the Commandments 2) the divine mandates 3) the given vocation 4) the free, spontaneous, undertaken responsibility." (Microfilm No. 395, Frame No. 19.) All are treated in *Ethics* but the last has a special emphasis and urgency. This is all the more striking in light of its highly exceptional character for Bonhoeffer. It is of great significance that almost all references are in sections reflecting resistance and that its chief consideration is in the subsection on statecraft. Most telling of all, as will be shown, is that this theme first comes to the fore only after Bonhoeffer enters the conspiracy.

[91] *E,* p. 240.

[92] *CD,* p. 293. ("To resist the [governing] power is to resist the ordinance of God, who has so ordered life that the world exercises dominion by force and Christ and Christians conquer by service.")
A version of the two-kingdoms stance turns up in an interesting way at a time Bonhoeffer had left this behind. He prepared his own defence for the hearings held while he was in Tegel Military Prison. In the extant notes the following is addressed to his interrogator, Military Court Counsel Roeder.
". . . If people wish to know my view of the Christian's duty of obedience to the governing authorities, they should read my commentary on Romans 13 in my book, *The Cost of Discipleship.* The appeal to submit to the will and demands of authority for the sake of Christian conscience has probably seldom been expressed more strongly than there. That is my personal position in

hoeffer at this time.[93] But divine law can. Murder, for example, is a boundary that cannot be passed.[94] Bonhoeffer's reason is as christological as ever. Because Jesus is the Author, Giver, and Fulfiller of the divine law the disciple may never willfully and knowingly violate it.[95]

In *Ethics* this is no longer the case. Now "there is a freedom . . . from the whole of the divine law, a freedom which breaks this law, but only to give effect to it anew." [96] The freedom is grounded in Jesus as the Redeemer. "It is precisely by Him that [responsible action] will be set free from the [divine] law for the responsible deed." [97]

In other words, from *The Cost of Discipleship* to *Ethics* an opening has occurred, an opening for a rare but real exception to keeping the divine law.

The shift can be followed in more generalized terms. In *The Cost of Discipleship* the key word is single-minded obedience. This is what is commanded. But in *Ethics* it is freedom, permission, liberty [98] that are commanded. Bonhoeffer certainly does not drop obedience as a key term for Christian ethics, but now he always adds "and freedom" when speaking of obedience; too, he now speaks of a real tension between obedience and freedom.[99] They stand in tension with and complement each other. "The man of responsibility stands between obligation and freedom." [100] In *The Cost of Discipleship* there is no tension between freedom and obedience; it is the latter which is commanded, not the former. The shift can be summarized in this way: in *The Cost of Discipleship* the linkup of responsibility is with single-minded obedience; in *Ethics* it is with freedom.[101]

This formulation is overly sharp in that obedience to divine law is also a strong boundary in *Ethics,* as has been shown. But the formulation does point to a change extremely important in light of Bonhoeffer's clandestine resistance activity; namely, the change from divine law as an *absolute* boundary in ethics to a very strong *secondary* one. The difference is the wedge that opens the way for the exception. In Bonhoeffer's case, the exception was tyrannicide.

---

this matter. I cannot judge what such personal arguments mean legally, but I cannot imagine that they can simply be ignored." (Dietrich Bonhoeffer, *Widerstand und Ergebung,* ed. Eberhard Bethge [Munich: Chr. Kaiser Verlag, 1970], p. 75.)

[93] *CD,* p. 289. ("No law of the world can interfere with this fellowship [of the Church]. . . . The Church can never tolerate any limits set to the love and service of the brethren.") However, and in accord with Bonhoeffer's exegesis of Romans 13, the breaker of the law is to endure with patience any consequent suffering meted out by the state. Though laws must sometimes be broken for the sake of serving others, rebellion and revolution are categorically ruled out here by Bonhoeffer. (*Ibid.,* p. 291.) The Christian does not even ask for the rights accorded other citizens. (*Ibid.,* p. 156.) The Church cannot tolerate limits set against love of neighbor but "the Christian life is a life of crucifixion." (*Ibid.,* p. 342.)

[94] *CD,* p. 143. [95] *Ibid.* [96] *E,* p. 261. [97] *Ibid.* [98] *Ibid.,* p. 281. [99] *Ibid.,* p. 253.
[100] *Ibid.*
[101] A draft for *Ethics* written in 1941–42 includes the sentence: "The content of the responsibility of Jesus Christ for men is love; its form is freedom." ("Die Geschichte und das Gute," *GS* III, 466.)

It must be emphasized that in both cases the final referent is not divine law but Jesus Christ. In *The Cost of Discipleship* it is because Jesus Christ is the Author, Giver, and Fulfiller of divine law that it is an impassable boundary. In *Ethics* Bonhoeffer found Jesus Christ as the Responsible Man par excellence, the Bestower of Freedom, and the Redeemer of the man who incurs guilt in venturing the deeds of free responsibility. Now divine law becomes a passable boundary in those rare moments of *necessità* when it is imperative to transgress this boundary in order to meet the claims of God and neighbor.

Acceptance of Guilt and Responsibility. If deputyship is the master mark of responsibility, acceptance of guilt (*Schulduebernahme*)[102] is the heart of deputyship. As noted above, Bonhoeffer moves *directly* from discussing the deed of free responsibility to discussing the acceptance of guilt. Again the first and all-important fact is the christological one. Jesus did not seek first of all to be good or to preserve his innocence. Rather, he freely took upon himself the guilt of others. Responsible men should do the same.[103]

Essentially it is such an understanding that stands behind Bonhoeffer's move away from the ascetic direction of his earlier pacifism to the new direction of actively sharing in the guilt of his fellowmen and his nation through conspiracy. With the acceptance of guilt Bonhoeffer shifts from the pacifism and indeed the whole tone of the last half of *The Cost of Discipleship* to solidarity with the responsible and guilty men who stand behind the pages of *Ethics*. With them he bears the responsibility for Germany's actions as well as the heavy burden of rectifying them; he joins the conspiring but responsible men who, in their very effort to undo Hitler, become guilty through entanglement in an ambiguous mesh of evil. And he also bears the guilt of the German Church and his own bourgeois heritage. Through this personal *Schulduebernahme* on behalf of all these, Bonhoeffer moves away from his momentary fascination with saintliness into the deeper dimensions of deputyship where guilt is not merely accepted through sympathetic understanding, but rather is borne through assertive and often agonizing action. Often, however, this is not guilt directly resultant from his own actions but one that knows the dimensions of "collective" guilt.[104] Yet in any case the sinner is to follow the Sinless One in taking on the guilt of other men whether that guilt is directly the sinner's or not.

To maintain one's innocence in a setting such as that of the Third Reich, even to the point of *not* plotting Hitler's death, would be irresponsible action.

---

[102] *Schulduebernahme* is a strong word in German. "Acceptance" is a good translation if the reader recognizes the force of Bonhoeffer's term. It is acceptance as a full transfer and taking possession of guilt; it is taking guilt upon oneself as one's own.

[103] *E*, p. 241; *ibid.*, pp. 110 ff. Excerpts follow later in this chapter.

[104] See "The Confession of Guilt," *ibid.*, pp. 113 ff.

To refuse to stand with others trying desperately to topple the perpetrators of mass crimes, to refuse to engage oneself in the demands of *necessità*, would be the selfish act of one who cared for his own innocence, who cared for his own guiltlessness, more than he cared for his guilty brothers. It would be a rejection of deputyship as *the* form of the responsible life and of acceptance of guilt as the heart of deputyship. If responsible men have no choice but to infiltrate Hitler's war machinery, the Christian does not forsake them but joins them. And if in the process he becomes a martyr he will be not a saintly martyr but a guilty one. He may have to forfeit every taint of perfectionism in his pacifism. He may have to join the grotesque, evil enterprises of his very enemy. He may even have to consider and carry out tyrannicide, or actively support those who do. He will bear his colleagues' burdens and share their sinfulness even when they are not related directly to his own actions. And he will do so as an extraordinary form of the *imitatio Christi* in a demonic society.

The preceding paragraphs have abandoned the exposition of Bonhoeffer's writings in an attempt to move ahead somewhat and mirror Bonhoeffer's move from passive to active resistance as this turns upon his theme of the acceptance of guilt. But we must backtrack and show both the theological undergirding and the ethical outcome of this theme.

. . . Jesus is not concerned with the proclamation and realization of new ethical ideals; He is not concerned with Himself being good (Matt. 19:17); He is concerned solely with love for the real man, and for that reason He is able to enter into the fellowship of the guilt of men and take the burden of their guilt upon Himself. Jesus does not desire to be regarded as the only perfect one at the expense of men; He does not desire to look down on mankind as the only guiltless one while mankind goes to its ruin under the weight of its guilt; He does not wish that some idea of a new man should triumph amid the wreckage of a humanity whose guilt has destroyed it. He does not wish to acquit Himself of the guilt under which men die. A love which left man alone in his guilt would not be love for the real man. As one who acts responsibly for the historical existence of men Jesus becomes guilty.[105]

Such is the christological fact. What it means for man follows.

. . . Jesus took upon Himself the guilt of all men, and for that reason every man who acts responsibly becomes guilty. *If any man tries to escape guilt in responsibility he detaches himself from the ultimate reality of human existence.* . . . He sets his own personal innocence above his responsibility for men, and he is blind to the irredeemable guilt which he incurs precisely in this; he is blind also to the fact that real innocence shows itself precisely in a man's entering into the fellowship of guilt for the sake of other men. Through Jesus Christ it becomes an essential part

[105] *E.*, pp. 240-41.

of responsible action that the man who is without sin loves selflessly and for that reason incurs guilt.[106]

The taking on of guilt is not only sympathy and understanding for another's deeds. Nor is it only intercession for others before God. It is full vicarious action, i.e., he who does so answers for the other and bears the consequences. It is real acceptance of real guilt.

When a man takes guilt upon himself in responsibility, and no responsible man can avoid this, he imputes this guilt to himself and to no one else; he answers for it; he accepts responsibility for it. He does not do this in the insolent presumptuousness of his own power, but he does it in the knowledge that this liberty is forced upon him and that in this liberty he is dependent on grace. Before other men the man of free responsibility is justified by necessity; before himself he is acquitted by his conscience; but before God he hopes only for mercy.[107]

The section on the structure of the responsible life ends with both the strong assertion of freedom to do the illegal deed and the reticence to make free responsibility itself normative,[108] a matter already noted above. Bonhoeffer recognized the narrowness of the ledge he was walking. He, the advocate of passive resistance and nonviolence, knew what moral turbulence[109] was churning among the conspirators when finally they had to turn to the very weapons they despised—deception and violence—for use against the enemy who employed them ruthlessly, skillfully, and, for the conspirators, so repulsively. Now the same vile acts were used in the causes of both criminality and justice. The same tools were to serve both Nazism and civility. Yet one set was for the eventual hallowing of the law and the other for the further rule of utter brutality, cynicism, and arbitrariness. Thus the extant portion of this section of *Ethics* concludes as follows:

. . . Whether an action arises from responsibility or from cynicism is shown only by whether or not the objective guilt of the violation of the law is recognized and acknowledged, and by whether or not, precisely in this violation, the law is hallowed. It is in this way that the will of God is hallowed in the deed which arises from freedom. But since this is a deed which arises from freedom, man is not torn asunder

[106] *Ibid.*, p. 241. Emphasis mine. Note Bonhoeffer's continual ontological grounding of these themes. This characterizes all of Bonhoeffer's theology, but it is easily overlooked because he used the vocabulary of personalism and sociality and not ontology. Bonhoeffer was clear in his intents from his earliest writings on. "The sphere of the entity, of 'there is,' of frozen ontological concepts, is thawed into motion by the sociological category [of the person]" (*AB*, p. 16). "The problem is . . . the metaphysic of sociality" (*CS*, p. 26).

[107] *E*, p. 248. The last sentence might be considered a summary of Bonhoeffer's rationale for his active resistance.

[108] *Ibid.*, p. 262.

[109] See the portions excerpted later from "After Ten Years," *LPP*, pp. 1 ff.

in deadly conflict, but in certainty and unity with himself he can dare to hallow the law truly even by breaking it.[110]

The Guilt Accepted. If the understanding of the acceptance of guilt is crucial to Bonhoeffer's pivotal move from pacifism to active resistance, then some considerations about the nature of this guilt are in order.

The passages in *Ethics* speak of guilt in very general terms.[111] Yet Bonhoeffer's own experience of guilt is terrifyingly specific. And while his formulations intend to include far more than his own experience, that experience itself is not omitted as a formative force—on the contrary! What then is the guilt in Bonhoeffer's own setting which stands behind these passages?

Bonhoeffer was conscious of a guilty church even before Hitler came to power. A 1932 sermon includes the ominous sentences:

. . . Must it be that Christendom, which began so revolutionary, is now conservative for all time? [Must it be] that every new movement must break ground without the Church, that the Church always comprehends twenty years later what has actually happened? If it must really be so, then should we be surprised if times come for our Church when the blood of martyrs will be called for? But this blood, if we then really have the courage and fidelity to shed it, will not be so innocent and clear as that of the first witnesses. Our blood will be heavily burdened with our own great guilt, the guilt of the useless servant.[112]

This was before the first crimes were ground out by Hitler's machinery. Bonhoeffer knew of these crimes from the days of their occurrence up to and even after the time of his arrest. The first seven years of this exercise in terror hang as the backdrop for "The Confession of [the Church's] Guilt" written in September, 1940. The reader should not overlook that it was penned at the zenith of Hitler's successes abroad and his popularity at home.

The Church confesses that she has not proclaimed often and clearly enough her message of the one God who has revealed Himself for all times in Jesus Christ and who suffers no other gods beside Himself. She confesses her timidity, her evasiveness, her dangerous confessions. She has often been untrue to her office of guardianship and to her office of comfort. And through this she has often denied to the outcast and to the despised the compassion which she owes them. She was silent when she should have cried out because the blood of the innocent was crying aloud to heaven.[113] She has failed to speak the right word in the right way and at

---

[110] *E*, p. 262.

[111] As with the use of the term "law," "guilt" is employed freely by Bonhoeffer without precision of meaning. Here again it is necessary to attempt to gain some illumination by doing biographical and historical research. One should also remember that Bonhoeffer's essays in *Ethics* were drafts and were never completed to his own satisfaction. ("18 November 1943," *LPP*, p. 70.) For further discussion of "guilt," see pp. 171 ff.

[112] "4. Sonntag nach Trinitatis, 19. Juni 1932," *GS* IV, 71.   [113] The Jews above all.

the right time. She has not resisted to the uttermost the apostasy of faith, and she has brought upon herself the guilt of the godlessness of the masses.

The Church confesses that she has taken in vain the name of Jesus Christ, for she has been ashamed of this name before the world and she has not striven forcefully enough against the misuse of this name for an evil purpose.[114] She has stood by while violence and wrong were being committed under cover of this name. . . .

The Church confesses that she has witnessed the lawless application of brutal force, the physical and spiritual suffering of countless innocent people, oppression, hatred and murder, and that she has not raised her voice on behalf of the victims and has not found ways to hasten to their aid. She is guilty of the deaths of the weakest and most defenceless brothers of Jesus Christ. . . .

The Church confesses herself guilty towards the countless victims of calumny, denunciation and defamation. She has not convicted the slanderer of his wrongdoing, and she has thereby abandoned the slandered to his fate. . . .

The Church confesses herself guilty of breaking all ten commandments, and in this she confesses her defection from Christ. . . . By her own silence she has rendered herself guilty of the decline in responsible action, in bravery in the defence of a cause, and in willingness to suffer for what is known to be right. She bears the guilt of the defection of the governing authority from Christ.[115]

As noted above, Bonhoeffer's basic disappointment with the Confessing Church was its not-being-for-others. This denied the singular essence of the Church. It must not be glossed over that this disillusionment with the Confessing Church came at a time that overlapped Bonhoeffer's contact with members of the military/political conspiracy.[116] Some of these men were Christians, some not. But Bonhoeffer found many among them who did what he and others had hoped and worked for in the Confessing Church: here were men who acted for others and for their nation even when discovery of such action would (and did) mean certain death; men whose action "corresponded with reality" as Bonhoeffer understood reality; men who bore enormous burdens of responsibility in noble fashion; men who felt the weight of guilt because of the crimes committed in Germany's name; men who took this guilt upon themselves and sought to make amends for the suffering left in the wake of the guilty deeds; men who were free enough to undertake the necessary but horrendous plotting of tyrannicide even though such plotting was contrary to all they considered the normal proper bearing of peaceful men. The simultaneous disappointment with the Confessing Church (as well as the Ecumenical Church) and the discovery of Christ's form in quite another community of suffering and deputyship was of incomparable importance to the expansion of the christological horizons in Bonhoeffer's theology. Further evidence is per-

---

[114] The Nazi program of "Practical Christianity" and the various programs of the "German Christians."

[115] E, pp. 113-15.   [116] Biography, pp. 524 ff.

haps necessary to substantiate this claim firmly, yet this fact should be mentioned in the context of Bonhoeffer's experience of the Church's guilt. (Incidentally, we shall meet this same double movement behind the theology of the prison letters.)

The mention of these men introduces the second element of the guilt Bonhoeffer took upon himself, that of his nation. How he regarded this is concealed in the meaning he gave the resistance movement. He saw this most political movement in a most unpolitical way, namely, as an act of repentance.

Among other places this is revealed in Bonhoeffer's important mission for the resistance movement, the visit to Sweden in 1942. In Sigtuna, George Bell, Bishop of Chichester, received a detailed account of the plans and personalities of the resistance from Bonhoeffer and Hans Schoenfeld, who represented another arm of the movement. Bell passed it along in person to Anthony Eden and Sir Stafford Cripps of the British Government, and Ambassador J. G. Winant of the U.S.A. The request for help from the Allies was negative, however.

In the report of the Sigtuna meeting Bell writes of Bonhoeffer's stance.

After Schoenfeld had spoken on this and other matters [postwar German boundaries], Bonhoeffer intervened. He was obviously distressed in his mind as to the lengths to which he had been driven by force of circumstances in the plot for the elimination of Hitler. The Christian conscience, he said, was not quite at ease with Schoenfeld's ideas. "There must be punishment by God. We should not be worthy of such a solution. We do not want to escape repentance. Our action must be understood as an act of repentance." [117]

Visser 't Hooft was another confidant to whom Bonhoeffer had given the resistance plans for delivery to the Allies. And he recalls the identical understanding of resistance and of Germany's defeat which Bonhoeffer had shared with Bell. Bonhoeffer told a circle of friends in Geneva: "Only in defeat can we atone for the terrible crimes we have committed against Europe and the world." [118]

These are not faulty recollections from chance meetings. They come from friends close to Bonhoeffer in settings revolving around Bonhoeffer's resistance assignments. But if the occasional nature of some of these remarks and the fact that Bonhoeffer was speaking to foreigners gives cause to doubt that he actually viewed the resistance activity in this way, one need only turn to the reminiscences of those countrymen who shared his confidence and trust. One

[117] George Bell, Bishop of Chichester, "The Background of the Hitler Plot," *Contemporary Review*, October, 1945, p. 206.

[118] Willem A. Visser 't Hooft, "An Act of Penitence," *I Knew Dietrich Bonhoeffer: Reminiscenses by His Friends,* eds. Ronald Gregor Smith and Wolf-Dieter Zimmermann (New York: Harper, 1966), p. 194.

such comes from Bonhoeffer's landsman, Oscar Hammelsbeck. He was both a confidant of Bonhoeffer's in matters of the military/political conspiracy and a partner in numerous theological and political discussions from 1937-1943.[119] From their exchanges Hammelsbeck concludes that Bonhoeffer's active resistance to Hitler was a consequence of "his moral conviction that 'the structure of responsible action includes both readiness to accept guilt and freedom' (*Ethics*, p. 240)." [120]

In Bonhoeffer's eyes his class was guilty as well as his nation. He held his upper bourgeois heritage in high esteem[121] and drank deeply from it for his opposition to Nazism.[122] But he was especially aware of the fatal sins of omission that allowed Hitler his course.[123] One such was the lack of civil courage which prevented the necessary free and responsible action that the times demanded.[124] His class knew civil *legal* responsibility well. But civil courage for the illegal but responsible deed it did not. Thus when Bonhoeffer writes of "sins of strength" [125] he asks whether the bourgeois community's sin is not the fear of free responsibility.[126] And there is the letter to his fiancee: "How many 'scruples' (*Bedenklichkeiten*) repeatedly prevent our class from acting. I believe that the weakness of our class is based on its justified or unjustified scruples. Simple people are different. They make more mistakes, but they also do more good, because their road to action does not lead through scruple." [127] The recollection of a fellow inmate at Tegel Prison is appropriate here as well. After the war he reported on his conversations with Bonhoeffer. Included

[119] Oscar Hammelsbeck, "In Discussion with Bonhoeffer," *I Knew DB*, p. 179.

[120] *Ibid.*, p. 182. In a letter to the author Dr. Hammelsbeck says: "Your question about the place of acceptance of guilt and responsibility in Bonhoeffer's move to active resistance goes to the center of my relationship with Dietrich Bonhoeffer. . . . You are certainly correct that 'acceptance of guilt' and 'deputyship-laden responsibility' were decisive for Bonhoeffer." (Letter of February 19, 1969, from Dr. Oscar Hammelsbeck, Heiligenkirchen, West Germany.)

[121] "2 March 1944," *LPP*, pp. 60-61.

[122] One indication is that the entire Bonhoeffer family vehemently opposed Hitler from the very beginning, and Dietrich was the only one among them to do so from fundamental and explicit theological tenets. The common familial elements (and to a large extent, class elements) which made for resistance are beautifully and movingly expressed in the farewell letter of Klaus Bonhoeffer (brother of Dietrich) to his children shortly before his execution. This is published in: Dietrich and Klaus Bonhoeffer, *Auf dem Wege zur Freiheit: Gedichte und Briefe aus der Haft*, ed. Eberhard Bethge (Berlin: Lettner Verlag, 1954), pp. 43-48.

[123] In Tegel Bonhoeffer reflected at length upon his bourgeois heritage. Most of this is in the form of an incomplete novel and play. In the former a member of a bourgeois family comments on the sad state of affairs in the nation. "It was not the guilt of the young . . . that the elderly let things take their course with such lack of insight and with such indifference— that was the worst of all." (Dietrich Bonhoeffer, "Romanversuch" [unpublished portion; Tegel Prison], p. 4. Used with the permission of Eberhard Bethge.)

[124] "After Ten Years," *LPP*, p. 5.

[125] Those at the heart of a man's or community's strong points and acclaimed excellence.

[126] "8 July 1944," *LPP*, p. 183.

[127] Maria von Wedemeyer-Weller, "The Other Letters from Prison," *Union Seminary Quarterly Review*, Fall, 1967, pp. 25-26.

is this statement: "[Bonhoeffer] related that . . . the leading German families had, in part, atoned for their guilt in that they attempted to do away with Hitler, although much too late."[128]

Bonhoeffer was thus poignantly conscious of the guilt of his church, nation, and class in the sordid crucifixions carried out in the Third Reich. If there were to be martyrs they would indeed be guilty martyrs. They, too, were guilty in various ways and degrees for the rise of the Third Reich.

Acceptance of guilt meant taking on this collective guilt as one's own even when it was not directly resultant from one's own actions, even when one vehemently opposed the very causes that gave rise to it. Acceptance of guilt was not passive but was rather a dimension of vicarous action; it was deputy-ship among sinners. In Bonhoeffer's particular case it included exercising solidarity with those who were constrained to do evil, who were constrained to break not only state law but divine law in order to eliminate the *Fuehrer* who had become the *Verfuehrer*.[129] Responsibility called for the real acceptance of real guilt, one's own and others'. Bonhoeffer took the step of *Schulduebernahme* and with it left behind the ascetically tinged pacifism of *The Cost of Discipleship,* as will be shown in detail later. With this step he entered the ambiguous entanglements of the military/political conspiracy.

The Biography of Acceptance of Guilt. There is a relative paucity of biographical data for the move into the labyrinth of active conspiracy, but there is enough to post the way Bonhoeffer traveled.

When Bonhoeffer went to the United States in 1939 he was still a pacifist. He and Paul Lehmann discussed a book Bonhoeffer had read on the crossing, Hermann Rauschning's analysis of Nazism, *The Revolution of Nihilism: Warning to the West.* Lehmann told Bonhoeffer that this book was an important influence in moving him from advocating pacifism to advocating revolution. Bonhoeffer replied that the book had actually confirmed his pacifism. The discussion then turned to the question of how to live in a setting of turbulent change. But the point is that Bonhoeffer was a self-proclaimed pacifist as late as mid-1939.[130]

---

[128] Professor Gaetano Latmiral, "Letter to Dr. Gerhard Leibholz," from excerpts published in the *Biographie,* p. 955. Dr. Leibholz is the husband of Bonhoeffer's twin sister.

The reader may also wish to see additional sources such as the poem "The Past" (*LPP,* pp. 215 ff.) and the "Dramenfragment" (*GS* III, 478 ff.).

[129] The reference is to Bonhoeffer's 1933 radio address in which he warned that the "leader" (*Fuehrer*) might become the "deceiver" (*Verfuehrer*) if Hitler's office (*Amt*) were not properly understood and limited. See "Der Fuehrer und der einzelne in der jungen Generation," *GS* II, 22 ff.

[130] Interview with Paul Lehmann, March 13, 1968, Union Theological Seminary, New York. On another occasion Dr. Lehmann wrote: "His pacifism may have been rooted in an inbred Lutheran disquiet about the anarchy to which revolutionary social change is prone. If so, it was due no less to his unwillingness to accept life in this world as a mere 'holding action' until the

In New York Bonhoeffer wrestled with the question of remaining in the States or returning to Germany. A most illuminating diary entry makes transparent just how christological Bonhoeffer's decision was and how heavily the question of the place of responsibility weighed in that decision. The entry of June 9 reads in part:

> . . . Great projects always simply lead us to where we stand ourselves. But we ought only be found where He is. Indeed we can be nowhere else than where He is. Whether you are working over there, or I in America, we are all only where He is. . . . Or have I run away from Him after all, from the place He expects me to be? The place where He is for me? [131]

Bonhoeffer soon decided he had "run away . . . from the place He expects me to be." Responsibility as a theme resonates clearly in the oft-cited letter of June, 1939, to Reinhold Niebuhr; the acceptance of guilt echoes throughout these sentences as well.

> . . . Sitting here in Dr. Coffin's garden I have had the time to think and to pray about my situation and that of my nation and to have God's will for me clarified. I have come to the conclusion that I have made a mistake in coming to America. I must live through this difficult period of our national history with the Christian people of Germany. I will have no right to participate in the reconstruction of Christian life in Germany after the war if I do not share the trials of this time with my people. My brothers in the Confessional Synod wanted me to go. They may have been right in urging me to do so; but I was wrong in going. Such a decision each man must make for himself. Christians in Germany will face the terrible alternative of either willing the defeat of their nation in order that Christian civilization may survive, or willing the victory of their nation and thereby destroying our civilization.

---

triumph of the spirit in the second coming of Christ." (Paul Lehmann, "Paradox of Discipleship," *I Knew Dietrich Bonhoeffer*, p. 44.) There is a great deal in Rauschning's prophetic book that could well have served to confirm a pacifism such as Dr. Lehmann describes. For example, Rauschning uses the word "revolution" as a sweeping category designating violent destruction of all order. (Hermann Rauschning, *The Revolution of Nihilism: Warning to the West*, trans. E. W. Dickes [New York: Longmans, Green and Co., 1939], passim.) He speaks of "dynamism" as "the will to anarchy" (*ibid.*, p. 267) and says that this dynamism combined with violent means is the motor of Nazism. Rauschning also sees the answer to the nihilist revolution only in the development of an "ethical and religious *fronde*" (*ibid.*, pp. 118 ff.). The battle is pictured as one of life and death between Nazism on the one hand and "the European society of nations," "civilization of the West," and "Christianity" on the other (*ibid.*, p. 67). Again and again the Nazi "revolution" (Rauschning's designation) is one of violence, nihilism, and anarchy, and the opposition necessary to stop it must be a politics profoundly informed by ethical and religious truths. While there may have been much in this book with which Bonhoeffer may have taken issue, it is also clear that there is much that could well have given him reason to say it confirmed his pacifism, given Dr. Lehmann's suggestive conjectures about the roots of that pacifism.

[131] "Tagebuch der Amerikareise," *GS* I, 293-94.

I know which of these alternatives I must choose; but I cannot make the choice in security.[132]

The diary mirrors both the struggle and the decisive lines forming Bonhoeffer's decision to return.

. . . It is unbearable here for a German; one is simply torn in two. To be here during a catastrophe is simply unthinkable unless matters are so ordained. . . . We cannot part ourselves from our destiny, least of all here abroad.
. . . It is strange how strongly these particular thoughts have affected me these past few days and *how difficult it is for any thoughts about the Una Sancta to make headway.*[133]
. . . By chance I read from II Tim. 4 today: "Do your best to come before winter" —Paul's request of Timothy. Timothy is to share the suffering of Paul and not be ashamed. "Do your best to come before winter"—otherwise it could be too late. That has been pursuing me all day. We are like the soldiers home on leave who feel constrained to return regardless of what may be expected back in action. Not as if we were essential, as if we were necessary (to God?), but simply because that is where our life is and because if we are not back there in the fight, we leave our life behind, we destroy it. It is not a matter of something pious, more like some vital urge. God acts not only through pious feelings, but also through such vital ones. "Do your best to come before winter"—it is not a misuse of Scripture if I let that be said to *me*. May God give me grace to do it.[134]

[132] Reinhold Niebuhr, "The Death of a Martyr." Reprinted from the June 25, 1945 issue of *Christianity and Crisis,* p. 6, by permission of Christianity and Crisis, Inc. In virtually every use of this letter the fact is not mentioned that the letter itself is not extant and that Dr. Niebuhr prefaced these words with: "[Bonhoeffer] wrote something to the effect . . ." (*ibid*). Niebuhr's recollection is not exact. He says Bonhoeffer wrote after the war had begun. (*Ibid.*) This is an impossibility since Bonhoeffer left New York in early July, two months before the invasion of Poland. But the general formulation of the choice Bonhoeffer faced and the reflected theme of responsibility for the future of his nation and church are surely genuine. Dr. Niebuhr's memory for essentials, if not for exact chronology, is trustworthy and virtually the same content is present in other documents. One identical account comes from a friend with whom Bonhoeffer spoke about the decision to return. See Hellmut Traub, "Two Recollections," *I Knew DB,* pp. 156-61. Traub's conversation with Bonhoeffer took place in the late summer of 1939.
[133] "Tagebuch der Amerikareise," *GS* I, 306. Emphasis in the original. The entry is dated 22 June 1939. The translation in *The Way to Freedom* is fully incomprehensible. "Waehrend einer Katastrophe hier zu sein, ist einfach undenkbar . . ." ("To be here during a catastrophe is simply unthinkable . . .") is translated as: "Whereas a catastrophe here is quite inconceivable . . .". (Dietrich Bonhoeffer, *The Way to Freedom,* ed. Edwin Robertson, trans. Edwin Robertson and John Bowden [New York: Harper, 1966], p. 235.) This fully destroys the identification of Bonhoeffer with Germany's fate. The translator here locates the catastrophe in the United States and thereby wholly confuses the passage. Otherwise it is clear: Bonhoeffer cannot be parted from Germany's fate, even by the thoughts of now having access to the *Oekumene* (*Una Sancta*) for which he had worked in Germany.
[134] "Tagebuch der Amerikareise," *GS* I, 309. Emphasis in the original. The entry is dated 26 June 1939.

After analyzing in great detail the various factors involved in Bonhoeffer's decision, Bethge concludes:

What had really caused him to decide . . . to go back to Germany is not equally clear in all the letters and conversations of those days. It was simply his readiness to recognize that he now was and would have to remain a German in full acceptance of guilt and responsibility.[135]

A few long years later Bonhoeffer wrote from prison:

Now I want to assure you [Bethge] that I have not for a moment regretted coming back in 1939—nor any of the consequences, either. I knew quite well what I was doing, and I acted with a clear conscience. I have no wish to cross out of my life anything that has happened since, either to me personally . . . or as regards events in general. And I regard my being kept here . . . as being involved in the part that I had resolved to play in Germany's fate.[136]

The themes of responsibility and acceptance of guilt are expressed here as "the part I had resolved to play in Germany's fate"; not wishing to "cross out . . . anything that has happened since" includes Bonhoeffer's activity in the military/political conspiracy. Bonhoeffer is saying, at the very least, that he anticipated closer contact with the underground even though he did not yet know what "sort of personal decisions [would] be asked from me." [137]

But the most illuminating fact of all is this. On the return crossing Bonhoeffer wrote an essay later to become part of the section on the structure of responsible life in *Ethics;* it was the composition, "The Acceptance of Guilt." [138] He was writing biographically when he penned the following:

[135] *Biography*, pp. 558-59.

[136] "22 December 1943," *LPP*, p. 99. Bonhoeffer's patriotism is best phrased and most forcefully expressed in his poetry. A good example is the final portion of "Der Tod des Mose" ("The Death of Moses"). The entire poem is biographical. It was composed after the failure of the attempt on Hitler's life in July, 1944, thus at a time Bonhoeffer had to reckon with his death. The last stanzas read:

> "God who punishes sin and willingly forgives,
> I have loved this people.
>
> That I have carried its disgrace and burdens,
> and seen its salvation—that is enough.
>
> Seize me, hold me! My staff is sinking;
> Faithful God, prepare my grave."
> (Dietrich and Klaus Bonhoeffer, *Auf dem Wege zur Freiheit*, p. 30.)

[137] "An G. K. A. Bell, Bischof von Chichester," *GS* I, 321. The letter is dated July 22, 1939.

[138] Information of the date of this essay is from the Rev. Otto Dudzus in an interview, October 11, 1968, in Cologne, Germany. My thanks also to Pastor Dudzus for drawing my attention to the passages in Bonhoeffer's American diary which show how central to his decision were his Christology and the motifs of responsibility and acceptance of guilt. Later I came across

. . . Jesus took upon Himself the guilt of all men, and for that reason every man who acts responsibly becomes guilty. If any man tries to escape guilt in responsibility he detaches himself from the ultimate reality of human existence. . . . He sets his own personal innocence above his responsibility for men, and he is blind to the irredeemable guilt which he incurs precisely in this; he is blind also to the fact that real innocence shows itself precisely in a man's entering into the fellowship of guilt for the sake of other men.[139]

What has happened here? Bonhoeffer, the pacifist, after severe disappointment with the Confessing Church's abbreviated efforts toward domestic peace, and the Ecumenical Church's toward international peace, began,[140] in the new setting, to perceive that a continued adherence to a thoroughgoing pacifism was a version of the ethics of private virtuousness, i.e., "setting his own personal innocence above his responsibility for men." He began to regard his pacifism as an illegitimate escape, however legitimately it may have expressed conformation to Christ before this. A thoroughgoing pacifism would invariably have led to fewer contacts with, and less active support for, the very men who embodied the responsibility and acceptance of guilt which the form of Christ in the present extraordinary circumstances demanded. And because conscientious objection was virtually synonymous with subversion and even punishable by death during the Third Reich, the consistent maintenance of his own pacifist stand would not only have endangered his own tasks but would also have brought state suspicion and Gestapo investigation upon his own family and his friends in the conspiracy. It would have been highly irresponsible at a time when they were working hard to stop Hitler's crimes. Pacifism, in this setting, would have been a courageous witness, to be sure; but it would also have been a private act of pietism. In Bonhoeffer's own understanding it would even have been selfish, however understandable, because it would not have been above all for others.

Bonhoeffer has again viewed the change christologically. If Jesus did not seek first of all to be good or to preserve his innocence, if he instead refused to shun the fellowship of guilt and took upon himself the guilt of others, if he

---

confirmation of Dudzus' dating of "The Acceptance of Guilt" in: Eberhard Bethge, "Dietrich Bonhoeffer: Person und Werk," *Die muendige Welt* (Munich: Chr. Kaiser Verlag, 1955), I, 12. Bethge also writes: "[Bonhoeffer] had gone west in order to avoid taking up the sword and he returned in order to take it up after all" (*ibid.,* p. 11). Bonhoeffer had gone to the States to escape the conscription dilemma, and he returned knowing his contacts with the conspiracy would increase.

[139] *E,* p. 241.

[140] No claim is made here for a dramatic decision focusing upon his self-acclaimed pacifism, only that a decisively formative decision was being made and understood in terms of responsibility and acceptance of guilt. This decision and these motifs then gradually affect the pacifism as they are played out in the contact with the men of the conspiracy.

stood in solidarity with those enmeshed in inescapable responsibilities that could not but incur guilt in an evil order—if he, true man, did this, then responsible men should do the same.

It was from a christological foundation, therefore, that Bonhoeffer sketched the structure of the responsible life with the lexicon of deputyship, correspondence with reality, conscience, acceptance of guilt, and freedom. Without a single exception the touchstone of content and direction is Jesus Christ, the Deputy, Reality Personified, the Origin and Goal of Conscience, the Bearer of Guilt and the Bestower of Freedom, even freedom to violate the divine law. This Jesus is the Responsible Person par excellence. It is he to whom we are to conform.

"After Ten Years"

The foregoing themes have now and then touched upon the topic of resistance in the course of their explication by Bonhoeffer. But as essays in theological ethics they were not intended to deal first of all with the actual relationships between theological reflections and the theories and facts of resistance. Such relationships are in fact present at every turn, at times obvious, more frequently veiled. Now the task is to trace these actual, inseparable ties; the task is to draw tightly the acclaimed lines between the theology and ethics of Bonhoeffer and his reflection on resistance.

"After Ten Years," *the* document expressing the spirit and thought of the conspirators, comes from Bonhoeffer's hand. It was a Christmas gift for those resisters closest to Bonhoeffer, written in the winter of 1942 when the race between arrest and success was close. This was also a time Bonhoeffer knew that the Reich Security Head Office was gathering evidence against him. The essay survived the police and bombs in the beams of a house and is now printed as the opening piece in *Letters and Papers from Prison*.[141]

Bonhoeffer's essay is "an account of what we have experienced and learnt in common during these years." [142] "These years" are the ten years of Hitler's reign; "we" are Bonhoeffer and the resisters close to him.

In this tract free responsibility as a theme follows on the heels of a short treatment of the ethics of duty. Free responsibility is interjected here and contrasted with duty for good reason: the ethics of duty was the chief impediment to decisive action against Hitler's continued tyranny.

One example that recurs again and again in the history of German resistance will suffice to underscore the point. The major obstacle preventing a strike by

---

[141] "After Ten Years," *LPP*, pp. 1-17. The information about the essay is taken from the editor's preface, p. xxii.

[142] After Ten Years," *LPP*, p. 1.

the generals against Hitler was their doctrine of command and obedience and their fidelity to oaths, both of which were grounded in a widely held and deeply rooted ethic of duty.[143] These generals were not only in the best position to eliminate Hitler, they were in fact the seat of continued strong dissent from his policies. They did not suffer a lack of severe disagreement with Hitler. Nor can it be said that they lacked commitment to the conviction that he should be ousted in one way or another. What they lacked was an ethic of free responsibility. What they adhered to, on the contrary, was an ethic of duty-as-command-and-obedience and ultimate fidelity to oaths. As a result the generals continued "to do [their] duty by the devil"[144] until Stauffenberg undertook the venture of free responsibility, much too late.

Given this experience of vacillation among the most powerful dissenters from Hitler's politics, it is no surprise that Bonhoeffer confers such importance upon the deed of free responsibility as one of the four main marks of the structure of responsible life.

The thoughts on "Civil Courage" in the Christmas essay comprise a lengthy footnote on Bonhoeffer's critique of the duty ethic. His lines contain a crucial admission that must have been painful for someone whose devotion to his land was as intense as Bonhoeffer's.

. . . In recent years we have seen a great deal of bravery and self-sacrifice, but civil courage hardly anywhere, even among ourselves. To attribute this simply to personal cowardice would be too facile a psychology; its background is quite different. In a long history we Germans have had to learn the need for and the strength of obedience. In the subordination of all personal wishes and ideas to the tasks to which we have been called, we have seen the meaning and greatness of

---

[143] Every history of the military resistance reiterates this point. Here perhaps it is important to mention that Bonhoeffer could become very angry at the generals' failure to act. Further, in the view of a close friend, Franz Hildebrandt, Bonhoeffer's involvement in resistance is probably best understood politically as part of a civil police action to oust rule by a mob of criminals. This civil action in a time of "necessity of state" (*E*, p. 238) should have been taken early by the Army but was not. So it was necessary for civilians to enjoin resistance as civil police action. (Interview with Dr. Franz Hildebrandt, Edinburgh, Scotland, September 17, 1968.) Precisely this reason was clear in Bonhoeffer's conversations with Winfried Maechler. The latter recalls several instances when Bonhoeffer was angry at the generals for their failure to oust Hitler. One was the Fritsch crisis. In January, 1938, Colonel General von Fritsch, the Commander in Chief of the Army, was dismissed by Hitler on a phony charge of homosexual acts. Hitler seized the occasion to fully subordinate all three fighting services to himself and to purge the Army, Navy, and Air Force of higher officers known to be hostile to Nazi policies. The generals nonetheless failed to strike, resign, or carry out some other act that might have toppled Hitler. Bonhoeffer, through Dohnanyi, knew the details of the Fritsch affair and was angry about the inaction of these officers who were, in fact, themselves angry at the arbitrary and underhanded removal of their chief. The Army's failure to carry out the necessary civil police action was a compelling reason, according to Bonhoeffer, for civilians to join political resistance. (Interview with Winfried Maechler, West Berlin, Germany, February 22, 1969.)

[144] "After Ten Years," *LPP*, p. 3.

our lives. We have looked upwards, not in servile fear, but in free trust, seeing in our tasks a call, and in our call a vocation. . . . Calling and freedom were to him [the German] two sides of the same thing. But in this he misjudged the world; he did not realize that his submissiveness and self-sacrifice could be exploited for evil ends. . . . The fact could not be escaped that the German still lacked something fundamental: he could not see the need for free and responsible action, even in opposition to his task and his calling; in its place there appeared on the one hand an irresponsible lack of scruple, and on the other a self-tormenting punctiliousness that never led to action. Civil courage, in fact, can grow only out of the free responsibility of free men. Only now are the Germans beginning to discover the meaning of free responsibility. It depends on a God who demands responsible action in a bold venture of faith, and who promises forgiveness and consolation to the man who becomes a sinner in that venture.[145]

Here is "what we have experienced and learnt in common these years" [146] —the discovery of free responsibility and a God whose concrete command is freedom, permission, liberty; a God whose promise is forgiveness and consolation to those who incur guilt in being deputies.

Nevertheless, Bonhoeffer immediately counters an ethic in which unbound freedom is normative. Certainly the man of unbound freedom knows the necessary deed and can practice the art of compromise as well. He might also be clearly cognizant that compromise may prove the wrong tack and that a fruitful radicalism may be the demand of the hour instead. He is free to move in any and all of these directions. Yet his freedom may prove his undoing in that "he will assent to what is bad so as to ward off something worse, and in so doing he will no longer be able to realize that the worse, which he wants to avoid, might be the better." [147]

With these enigmatic lines Bonhoeffer stops short here of his standing criticism of an ethic that makes free responsibility normative, i.e., an ethic that ignores law as a generally binding boundary. Later in the same essay, however, he concludes that the exceptional act must never be made the normative one, that necessity must not become a principle. The content is unmistakably that of *Ethics*. But now the thoughts are part of the report on the lessons learned from opposition to Hitler.

It is true that all historically important action is constantly overstepping the limits set by these laws. But it makes all the difference whether such overstepping of the appointed limits is regarded in principle as the superseding of them, and is therefore given out to be a law of a special kind, or whether the overstepping is deliberately regarded as a fault which is perhaps unavoidable, justified only if the law and the limit are re-established and respected as soon as possible. It is not necessarily

[145] *Ibid.,* pp. 4-5.   [146] *Ibid.,* p. 1.   [147] *Ibid.,* p. 4.

hypocrisy if the declared aim of political action is the restoration of the law, and not mere self-preservation. The world is, in fact, so ordered that a basic respect for ultimate laws and human life is also the best means of self-preservation, and that these laws may be broken only on the odd occasion in case of brief necessity, whereas anyone who turns necessity into a principle, and in so doing establishes a law of his own alongside them, is inevitably bound, sooner or later, to suffer retribution.[148]

An ethic of private virtuousness is equally unacceptable because of its flight to avoid "the contamination arising from responsible action."[149] While the man of private virtue refuses to dirty his hands in the public arena, injustice will roll on. Thus, "in spite of all that he does, what he leaves undone will rob him of his peace of mind. He will either go to pieces because of this disquiet, or become the most hypocritical of Pharisees."[150]

(It should be noted in passing that such a statement contains an implicit, though only partial, critique of Bonhoeffer's own stance in *The Cost of Discipleship*. Specifically, there is an implicit criticism of his pacifism had he carried through with a consistent, conscientious objection to military service just at the time when requests were being made of him by the conspirators, just at a time when such a witness, noble as it might have been, would have endangered the resistance work of his family and friends. What Bonhoeffer would have left undone would have robbed him of the peace of mind he sought in going to America.)[151]

"After Ten Years" is an account of the resistance experience and not an essay in Christology or theological ethics. Nevertheless, Bonoeffer does not omit deep-running themes of his christological ethic.

. . . We are not Christ, but if we want to be Christians, we must have some share in Christ's large-heartedness by acting with responsibility and in freedom when the hour of danger comes, and by showing a real sympathy that springs, not

---

[148] *Ibid.*, pp. 10-11.

[149] *Ibid.*, p. 4. The notes written at this time include: "Do the necessary, rather than wish to be good." (Microfilm No. 395, Frame No. 108.)

[150] "After Ten Years," *LPP*, p. 4.

[151] In the Christmas essay Bonhoeffer treats more than the ethics of duty, unbound freedom, and private virtue as inadequate for men trying to stand fast in the face of Nazism. The exposition above does not cover more, however, and the reader may wish to consult Bonhoeffer's brief and acute remarks on "reason," "conscience," and "moral fanaticism" in *LPP*, pp. 2-4. The conclusion of the whole is worth quoting:

"Who stands fast? Only the man whose final standard is not his reason, his principles, his conscience, his freedom, or his virtue, but who is ready to sacrifice all this when he is called to obedient and responsible action in faith and in exclusive allegiance to God—the responsible man, who tries to make his whole life an answer to the question and call of God. Where are these responsible people?" (*Ibid.*, p. 4.)

from fear, but from the liberating and redeeming love of Christ for all who suffer. Mere waiting and looking on is not Christian behavior. The Christian is called to sympathy and action, not in the first place by his own sufferings, but by the sufferings of his brethren, for whose sake Christ suffered.[152]

A careful reading of this paragraph uncovers the motifs of responsibility, freedom, suffering, and acting for others (deputyship), all understood from Christ's *pro nobis Sein*.

The paragraph "Of Suffering" must not be passed over.

It is infinitely easier to suffer in obedience to a human command than in the freedom of one's own responsibility. It is infinitely easier to suffer with others than to suffer alone. It is infinitely easier to suffer publicly and honourably than apart and ignominiously. It is infinitely easier to suffer through staking one's life than to suffer spiritually. Christ suffered as a free man alone, apart and in ignomiy, in body and spirit; and since then many Christians have suffered with him.[153]

Because Bonhoeffer is writing of the experiences of those participating in the resistance movement, it is not unjust to consider this an allusion to the character of their suffering. Comparison can be made with the suffering of other patriots as the mass media and mass opinion knew it. The soldier, for example, suffered in obedience to a human command, with others, publicly, honorably, and through staking his life. The contrasting closeness of Christ's suffering to that of the resistance is not a confusion of Christ and Christians by Bonhoeffer ("We are not Christ, but if we want to be Christians . . .");[154] rather it is a statement for the inner security and resolution of others as well as himself, uttered by one very much aware of his pastoral function in this extraordinary community.[155]

Responsibility as responsibility for the future emerges as a major motif in this report. The life of the future generation was very much on the minds of those who had to reckon with their own deaths at any moment. ("We still love life, but I do not think that death can take us by surprise now.")[156]

. . . There remains for us only the very narrow way . . . of living every day as if it were the last, and yet living in faith and responsibility as though there were to be a great future. . . . Thinking and acting for the sake of the coming generation, but being ready to go any day without fear or anxiety—that, in practice, is the spirit in which we are forced to live. It is not easy to be brave and keep that spirit alive, but it is imperative.[157]

---

[152] "After Ten Years," p. 14.   [153] *Ibid.*, pp. 14-15.   [154] Reference is to the quotation above.

[155] Bethge says Bonhoeffer regarded it his pastoral duty to free the consciences of conspirators for executing the necessary action. (Interview with Eberhard Bethge, October 10, 1968, Rengsdorf, West Germany.)

[156] "After Ten Years," *LPP*, p. 17.   [157] *Ibid.*, p. 15.

In that setting faith and responsibility meant throwing innocence to the winds. Morally sensitive men found themselves doers of evil in order to prevent evildoers from doing even worse. But walking the path of guilt, however necessary, left its imprints, its scars. The technique and morality of conspiracy had its hideous effects. There are few paragraphs in the extant literature of morally sensitive conspirators which so poignantly portray their state of heart and mind as do Bonhoeffer's final lines.

We have been silent witnesses of evil deeds; we have been drenched by many storms; we have learnt the arts of equivocation and pretence; experience has made us suspicious of others and kept us from being truthful and open; intolerable conflicts have worn us down and even made us cynical. Are we still of any use? What we shall need is not geniuses, or cynics, or misanthropes, or clever tacticians, but plain, honest, straightforward men. Will our inward power of resistance be strong enough, and our honesty with ourselves remorseless enough, for us to find our way back to simplicity and straightforwardness? [158]

"After Ten Years" in Ethics

A portion of "what we have experienced and learned" was drafted by Bonhoeffer before he presented it to the resisters in the Christmas essay. The treatment of the ethics of duty, unbound freedom, private virtue, and other stances that failed [159] was undertaken earlier. But again it was a setting directly tied to the conspiratorial activity of the Military Counter-Espionage Service (*Abwehr*).

In late 1939 and again in 1940 Hans Oster, second in command of *Abwehr,* "betrayed" Germany by informing the Dutch about the impending invasion of their country. Bonhoeffer knew the details of this and other "treasonous" moves through Hans von Dohnanyi, Oster's right hand man. He underwrote them as supreme acts of free responsibility.[160] Bethge, a constant companion of Bonhoeffer in these days, relates that Oster's act was judged by Bonhoeffer to be the fitting one in a situation in which all ability to move was caught in a paralysis of conscience. It was a *Grenzfall* in which "treason had become true patriotism" and the patriot had to do "what was normally . . . treason." [161] "An officer saw the diabolical reversal of all values, and acted entirely alone so as not in any circumstances, after his experiences in Poland, to pave the way for new outrages in other countries—and the pastor approved of what he did." [162]

---

[158] *Ibid.,* p. 17.   [159] See pp. 63-66, including note 151, p. 66.
[160] *Biography,* p. 579.   [161] *Ibid.*   [162] *Ibid.*

It was at this time and in reflection upon this action (as well as others) that Bonhoeffer began to write the section entitled "Ethics as Formation." Included is:

> . . . What is worse than doing evil is being evil. It is worse when a liar tells the truth than when a lover of truth lies. It is worse when a misanthropist practises brotherly love than when a philanthropist gives way to hatred. Better than truth in the mouth of the liar is the lie. . . . The most shining virtues of him who has fallen away are as black as night in comparison with the darkest lapses of the steadfast.[163]

Here is the contrast of Hitler with Oster and the "good" deeds of the Nazis with the "evil" deeds of the conspiracy.

It was also at this time that Bonhoeffer sketched the various ethical schemes that, however meritorious in certain respects, collapsed in the struggle against Nazism; these were moral schemes by which "the *best* of men go under." [164] These schemes are taken up again in "After Ten Years." They need not be reviewed again here, but it is important to note that these meditations were begun as reflection upon Bonhoeffer's knowledge of conspiratorial events. And it is important to note they are later recorded as part of the lessons learned from conspiracy. (Parenthetically, General Oster was one for whom the Christmas essay was written.) It is even more noteworthy that this reflection introduces a critically important section of *Ethics,* "Ethics as Formation." [165] In other words, the hammering out of Bonhoeffer's own stance takes place within his reflection upon the stances of other opponents of Nazism, and it takes place in direct response to the work of the members of the military/political resistance. Not least of all it was there he saw the painful and necessary deed of free responsibility carried out, exemplified in actions such as Oster's; it was there, too, that deputyship was exercised in the profane acts of secular men and guilt taken on for the sake of neighbor and nation. "After Ten Years" found its way into *Ethics* even before the essay, "After Ten Years," was written.

---

[163] *E,* pp. 64-65. Trans. corrected. Among Bonhoeffer's notes for *Ethics* is one quoting Bismarck: "I hate him who forces me to lie." (Microfilm No. 395, Frame No. 33.)

[164] *E,* p. 67. Emphasis mine.

[165] *E,* pp. 64 ff. Bonhoeffer is eloquent when he writes about the Third Reich at the beginning of this section of *Ethics*: "Today there are once more villains and saints, and they are not hidden from the public view. Instead of the uniform grayness of the rainy day we now have the black storm-cloud and the brilliant lightning-flash. The outlines stand out with exaggerated sharpness. Reality lays itself bare. Shakespeare's characters walk in our midst. But the villain and the saint have little or nothing to do with systematic ethical studies. They emerge from primeval depths and by their appearance they tear open the infernal or the divine abyss from which they come and enable us to see for a moment into mysteries of which we had never dreamed. What is worse than doing evil is being evil. It is worse when a liar tells the truth than when a lover of truth lies." (*Ibid.,* pp. 64-65.) Trans. corrected.

The Gestalt Christi *and Nazi Morality*

In the same section in which Bonhoeffer writes about the moral patterns of the opponents of Nazism he turns his critique to Nazi morality. Obviously this must be veiled for security reasons; it is also veiled because Bonhoeffer is writing for other times than his own. And in any case he is not seeking a justification of resistance in *Ethics* but is rather attempting to present a theological ethic for the postwar order; [166] he is "thinking and acting for the sake of the coming generation." [167] Thus, Nazism and resistance are hardly his sole preoccupation. But they are included in his broader strictures and must not be overlooked. Bonhoeffer certainly did not overlook them. He, the theologian and pastor, wrote these lines while employed as an espionage agent in Hitler's war machinery.

Bonhoeffer works from the *Gestalt Christi* in every move against the motifs of Nazi morality. Incarnation, crucifixion, and resurrection yield the content that undercuts the popular and horrifyingly effective tenets of Nazism.

The incarnation is an attack upon all despisers of men and all idolizers of men. God became man, the real man, and God sides with the real man against all who either deify or debase him.[168] The Nazi "quest for the superman," the Nazi endeavor "to outgrow the man within the man," the Nazi "pursuit of the heroic," the Nazi "cult of the demigod" [169]—all these are heretical because the incarnation means that God says "yes" to the real man and no other.[170]

Hitler personified both contempt for man and idolization of man. The masses responded likewise. Bonhoeffer writes so passionately here that the full portrait must be cited. The first sentence gives away the leverage point in Bonhoeffer's stand—his vision of man in the incarnation.

The news that God has become man strikes at the very heart of an age in which both the good and the wicked regard either scorn for man or the idolization of man as the highest attainable wisdom. The weaknesses of human nature are displayed more clearly in a time of storm than in the smooth course of more peaceful periods. In the face of totally unexpected threats and opportunities it is fear, desire, irresolution and brutality which reveal themselves as the motives for the actions of the overwhelming majority. At such a time as this it is easy for the tyrannical despiser of men to exploit the baseness of the human heart, nurturing it and calling it by other names. Fear he calls responsibility. Desire he calls keenness.

---

[166] Among the titles Bonhoeffer was considering for his book on ethics were: "The Foundations and Structure of a Future World" and "The Foundations and Structure of a United West." (*Ethik,* "Vorwort," p. 12.)

[167] "After Ten Years," *LPP,* p. 15.

[168] *E,* p. 71. [169] *Ibid.,* p. 81.

[170] *Ibid.,* p. 72. Again Bonhoeffer's terminology is not defined. When he says "the real man" the reader can readily see what is excluded. But what is included is not precise. This impression holds across the board for Bonhoeffer's use of "reality" and its derivatives.

Irresolution becomes solidarity. Brutality becomes masterfulness. Human weaknesses are played upon with unchaste seductiveness, so that meanness and baseness are reproduced and multiplied ever anew. The vilest contempt for mankind goes about its sinister business with the holiest of protestations of devotion to the human cause. And, as the base man grows baser, he becomes an ever more willing and adaptable tool in the hands of the tyrant. The small band of the upright are reviled. Their bravery is called insubordination; their self-control is called pharisaism; their independence arbitrariness and their masterfulness arrogance. For the tyrannical despiser of men popularity is the token of the highest love of mankind. His secret profound mistrust for all human beings he conceals behind words stolen from a true community. In the presence of the crowd he professes to be one of their number, and at the same time he sings his own praises with the most revolting vanity and scorns the rights of every individual. He thinks people stupid, and they become stupid. He thinks them weak, and they become weak. He thinks them criminal, and they become criminal. His most sacred earnestness is a frivolous game. . . . In his profound contempt for his fellow-men he seeks the favor of those whom he despises, and the more he does so the more certainly he promotes the deification of his own person by the mob. Contempt for man and idolization of man are close neighbors.[171]

"The Despiser of Men"—this division of "Ethics as Formation"—ends as it began: "And again, the reason why we can live as real men and can love the real man at our side is to be found solely in the incarnation of God, in the unfathomable love of God for man." [172]

"The Successful Man" is the next short essay. It, too, is a reference to Hitler. Again Bonhoeffer works from the *Gestalt Christi* for his critique, this time basing it in the crucifixion.

A few words about the background of the essay are necessary. In June, 1940, France fell to Hitler's armies. With that Hitler attained success hardly imagined even by Germans. It was in fact the zenith of his power abroad (not synonymous with expansion of the Reich) and the height of his popularity at home. His military success made it plain the resisters had miscalculated severely. They had expected the collapse of the regime as a consequence of this foolish campaign to the west.[173] After the fall of France Bonhoeffer began to speak at this meeting and that about a historical "yes" to Nazism.[174] In September he wrote the essay on "The Successful Man." [175]

. . . The successful man presents us with accomplished facts which can never again be reversed. What he destroys cannot be restored. What he constructs will

---

[171] *E*, pp. 72-73. Dr. Bethge confirmed this as Bonhoeffer's portrait of Hitler and the blindly obedient masses. (Interview with Eberhard Bethge, October 10, 1968, Rengsdorf, West Germany.)

[172] *Ibid.*, p. 74.   [173] *Biography*, p. 586.

[174] Wilhelm Niesel, "From Keelson to Principal of a Seminary," *I Knew DB*, p. 147.

[175] *Biography*, p. 588.

acquire at least a prescriptive right in the next generation. No indictment can make good the guilt which the successful man has left behind him. The indictment falls silent with the passage of time, but the success remains and determines the course of history.[176]

Bonhoeffer was speaking of a historical "yes" and not a theological or an ethical one. "So far we have been talking about facts and not about valuations."[177] Bethge is surely right in saying that this historical state of affairs just at the time Bonhoeffer began his first resistance assignments represents a piece of pragmatism and a lesson in political realism which Bonhoeffer felt he must learn, and which was missing almost in toto in *The Cost of Discipleship* and in the Confessing Church.[178]

But realism about the escalated power and prestige of Hitler was not capitulation. When Bonhoeffer does talk about valuations he takes the measure of Hitler's success from the judgment that the crucifixion brings to all standards of success. The poignancy of Bonhoeffer's remarks is heightened when one recalls that Hitler's paeans of self-glorification incessantly proclaimed his victories the sure signs of divinely ordained destiny. Brute success meant divine sanction. Bonhoeffer, to the contrary, writes that "the figure of the Crucified invalidates all thought which takes success for its standard."[179]

[Jesus] is not concerned with success or failure but with the willing acceptance of God's judgment. Only in this judgment is there reconciliation with God and among men. Christ confronts all thinking in terms of success and failure with the man who is under God's sentence, no matter whether he be successful or unsuccessful.[180]

In the next meditation, "The Idolization of Death," the resurrection is the base point for Bonhoeffer's rejection of Nazi ideology and morality.

The miracle of Christ's resurrection makes nonsense of that idolization of death which is prevalent among us today. Where death is the last thing, fear of death is combined with defiance. Where death is the last thing, earthly life is all or nothing. Boastful reliance on earthly eternities goes side by side with a frivolous playing with life. A convulsive acceptance and seizing hold of life stands cheek by jowl

---

[176] *E*, pp. 75-76. [177] *Ibid.*, p. 76.

[178] *Biography*, pp. 588-89. Sentences from a draft for *Ethics* written at the height of Bonhoeffer's resistance activity show new themes brought forward in and by resistance. "That the love of God for the world also encloses political action, that the worldly gestalt of Christian love can therefore take in the gestalt of those fighting for self-assertion, power, success and security can only be comprehended there where the incarnation of the love of God is taken seriously." ("Die Geschichte und das Gute," *GS* III, 477.) "Political action means to perceive responsibility. It cannot take place without power. Power enters the service of responsibility." (*Ibid.*) In *The Cost of Discipleship* love and power are virtually antithetical.

[179] *E*, p. 77. [180] *Ibid.*

72

with indifference and contempt for life. There is no clearer indication of the idolization of death than when a period claims to be building for eternity and yet life has no value in this period, or when big words are spoken of a new man, of a new world and of a new society which is to be ushered in, and yet all that is new is the destruction of life as we have it. The drastic acceptance or rejection of earthly life reveals that only death has any value here. To clutch at everything or to cast away everything is the reaction of one who believes fanatically in death.[181]

Bonhoeffer goes on to say the resurrection has broken the power of death and thereby granted it only limited rights. The Nazi idolization of death, so acutely analyzed in the above quotation, is thereby relativized; it cannot belong to the man being formed in Christ.[182]

To summarize: "Ethics as Formation" begins with the picture of life in the Third Reich ("Today there are once more villians and saints . . .") and the sketches of reason, moral fanaticism, conscience, duty, absolutized freedom, and private virtuousness as ethical postures that fail to range themselves so as to strike at the heart of evil. It ends with the Church's confession of guilt for the rise of the Reich and the silence before its crimes. Between, Bonhoeffer turns to the *Gestalt Christi* for the resources to combat Nazi themes (and others)— "The Despiser of Men," "The Successful Man," "The Idolization of Death." In all cases the ethics of conformation here taking shape proceeds from the *Gestalt Christi* for its censure of Nazi morality.

[181] *Ibid.,* pp. 78-79. The adverb "today" occurs frequently in *Ethics* and should not be overlooked. It ties Bonhoeffer's reflection to his environment—Nazism, resistance, and the war.
[182] *Ibid.,* p. 79.

3
Letters and Papers from Prison and Resistance

Preliminaries

Paul Lehmann provides a significant help for all students of Bonhoeffer's life and writings when he suggests that Bonhoeffer possessed "a kind of incipient openness to what was at the other extreme of one's experience, to try to take it in, not to try to control it, but in order to learn from it what one could learn for one's own experience."[1] Bonhoeffer's biography could be written around this sentence by showing how the riches of his own heritage were interlaced with his amazing appropriation of other resources (and precisely at the time all the forces about him were rooted in a narrow nationalism). That definitive biography has been written, however; and here the point is to use a modified version of Lehmann's insight as the starting point for this discussion of *Letters and Papers from Prison* and resistance. To be faithful to Bonhoeffer's language the formulation can best be stated in christological terms: what moved the Bonhoeffer of the 1930s and 1940s was an openness, even eagerness, to search for Jesus Christ among new claims.

As academician he began his Christology lectures at the university with the inquiry about "The Present Christ"[2] and asked: "If we look for the place of Christ, we are looking for the structure of the 'Where?' within that of the 'Who?'"[3] As pastor and teacher battling in the *Kirchenkampf* he began

---

[1] Paul Lehmann, "Dietrich Bonhoeffer," January Lecture Series (New York: Union Theological Seminary, 1968), p. 3. (Mimeographed.)

[2] *CC*, pp. 43 ff.   [3] *Ibid.*, p. 61.

The Cost of Discipleship: "Behind all the slogans and catchwords of ecclesiastical controversy . . . there arises a more determined quest for him who is the sole object of it all, for Jesus Christ himself. . . . What is his will for us today?"[4] And as prisoner he wrote in the first of the famous theological letters: "What is bothering me incessantly is the question . . . who Christ really is for us today?"[5] The continuing search for Christ among new claims is clear.

Among the new claims were those of the military/political resistance. The American diary dramatizes Bonhoeffer's early grapplings with the question of Christ and these new claims. "Great projects always simply lead us to where we stand ourselves. But we ought only be found where He is . . . we are all only where He is. . . . Or have I run away from Him after all, from the place where He expects me to be?"[6] "Where He is" turned out to be with those Germans who were opening their mouths "for the dumb, for the rights of all who are left desolate."[7] The new claims turned out to be those "involved in the part that I had resolved to play in Germany's fate."[8]

For a German Lutheran pastor to become a conspirator was indeed a matter of new claims. The search for Jesus Christ in such environs was fully unprecedented. Yet precisely there Bonhoeffer sought the contemporary form of the *Gestalt Christi* and found Jesus to be "the responsible person par excellence,"[9] the bearer of guilt, the bestower of freedom.

Bonhoeffer's search for Jesus among these new claims wound through the incomplete essays on ethics, as I have sought to demonstrate above. But it did not end there. In Tegel Prison Bonhoeffer had the time, albeit forced and unpleasant, to search further among those claims which had in fact brought him to his cell. He continued in quest of "who Christ really is for us today." He made some discoveries in the process. Yet these, too, were rooted at least in part in the experiences consequent upon his return from America to take up the new claims.

Bonhoeffer's continuing christological search in the prison letters is the concern here, although only insofar as it is tied to resistance.[10] This excludes a

---

[4] *CD*, p. 37.   [5] "30 April 1944," *LPP*, p. 139.

[6] "Tagebuch der Amerikareise," *GS* I, 293-94.

[7] Proverbs 31:8, a favorite verse of Bonhoeffer's, referring above all to the Jews.

[8] "22 December 1943," *LPP*, p. 99.   [9] *E*, p. 225.

[10] Even reflection on resistance will be curtailed somewhat. Interesting but less essential items will be omitted. For example, there are code words and allusions to events in the resistance movement, including the impending assassination attempt (e.g., *LPP*, 71, 72, 184, 186). "Tossing in expectation of great events . . . powerlessly trembling for friends at an infinite distance" was written just days before the assassination attempt that Bonhoeffer knew was in the offing. (*Ibid.*, p. 189.) Nor was it a datum of coincidence that Bonhoeffer collected passages from the Old Testament about men telling lies "vigorously and to the glory of God" (*ibid.*, p. 86) just at the time he himself was telling them vigorously to protect the ongoing resistance work, as well as to protect men already arrested. This was also the time he wrote

great deal. No compendium of what Bethge calls "The New Theology"[11] will be attempted. Only selected themes will be extracted, though they are the most provocative ones. The contention is thus a limited but firm one: the theology of the prison letters is intimately tied to the experience of resistance.

Christology and Resistance in the Prison Letters

"Who is *Christ* for us today?"

Christology in the prison letters can be handled with a certain economy because it shows the strongest possible continuities with Bonhoeffer's earlier christological creed. "The man for others"[12] is vividly the Christ of the *theologia crucis*.

> Men go to God when he is sore bestead,
> Find him poor and scorned, without shelter or bread,
> Whelmed under the weight of the wicked, the weak, the dead;
> Christians stand by God in his hour of grieving.[13]

Nor has the Christo-universalism been set aside. Bonhoeffer continues to see all reality in Christ and attempts to understand "secular" behavior in terms of Christ's taking form among men. "The question how there can be a 'natural piety' is at the same time the question of 'unconscious Christianity,' with which I am more and more concerned."[14] "One has to live for some time in a community to understand how Christ is 'formed' in it."[15]

This is Bonhoeffer's Christology of long standing. A distinctive accent is present in *Letters and Papers from Prison,* however. It is the messianic sufferings of Jesus *in the secular life* as *the* mark of his being-for-others. We noted above that the suffering being-for-others is not itself a new theme; *The Cost of Discipleship* throbs with it. What makes the accent distinctive is thus not the *pattern* of Christ's life, but the *place* where it is lived out. It is not the *way* of Jesus which has changed so much since Bonhoeffer's early writings,[16] but

---

the essay "What is Meant by 'Telling the Truth'?" (*E*, pp. 363 ff.) These and other connections to resistance will be neglected above in favor of more general correlations of theology and the biography of resistance.

[11] *Biography*, pp. 757 ff. These are great pages, and every student of contemporary theology ought to read them with extraordinary care.

[12] "Outline for a Book," *LPP*, p. 202.   [13] "Christians and Pagans," *LPP*, p. 192.

[14] "27 July 1944," *LPP*, p. 197. See, however, the discussion on pp. 169-71.

[15] "16 July 1944," *LPP*, p. 186.

[16] See pp. 19-21 above where the essence of Christ, man, and the Church in Bonhoeffer's early writings is clearly being-there-for-others; this is stamped above all by deputyship. The "Outline for a Book" in *Letters and Papers from Prison* repeats our earlier discussion in compact form. (*Ibid.*, p. 202.) The reader must not overlook the phrase "the *being* of Jesus." The German is *"Sein,"* and it carries Bonhoeffer's ontology. Being-for-others is the way "reality" is "realized."

the *where*. This follows for the Christian life as well, surely no surprise for a thinker so christocentric as Bonhoeffer.

The Christian, unlike the devotees of the redemption myths, has no last line of escape available from earthly tasks and difficulties into the eternal, but, like Christ himself ("My God, why has thou forsaken me?"), he must drink the earthly cup to the lees, and only in his doing so is the crucified and risen Lord with him, and he is crucified and risen with Christ. This world must not be prematurely written off; in this the Old and New Testament are one. Redemption myths arise from human boundary-experiences, but Christ takes hold of a man at the centre of his life.[17]

In *Letters and Papers from Prison* the Christology of suffering for others in the secular life is normative for the Christian life. "It is not the religious act that makes the Christian, but participation in the sufferings of God in the secular life." [18]

So it is the secular life, i.e., the place rather than the pattern of the suffering of Christ and of the Christian life, which becomes the distinctive emphasis. *The Cost of Discipleship* and *Letters and Papers from Prison* both speak of the *imitatio Christi* [19] but the prison letters make the difference very clear.[20]

---

[17] "27 June 1944," *LPP*, p. 176. [18] "18 July 1944," *LPP*, p. 190.
[19] *CD*, p. 344; *LPP*, pp. 96, 99.
[20] To be more precise a sharp ambivalence is present in *The Cost of Discipleship* which is not present in *Letters and Papers from Prison*. It shows up most clearly in the pictures of the Church, but it is also the case for the Christian life in general. In the first part of *The Cost of Discipleship* the Church comes to its form in the world through its suffering for the world. Deputyship is the essence of the Christian life; its pattern is that of the *theologia crucis*. Christian life is participation in the *missio Jesu*. The following could have been a portion of the prison letters.
"Suffering means being cut off from God . . . [Jesus] bears the whole burden of man's separation from God, and in the very act of drinking the cup he causes it to pass over him. He sets out to overcome the suffering of the world, and so he must drink it to the dregs. Hence while it is still true that suffering means being cut off from God, yet within the fellowship of Christ's suffering, suffering is overcome by suffering, and becomes the way to communion with God. Suffering has to be endured in order that it may pass away . . .
"For God is a God who bears. The Son of God . . . bore the cross. . . . In the same way his followers are also called upon to bear, and that is precisely what it means to be a Christian." (*CD*, p. 102.)
Had Bonhoeffer carried through with this to the end, the quotation above from the prison letters ("The Christian, unlike . . .") might have been a paragraph in *The Cost of Discipleship*. But in the second part of that book a rather drastic turn is made. Instead of the Church coming to its form through its suffering for the world, the Church comes to its suffering in the world through its form. Here the Church "must claim a definite sphere in the world for itself, and so define clearly the frontier between itself and the world." (*Ibid.*, p. 314.) Here is the Church's strong separation and clear distance from the world: "Like a sealed train travelling through foreign territory, the Church goes on its way through the world." (*Ibid.*, p. 313.) How sanctification is possible "only within the visible Church." (*Ibid.*, p. 314.) "By pursuing sanctification outside the Church we are trying to pronounce ourselves holy." (*Ibid.*, p. 315.) Here the world is indeed "prematurely written off" as *the* place where formation to Christ takes place. These sentences could find no place in *Letters and Papers from Prison* and their content

I remember a conversation that I had in America thirteen years ago with a young French pastor. We were asking ourselves quite simply what we wanted to do with our lives. He said he would like to become a saint (and I think it is quite likely that he did become one). At that time I was very impressed, but I disagreed with him, and said, in effect, that I should like to learn to have faith. For a long time I did not realize the depth of the contrast. I thought I could acquire faith by trying to live a holy life, or something like it. I suppose I wrote *The Cost of Discipleship* as the end of that path. Today I can see the dangers of that book, though I still stand by what I wrote.[21]

I discovered later, and I am still discovering right up to this moment, that it is only by living completely in this world that one learns to have faith. One must completely abandon any attempt to make something of oneself, whether it be a saint, or a converted sinner, or a churchman (a so-called priestly type!), a righteous man or an unrighteous one, a sick man or a healthy one. By this-worldliness I mean living unreservedly in life's duties, problems, successes and failures, experiences and perplexities. In so doing we throw ourselves completely into the arms of God, taking seriously, not our own sufferings, but those of God in the world—watching with Christ in Gethsemane. That I think is faith, that is *metanoia;* and that is how one becomes a man and a Christian (cf. Jer. 45!).[22]

This letter was written the day after the failure of Count Stauffenberg and the resistance movement to assassinate Hitler. Bonhoeffer knew of the failure and now had to reckon with the probability of his own death. On the evening of July 21 he wrote the poem "Stations on the Road to Freedom." The last stanza is "Death." [23]

---

is later judged negatively by Bonhoeffer. (See the letter of 21 July quoted above.) Thus the ambivalence is sharp in *The Cost of Discipleship* and only part of its picture of the Church and the Christian life appears again in *Letters and Papers from Prison.*

[21] The single quotation from Karl Marx among Bonhoeffer's wartime notes is appropriate here: "It is easy to be a saint if one does not wish to be a man." (Microfilm No. 395, Frame No. 60.)

[22] 21 July 1944," *LPP,* p. 193. The young French pastor mentioned was Jean Lasserre, a close friend of Bonhoeffer's at Union and a major influence for Bonhoeffer's pacifism. (*Biography,* pp. 111 ff.) Lasserre has no recollection of the specific conversation mentioned in this letter. He does recall the subject of *sanctification* as an ongoing one with Bonhoeffer, however, and in that context may have stated his wish to become a saint. But Lasserre came to the issue of sanctification from a Calvinist "Social Gospel" background and so was seeking at Union to find the meaning of sanctification *in the midst of the world.* Since this is also part of Bonhoeffer's concern in *Letters and Papers from Prison,* the recollection about sainthood and criticism of himself in *The Cost of Discipleship* says much more about Bonhoeffer than it does about Lasserre. Bonhoeffer may, in the end, still be right about Lasserre, however, as the latter's major writing can be said to belong to the theology of *The Cost of Discipleship* which he himself influenced. The reader is referred to: Jean Lasserre, *War and the Gospel,* trans. Oliver Coburn (Scottsdale, Pa.: Herald Press, 1962). (The above information is from an interview with Jean Lasserre, West Berlin, Germany, November 16, 1968. Pastor Lasserre was in Berlin to deliver an address on passive resistance.)

[23] Susanne Dress-Bonhoeffer visited her brother in the same week this letter was written,

Come now, thou greatest of feasts on the journey to freedom eternal;
death, cast aside all the burdensome chains,
and demolish
the walls of our temporal body, the walls of our souls
that are blinded,
so that at last we may see that which here remains hidden.
Freedom, how long we have sought thee in discipline,
action, and suffering;
dying, we now may behold thee revealed in the Lord.[24]

The poem is not an aside to the letter. What holds them together is the resistance experience. Following the commentary on learning faith by "participation in the sufferings of God in the secular life," the letter continues. And here
the resistance experience is included as an indispensable element of Bonhoeffer's
theology and ethics.

. . . I am glad to have been able to learn this, and I know I have been able to
do so *only along the road that I have travelled.* So I am grateful for the past and
present, and content with them. You may be surprised at such a personal letter;
but if for once I want to say this kind of thing, whom should I say it to? May God
in his mercy lead us through these times; but above all may he lead us to himself.[25]

The reference to Jeremiah 45 at precisely the point of learning "how one
becomes a man and a Christian" [26] provides further documentation of the
place of resistance in Bonhoeffer's theological odyssey. As is clear from all the
other uses of Jeremiah in *Letters and Papers from Prison*[27] the reference is to
Jeremiah 45:4-5:

Thus shall you say to him, Thus says the Lord: Behold, what I have built I am
breaking down, and what I have planted I am plucking up—that is, the whole
land. And do you seek great things for yourself? Seek them not; for, behold, I am
bringing evil upon all flesh, says the Lord; *but I will give you your life as a prize of
war in all places to which you may go.*[28]

---

i.e., shortly after the failure of July 20, 1944. She recalls discussing this poem with him. It
was a highly biographical one, and he wrote of "death" as the likely consequence of the failure
of the day before. (Interview with Susanne Dress-Bonhoeffer, West Berlin, Germany, February
20, 1969.)

[24] "Stations on the Road to Freedom," *LPP,* p. 195.

[25] "21 July 1944," *LPP,* p. 194. Emphasis mine.

[26] From the quotation, p. 78 above.

[27] "5 September 1943," *LPP,* p. 45; "30 April 1944," *LPP,* p. 139; "Thoughts on the
Baptism of D.W.R.," *LPP,* pp. 157-58. In all these Bonhoeffer uses verses 4-5 exclusively even
though he mentions only the chapter.

[28] Emphasis mine.

The pattern and the place of Christ and the Christian life were learned in part, ironically, "as a prize of war." This is the testimony of *Letters and Papers from Prison.* Jesus Christ was searched for and found among the new claims of the military/political resistance. This person and the pattern of his life, and thus the pattern of the Christian's life, we met before in "After Ten Years," as exemplified especially in the paragraph "Of Suffering." [29] This is the Christ and the Christian life whose profiles are also clear in "The Structure of Responsible Life" and particularly "The Acceptance of Guilt." This is the Christ and the Christian life standing behind the wrestling in the American diary. It is the Christ and the Christian life taking form in the resistance document that exposes the transition from *The Cost of Discipleship* to *Ethics.*

In short, the person of Christ and the pattern of the Christian life are not new in an essential way in *Letters and Papers from Prison.*[30] Their basic outlines are those mirrored in the resistance reflection traced through *Ethics* and "After Ten Years." The most formative tenets go back even further to the early writings. What has altered is the *place* of being-for-others. It is increasingly a matter of "drinking the *earthly* cup to the lees." [31]

An objection can be raised immediately: "the earthly cup" represents the contrast of *Letters and Papers from Prison* with *The Cost of Discipleship,* but it does not represent the contrast of the prison letters with *Ethics. Ethics,* it might be alleged, proclaims the "this-worldliness" of faith as emphatically as does *Letters and Papers from Prison.*

Yet there is a difference, and that introduces the next topic.

The World Come of Age and Religion

"Who is Christ for us *today?*"

"The question is: Christ and the world that has come of age."[32]

"Today" is the time of the world come of age. This is a double movement for Bonhoeffer: the increase of human autonomy through the maturation of reason and the decay of religion. Both spell "responsibility," as will be shown.

---

[29] See p. 67.

[30] Bethge is right, however, in intimating that a certain clarity and unity is present in the prison letters which did not show itself before. "Bonhoeffer's simplified description of Jesus as 'the man for others' does indeed show an insight gained only through prolonged effort." ("Editor's Foreword," *LPP,* p. xiv.) "It is the unity . . . of the three elements—theology, ecclesiology, and ethics—that so attracts one to Bonhoeffer." (*Ibid.,* p. xiii.) The unity is expressed as being-for-others in the theological letters and the sketch for a book. Yet whatever clarity is here gained, it is precisely in this that Bonhoeffer's theology in *Letters and Papers from Prison* is *not* new but astoundingly continuous in its basic tenets.

[31] Reference is to the quotation on p. 77 above. Emphasis mine.

[32] "8 June 1944," *LPP,* p. 170.

Bonhoeffer designates the increase of human autonomy by various forms of the German *"muendig."* [33] The person who is *"muendig"* is one who "speaks for himself." The reference is to the passage from adolescence to adulthood. One is no longer a minor but is on his own. He has "come of age." He is now fully responsible for his actions. The reader of Bonhoeffer in English should note carefully that *"muendig"* is thus a reference to moral *accountability* and not moral maturity. That is, Bonhoeffer is saying that man is fully responsible for his actions whether he acts childishly, immaturely, irresponsibly, or whatever. The world's adulthood is in part, then, Bonhoeffer's designation of man's irrevocable responsibility for his answers to life's questions, together with all the consequences. Man can no longer return to an adolescent dependence upon a father to whom final responsibility falls.[34]

Yet the element of moral accountability is emphasized less than rational maturity. The lexical aspect of *"muendig"* is significant, but the literary reference to Kant is even more so. Bonhoeffer's appropriation of "come of age" is from Kant's description of the Enlightenment as "the emergence of man from immaturity that he is himself responsible for. Immaturity is the incapacity to use one's own intelligence without the guidance of another person." [35]

Man, using his autonomous reason, can and does answer the questions of life; man can and does interpret natural and social processes, all without the tutelage of a divinity, without God as a working hypothesis. Further, man is accountable for the use of his reason and its behavioral expression. "World come of age," then, designates rational maturity and moral accountability. Especially the former is clear in a summary of Bonhoeffer's.

God as a working hypothesis in morals, politics, or science, has been surmounted and abolished; and the same thing has happened in philosophy and religion (Feuerbach!). For the sake of intellectual honesty, that working hypothesis should be dropped, or as far as possible eliminated.[36]

The decay of religion is also part of what Bonhoeffer means by the world's coming of age. To characterize religion he uses pejoratively such terms as *deus ex machina* (the God-of-the-gaps); provinciality (religion as a separated sector of one's life); metaphysics (thinking in two realms, the supernatural completing the natural); individual inwardness (pietism or other forms of ascetic escape); indispensability (a religious a priori as constitutive of human

---

[33] *"Muendigkeit"* means "adulthood"; *"muendigwerden"* means "coming of age"; *"muendiggewordene"* means "having come of age" or "come of age." Dietrich Bonhoeffer, *Widerstand und Ergebung,* ed. Eberhard Bethge, 11th ed. (Munich: Chr. Kaiser Verlag, 1951), pp. 217, 236, 241, 218, 331 respectively.

[34] "8 June 1944," *LPP,* p. 169.

[35] *Biography,* p. 770, citing Immanuel Kant's *Was ist Aufklaerung?* (1784).

[36] "16 July 1944," *LPP,* p. 187.

nature); and sanction (religion as a protector of privilege).[87] While each could be treated at length, almost all can be included in the following: religion in *Letters and Papers from Prison* refers to a particular way of thinking and behaving in an attempt to cope with human weakness and difficulties; more specifically, it is seeking to manage life in this way by using a peripheral dependence upon a supernatural power.[88]

Religion does *not* refer as such to the institutional elements of the Church—sermon, sacrament, Scripture, doctrine, prayer, etc. These may be interpreted in either a "religious" or "nonreligious" manner, depending upon whether they help men to "find God in what we do know [nonreligious interpretation], not in what we do not know" [39] [religious interpretation]; whether or not they help men to realize God's presence, "not in unsolved problems [religious interpretation] but in those that are solved" [40] [nonreligious interpretation]; whether they help men "to speak of God not on the boundary [religious interpretation] but at the center of life" [41] [nonreligious interpretation].[42]

---

[87] "30 April 1944," *LPP*, pp. 139-43; "8 June 1944," *LPP*, pp. 167-72; "30 June 1944," *LPP*, pp. 177-80; "8 July 1944," *LPP*, pp. 181-84; "16 July 1944," *LPP*, pp. 184-88; "18 July 1944," *LPP*, pp. 189-91; "Outline for a Book," *LPP*, pp. 200-204.

[88] My appreciation to Clifford Green, Department of Religion, Wellesley College, for a conversation yielding this compact definition of "religion" in the prison letters.

[39] "25 May 1944," *LPP*, p. 164. [40] *Ibid.* [41] "30 April 1944," *LPP*, p. 142.

[42] Documentation of the connection between Bonhoeffer's resistance activity and his thoughts taking shape on "religion" is found in *GS* II, 419-21. He wrote Bethge a letter while on the way to Munich in the early summer of 1942. Impending was a trip with Hans von Dohnanyi to the Vatican in order to make contact with the Allies for the resistance. This was but a month after Bonhoeffer's important meeting in Sweden with Bishop Bell. That is, this was written at the height of Bonhoeffer's activity for the resistance movement. In this letter of June 25, the resistance duties are what Bonhoeffer means by "my present activity in the worldly sector."

"My activities, which have lately been very much in the worldly sector, are occasion for reflection again and again. I am surprised that I live and can go on living without the Bible for days at a time. If I were to constrain myself to study it, I would not feel it to be out of obedience but auto-suggestion. I understand that such auto-suggestion might be and is a great help; yet by doing so I fear a falsification of a genuine experience and, when all is said and done, still would not discover genuine help anyway. But when I do open the Bible again, it is ever so new and pleasant, and I should just like to preach once again. I know that I need only open my own books to hear what might be said against all this. I do not want to justify myself and I recognize I have had more fertile days "spiritually." But I feel how resistance to everything "religious" grows within me—often to the point of an instinctive abhorrence, which is certainly not good. I'm not religious by nature. Yet I continually have to be thinking of God and of Christ, and I set a great store by integrity, life, freedom and compassion. It is just that I find the religious wrappings so uncomfortable. Do you understand? These thoughts and insights are hardly new, but since I think I shall be able to find my way through them, I'll let these things circulate awhile and won't offer resistance. I also understand my present activity in the worldly sector precisely in this way [i.e., non-religiously]. Please excuse these confessions; the long train ride is responsible. We must talk about these things in peace and quiet sometime."

This is two years before Bonhoeffer picks up "religion" in the prison letters and gives it much more clarity than here. But the tie to resistance is clear. Already in this letter Bonhoeffer

"World come of age," to summarize, is a necessary double movement of human autonomy and the decay of religion. The outcome of both ends of the movement is increased responsibility as man's reason matures, the God-of-the-gaps dies, and human destiny falls into human hands in ever greater measure.

Bonhoeffer acclaimed the world's coming of age. He saw it through the perspectives of the *theologia crucis* and in that way understood it as a historical movement centered in the cross which opened up the way for men to see, not the God of "religion," but the God of the Bible.

Here is the decisive difference between Christianity and all religions. Man's religiosity makes him look in his distress to the power of God in the world: God is the *deus ex machina*. The Bible directs man to God's powerlessness and suffering; only the suffering God can help. To that extent we may say that the development towards the world's coming of age outlined above, which has done away with a false conception of God, opens up a way of seeing the God of the Bible, who wins power and space in the world by his weakness. This will probably be the starting-point for our "secular interpretation." [43]

The cross is the way of God's taking up all things, including the most despondent godlessness, unto himself and reconciling them. The cross is God's way of freeing all things to be what they were intended from creation. Thus the world come of age is better understood on the basis of the Gospel and in the light of Christ than it understands itself in its godlessness.[44]

Jesus, "the suffering God," drank the earthly cup to the lees. He lived without religious illusions, without ascetic escapes, without the *deus ex machina*. He denied privilege. He broke through the bonds that held men. He freed men for the supreme responsibility of being-for-others. He met men at the center of their lives and in the midst of their knowledge and concerns, not on the periphery. He called them, "not to a new religion, but to life." [45] And he helped men be strong, "not by virtue of his omnipotence, but by virtue of his weakness and suffering." [46] It is on the basis of the Jesus of the *theologia crucis* that the world come of age is best understood. Indeed, this Jesus is the man-come-of-age par excellence. *"Muendigkeit"* is best understood on the basis of the utter *"Weltlichkeit"* of God-in-Christ.

"Who is Christ for *us* today?"

Bethge says that "us" for Bonhoeffer includes "the non-ecclesiastically minded co-conspirators in his family who were willing to serve a coming society. 'Us' refers to men who are related to each other in sharing guilt for the past and

is on the road about which Bethge comments: "Thus the basic point is how Bonhoeffer's life in the Resistance Movement and his non-religious interpretation mutually interpret each other" (*Biography*, p. 790).

[43] "16 July 1944," *LPP*, p. 188.   [44] "8 June 1944," *LPP*, p. 172.
[45] "18 July 1944," *LPP*, p. 191.   [46] "16 July 1944," *LPP*, p. 188.

in common destinies for the future." [47] Bethge is also certain that Bonhoeffer's purpose in setting out to redo theology under the rubric of "secular interpretation" was to verbalize theologically "the true character of Christ and the true character of those worldly, secularized men." [48] As mentioned earlier the impetus was partly the great disappointment of Bonhoeffer in the Confessing Church, on the one hand, and the discovery that the necessary Christian deeds demanded of that Church were being done by Christians *and* non-Christians in the military/political conspiracy, on the other. But the impetus was surely also, as Bethge suggests, the *character* of the men with whom Bonhoeffer grew up and with whom he worked in resistance. Bonhoeffer's tracing of the process of the world's coming of age could just as easily have been biographical as historical. He was privileged to grow up among people who were deeply conscious of human autonomy and who were convincing representatives of autonomous reason in many disciplines and occupations. They certainly did not require or use "God as a working hypothesis." Furthermore they were men who bore responsibility in noble fashion without using a God-of-the-gaps as the escape on the many occasions of failure. This was true of Bonhoeffer's immediate and extended family as well as other circles of intellectual aristocracy about him. [49]

The experience of *"Muendigkeit"* was intensified when Bonhoeffer joined the resistance. Here were men who, under threat to their own existence, acted for others in a state where compassion itself was a crime. They did not look to religion for some easy comfort. They did not turn to inwardness as an escape from the harsh reality of public responsibility, nor flee to some bastion in the

[47] Eberhard Bethge, "Bonhoeffer's Christology and His 'Religionless Christianity,' " *Union Seminary Quarterly Review*, Fall, 1967, pp. 65-66.

[48] Eberhard Bethge, "Turning Points in Bonhoeffer's Life and Thought," *Union Seminary Quarterly Review*, Fall, 1967, p. 19.

[49] In the unpublished part of the incomplete Tegel novel Bonhoeffer puts his familial experience of *"Muendigkeit"* and "unconscious Christianity" in the form of an exchange between two youths, Christoph and Ulrich.

" . . . Christoph looked at Ulrich: 'Do you mean we must have more religion if we want to be in a responsible position some day?' 'I mean, Christoph—really I am asking myself—no, I mean we must *be* Christian.' Christoph looked out on the lake, saw young Martin paddling around self-forgetfully on his raft, looked at the forest, then at the wide sky. 'A damned old-fashioned thought!' Ulrich did not answer. 'And just as uncomfortable.' Ulrich remained silent. A long pause set in. 'You spoke of your mother, Ulrich,' Christopher began again, 'and you know how much I like her—forgive my dumb outburst. But I am thinking of father and mother. It cannot be said that they are Christians, in any case not in the current sense of that word. They do not go to church; table prayer is there only for the sake of my kid brother and yet they are just as little affected by the spirit of perverted ambition, of empire-building, of titles and medals as your mother. To them a competent common laborer or simple craftsman is a hundred times dearer than some inflated Excellency.' 'Why is that?' Ulrich pondered. 'That is because they in reality, without knowing and expressing it, still live in Christianity, an unconscious Christianity.' " (Dietrich Bonhoeffer, "Romanversuch," p. 29 of a typewritten copy of the unpublished manuscript. Excerpt used with the permission of Eberhard Bethge.)

mind in order to close out the grimness around them. They did not seek surrogate fulfillments when their nation was folding, but planned as patriots for a new order. They did not generate a *deus ex machina* but sought to solve their problems with their own resources and live with the consequences. They suffered, and they understood Christ's suffering, in a most "nonreligious" way (even if via "unconscious Christianity").

Bonhoeffer acknowledged and admired their earthiness, their secularity, their integrity, their responsibility, and above all their "religionless Christianity."

Bonhoeffer's redoing his theology in view of the resistance experience and the character of his nonreligious colleagues leads to a dramatic break in his thought. It lies not between *Ethics* and *Letters and Papers from Prison* but within the prison letters themselves. The break occurs with the abandonment of his conception of the postwar order as "Christian civilization."

A picture of "Christian civilization" is precisely what Bonhoeffer sets out to sketch in *Ethics*.[50] The *Gestalt Christi* is *structurally determinative* for the entire order because the *Gestalt Christi* presents reality itself. The scheme of the mandates is a good example. They are "orders or 'institutions' of the reality of Christ" . . . which "are not in any sense products of history; they are not earthly powers, but divine commissions."[51] The "rights of the natural" and the shape of the penultimate, read off his christological ontology, could be cited as further examples. Even when Bonhoeffer speaks of "genuine worldliness" and "relative autonomy" late in *Ethics* it is nevertheless within a scheme of the "Christian civilization" of a "United West."[52] This is only to recall what was stated at the outset, that Bonhoeffer's is a christocratic understanding of reality out of which he now unfolds the "orders or 'institutions' of the reality of Christ" in the reality of the world.[53] Such is "Christian civilization."

When Bonhoeffer made his decision to return to Germany in 1939 he formulated the ensuing struggle as one for the survival of either "Christian civilization" or "Nazi Germany." The former was worth dying for, the latter worth dying against. "Christian civilization" was clearly understood by him as basic theological justification for entering the fray.[54] So Bethge rightly concludes that it is the manner of Bonhoeffer's theology at this time which made possible his first political moves.[55]

The manner of his theology (a structurally determinative Christology) per-

---

[50] Symptomatically, one of the titles he was considering for the book was "The Foundations and Structure of a United West." *Ethik*, "Vorwort," p. 12.

[51] *E*, p. 288.   [52] *Ibid.*, pp. 297-98 and a reference to note 50 above.   [53] *Ibid.*, p. 288.

[54] The references are many: examples include the letter to Niebuhr (*GS* I, 320); the conversations with Traub (*I Knew DB*, pp. 156 ff.); the letter of 1933 in which Bonhoeffer tells his grandmother the battle is "*Germanismus oder Christentum*" (*GS* II, 79); or the 1934 letter to Bishop Ammundsen in which the choice is "National Socialist or Christian" (*GS* I, 206).

[55] *Biography*, p. 763.

sists through the years of resistance and into the prison letters themselves. In November, 1943, he continues to speak of the reconstruction of "the life of the nations, both inwardly and outwardly, on the basis of Christianity." [56] A couple of weeks later he comments: "I sometimes feel as if my life were more or less over, and as if all I had to do now were to finish my *Ethics*." [57]

Although consistently neglected by Bonhoeffer scholars, it is an item of extreme significance that Bonhoeffer, once he returns to theological work (in 1944), does *not* work on *Ethics* but sets out to write a *new* book of a wholly different sort. A vastly altered mood [58] has replaced the self-confident effort of *Ethics* to lay the foundations and structures of a future order; in contrast, the new book insists upon asking the most fundamental questions of Christian faith in a deeply changed world. The first chapter is to be entitled "A Stocktaking of Christianity." It moves around a strong criticism of the Church, on the one hand, and the phenomenon of the world come of age, on the other. The second chapter on "The Real Meaning of the Christian Faith" leads off with "God and the secular" and ends with a plea for full intellectual honesty—not "What must I believe?" but "What do we really believe?" [59]

To be sure, Bonhoeffer is not less certain that Christ is Lord and that in some meaningful sense all reality is in him. The basic tenets of his Christology continue, as the outline for the new book shows.[60] But the shape of the *Gestalt Christi* "today" is much more questionable than in *Ethics*. Bonhoeffer speaks no longer of mandates but of the growth of human autonomy and the decay of religion. Ecclesiology is not abandoned, but, except for the essence of being-for-others, it is an open question.[61] If in 1943 Bonhoeffer could speak of reconstruction of the life of nations on the basis of Christianity, in the summer of 1944 he says "we are once again being driven back to the beginnings of our understanding" of basic Christian tenets themselves.[62]

What has happened, minimally, is that Bonhoeffer's return to systematic theological reflection has radically questioned his own christocratic conception of society and has brought him to that picture of the world come of age. Not the person of Christ or even the basic pattern of the Christian life is the new theme, but the *place* of their presence is.[63] The deep this-worldliness of *Ethics* has quite a different setting now—not in "Christian civilization" but in the world come of age. The difference between the following sentences is not small.

---

[56] "27 November 1943," *LPP*, p. 82. Trans. corrected.   [57] "15 December 1943," *LPP*, p. 90.

[58] See especially "Thoughts on the Baptism of D.W.R.," *LPP*, pp. 158, 161-62.

[59] "Outline for a book," *LPP*, pp. 201-3.   [60] *Ibid.*, p. 202.

[61] Contrast this with the rather extraordinary and strongly stated claims in *Ethics*, pp. 332 ff. where secular institutions are not regarded as capable of performing their proper services without an encounter with the Church and where only the Church can bring government to a proper understanding of itself.

[62] "Thoughts on the Baptism of D.W.R.," *LPP*, p. 161.

[63] The reader is reminded of the discussion, pp. 76-80 ff. above.

"The 'Christian' element . . . consists in man's being entitled and obliged to live as man before God." [64] "Before God and with God we live without God." [65]

But what has probably happened is even more. The break in Bonhoeffer's thought is simultaneously the breakup of his christological ontology *as a system*. *Ethics* is, in the end, a sophisticated, creative, modern version of a *Christendom* consciousness. But with the discernment of the world's coming of age that consciousness passes, and Bonhoeffer, who always jumps forward enthusiastically in a crisis, begins work on a new book about the ramifications of the new insights, as well as the continued meaning of the old.

The place of resistance in providing some of the material for the new discoveries is handled above and summarized below. Here I only add the second half of Bethge's accurate judgment. He was cited above with reference to "Christian civilization" as the mode of theology which made possible Bonhoeffer's political moves into resistance. The sentence goes on: "and these [moves] now influenced the new manner of his theology." [66] There is a definite break in Bonhoeffer's thought, and it has very specific ties to resistance.[67]

The conclusion of the look at *Letters and Papers from Prison* from the perspective of resistance is this: Just as the alliance of the sons of the Church and the sons of the Enlightenment was the catalyst for Bonhoeffer's "discovery" of the full orbit of the Lordship of Christ,[68] so now the intense experience of bearing responsibility together for the guilt of the past and for the shape of the future (all "nonreligiously") was part of the breakthrough to Bonhoeffer's last vision, the vision of discipleship as profound this-worldliness lived in the "world come of age" according to the pattern of "the man for others." "Thus the basic point is how Bonhoeffer's life in the Resistance Movement and his non-religious interpretation mutually interpret each other." [69]

In short, three components of the theological letters—Christ, world come of age, and religion—have lines leading directly to the resistance experience. In the leading question, "Who is *Christ* for *us today?*" Bonhoeffer's co-conspirators are part of the question and part of the answer. They helped him see Christ as "the man for others" in the very center of "life's duties, problems, successes and failures, experiences and perplexities." [70] They were indeed among "us" as their work with Bonhoeffer pushed him to make theological sense of their "religionless" and "unconscious" Christianity. And they were among those who showed Bonhoeffer "today" was the time of the "world come of age," with all the implications of that for redoing theology. The theology of *Letters and Papers from Prison* is in no small part Bonhoeffer's working through of the resistance experience.

---

[64] *E*, p. 297. [65] "16 July 1944," *LPP*, p. 188. [66] *Biography*, p. 763.
[67] The reader will want to view the critique, pp. 169 ff. in this light. [68] See pp. 32 ff. above.
[69] *Biography*, p. 790. [70] "21 July 1944," *LPP*, p. 193.

4
Summary and Conclusions of Part I

We can now summarize the form and content of Bonhoeffer's ethic as it took shape in the late thirties and early forties, and draw the pertinent conclusions about resistance. Although it may be somewhat artificial, this summary will separate form and content. The purpose is not only to highlight the admittedly interdependent elements by sorting them out, but also to prepare for the particular format used in the later critique.

Form

Bonhoeffer's is a thoroughly christocentric ethic in which the *Gestalt Christi* has correspondence with reality because reality itself has a christocratic structure.

It is an ethic of reality and realization in which the overriding thrust is toward concreteness. The goal is to bring to concrete expression in this world the cosmic reality given in Christ. To act in accordance with reality is to act in a manner fitting to the particular setting as that is viewed in light of Christ as *the* reality.

Ethics is done contextually because the ways Christ wins *Gestalt* among men vary with time and place.

Ethics is personalist-relational ethics. The supreme importance of the *Gestalt* of reality is that it is the *Gestalt Christi*. The concrete command is the command of Jesus Christ, true Man. He is the giver of forms among men. And he comes to men through other men; revelation is cast in human sociality.

The relational contextual ethic becomes increasingly "filled" in Bonhoeffer's writings. There is a move from an atomistic ethic to one with emphasis upon the range, coherence, and continuity of the *Gestalt Christi*. The outcome is a large place for the "natural," for the functioning of innate laws in the mandates, for the penultimate. There is a move, too, from a centeredness of Christ's presence in the Church to a centeredness of Christ's presence in the world (with the Church as a particular piece of world) and thus a shift of emphasis from an ethic of the disciple in the Church to an ethic of the Christian in the world.

The mandates play a structurally important role in Bonhoeffer's ethic because they are the media of conformation. They comprise the pre-ethical but moral environment that allows life to flow free of an overburdening by the ethical. The ethical as such occupies a peripheral location. It has a definite but rather unpredictable time and place; namely, when an accepted understanding of "who Christ is for us today" is subject to serious doubt. This occasion arises when the course of the structured flow of life in the mandates has been subjected to disruption and/or severe questioning, for one reason or another.

From a methodological standpoint the direction moves clearly from the question and answer about the indicative to the question and answer about the imperative. From: "How is Christ taking form among men here and now?" to: "What action on my part conforms to his action?"

The underlying assumption for Christian ethics is reconciliation, i.e., the recovered unity of God and the world in Christ, the bringing to realization of the ontological coherence of God's reality with the world's. The point of departure for Christian ethics is thus the Body of Christ, the community that knows and lives from this reconciliation.

The supreme ethical deed is the deed of free responsibility because this deed is the means of breakthrough to reality at the particular time and place of the ethical. The final judgment of the deed, however, lies in the hands of God. Ethics here is ethics out of justification by grace alone.

Content

Regardless of what date is chosen during the twelve years of resistance, Bonhoeffer's theology and ethics are thoroughly christological.[1] The heart of this is his Lutheran condescension theology expanded as a Christo-universal understanding of reality. In different words, Bonhoeffer's is a cosmological Christol-

---

[1] Among Bonhoeffer's notes for *Ethics* is a word-diagram that summarizes the entirety:

with

Life   as   Jesus Christ. (Microfilm No.

through   395, Frame No. 3.)

ogy of the *theologia crucis*. Incarnation, crucifixion, and resurrection are the dynamics of all reality and the forming forces of true selfhood. The *vita christiana* is a polyphonic life that lives from these dynamics.

The essence of Christ's person is his *pro nobis Sein,* "being-there" for man, nature, and history. "God is not free *of* man, but *for* man." [2] Likewise, to be a "man-for-others" is to be a real man. Too, the Church is only the Church in its being-for-others. This is ontologically true. Reality is so patterned.

Virtually all the christological tenets present in the forties were stated by Bonhoeffer in the early thirties on the eve of the *Kirchenkampf.* The decisive differences, however, are two.

The Christology of *Ethics* and especially *Letters and Papers from Prison* locates the arena of conformation in the very midst of the secular "life's duties, problems, successes and failures, experiences and perplexities." [3] Here is the first decisive difference: The drawing out of the Lordship of Christ over the world and of the *Gestalt Christi* within the world. This was latent in Bonhoeffer's Christology but, through *The Cost of Discipleship,* was developed almost entirely within an understanding of the Church as the locus of conformation. *"Christus als Gemeinde existierend"* [4] was broadened from "Christ existing as the fellowship of men in the Church" to "Christ existing as the whole human community."

The second decisive difference was the elaboration of the consistently held christological creed in the direction of ethics for the Christian in the world. The assertions of the early thirties are either silent where *Ethics* speaks vibrantly (e.g., the extremely important deed of free responsibility), or, more frequently the case, the earlier assertions fail to draw out for the Christian's public life and the profane behavior of secular men that which uniquely marks Christ's life and the life of the Church (e.g., deputyship and the acceptance of guilt). The gap between dogmatics and ethics is very large in 1930. They flow in and out of each other in 1940. The question of the 1933 Christology lectures is "Who is Christ?" The question of *Letters and Papers from Prison* is "Who is Christ for us today?" The difference is not moderate. It is the difference of a Christology with a latent ethic and a Christology with an activated ethic.

One contention of this portion of the study is that these two decisive differences are intimately related to Bonhoeffer's participation in resistance.

In the first instance (the expansion in Bonhoeffer's Christology), the document [5] showing the transition from *The Cost of Discipleship* to *Ethics* was demonstrated to be one explicitly about resistance.

In the second instance (the development of ethics out of Bonhoeffer's christological creed), the section of *Ethics* on "The Structure of Responsible Life" was exposited on its own terms and then tied to the resistance documents,

---

[2] *AB,* p. 90.   [3] "21 July 1944," *LPP,* p. 193.
[4] The key phrase of *The Communion of Saints.*   [5] *E,* pp. 55-59.

"After Ten Years" and "Ethics as Formation." When Bonhoeffer unfolded the structure of responsible life under the rubrics of acceptance of guilt, correspondence with reality, conscience, freedom, and the deed of free responsibility, he drew out or even introduced ethical themes not drawn out or introduced earlier, *even though* his Christology was virtually the same *in its basic outline*. Precisely these themes in their ethical dimensions were elicited from Bonhoeffer's Christology by the resistance movement.

Reference to "its basic outline" is intentionally broad because the experience of resistance also brought shifts and modifications in Bonhoeffer's Christology. This was shown in the pictures of Christ in *The Cost of Discipleship* and "The Structure of Responsible Life" as we traced the move of Bonhoeffer from passive to active resistance, from pacifism to conspiracy. Christ as the Bearer of Guilt and the Bestower of Freedom became especially dear to Bonhoeffer. The christological opening for an exceptional violation of divine law was crucial for the transition to active resistance and conspiracy.

The resistance experience also played its role in hammering out Bonhoeffer's ethic of conformation to the *Gestalt Christi*. "After Ten Years" and "Ethics as Formation" show that he developed his own alternative in the face of the highly regarded moral stances that buckled in the struggle against Hitler.

No claim is made here that the resistance experience gave Bonhoeffer his theological base. Hopefully, exactly the opposite has been shown—his theological base led him to and through resistance. But the resistance did forge the ethical consequences of his Christology. The form of the *Gestalt Christi* in the behavior of men in the world is uncovered by Bonhoeffer as he moves from his ecclesiastical vocation to the grotesque "vocation" as an agent in Hitler's war machinery. The contact with responsible men, both Christian and non-Christian, was decisive for a growing understanding of the Lordship of Christ, even though this Lordship had been asserted academically much earlier.

The critique of Nazi morality by Bonhoeffer always proceeded from the *Gestalt Christi* as a critique launched from the "facts" of incarnation, crucifixion, and resurrection.

Bonhoeffer's own ethic arranged itself around the unity of these dynamics of reality. And because this essential unity had to be maintained, it followed that certain extremes must necessarily be rejected *as normative,* extremes that could be considered normative only if incarnation (affirmation of the world) were detached from crucifixion (judgment of the world) or from resurrection (creation of a new world). Yet these far-ranging dynamics, including the extremes, are part and parcel of the *vita christiana,* and so Bonhoeffer did not rule out extreme behavior as occasional, necessary, and commanded. But it could never be regarded either as normal or normative. The deed of free responsibility became the classic example. It constituted Bonhoeffer's rationale for his work to put an end to Hitler and his regime.

The prison letters showed the influence of the resistance experience as Bonhoeffer had time and occasion to reflect upon the turbulence of those years. In *the* question of *Letters and Papers from Prison*—"Who is Christ for us today?"—"Christ," "us," and "today" all included the men and deeds of resistance. Too, the break noted in Bonhoeffer's thought led to the conclusion that while his theology made his first political moves possible ("Christian civilization"), his political moves in turn formed the new manner of his theology (Christ and the world come of age).

In conclusion it can be said that Bonhoeffer's own resistance was in fact his Christology enacted with full seriousness. From it he drew his understanding of what was occurring, what was to be done and what pattern this was to take. In the other direction, it must be concluded that the resistance was a catalyst for the development of Bonhoeffer's Christology, especially its ethic. He sought for Jesus Christ among new claims, and new claims showed him Jesus Christ.

EXCURSUS

The major study of Bonhoeffer's Christology is John A. Phillips' *Christ for Us in the Theology of Dietrich Bonhoeffer* (New York: Harper, 1967). It is certainly a weighty contribution to Bonhoeffer studies. But it is one of those rare books which is excellent *despite* its methodology and its thesis!

Regarding methodology, Phillips calls the *sine qua non* of Bonhoeffer studies "Bonhoeffer's freedom from the events of his life and of the time in which he lived." Until this detachment is achieved we shall not be able "to understand him and make use of his contribution." (*Ibid.,* p. 23.) As is clear in context, Phillips is here reacting to those interpretations of Bonhoeffer which think they have explained theological shifts and breaks in Bonhoeffer's thoughts by citing biographical turns and altered historical settings. When this is a *substitute* for theological analysis and explanation, the protest is wholly justified. But the swing to historical detachment as the *sine qua non* for understanding Bonhoeffer's theology is a corrective that is not a corrective, but a confusion. Indeed, it is a strange and unwarranted deviation from Bonhoeffer's own emphasis upon doing theology and ethics contextually, upon discovering "who Christ is *for us today.*" In any case, historical disengagement is not helpful as the methodological tool. I will not replay the conclusions of the chapter above, but I hope the unlikelihood of Phillips' *sine qua non* has been shown, without committing the error to which Phillips is rightly sensitive—avoiding a theological analysis by substituting a biographical and historical one.

Regarding Christology, we can fully agree with Phillips' initial starting point: "A liberated and many-sided but always *concrete* Christology . . . becomes our guide to the development of Bonhoeffer's theology"; and "to say that [Christology] was a constant motif of his thought does not mean that it remained an *idee fixe* by which he measured the utterances of fifteen years." (*Ibid.,* p. 28. Emphasis Phillips'.)

This is correct and helpful. The difficulty arises when Phillips fails to hold carefully enough to his own guide and proceeds to argue Christolog*ies,* two of them, as the guides. The insistence of this dissertation is that there is one, not two. The thesis here is Phillips' original—"a liberated and many-sided but always *concrete* Christology."

For Phillips, Bonhoeffer early held both a highly ecclesiological Christology and the beginnings of a wider one of the person and work of Jesus Christ outside the Church. The former is the prevailing one until *Ethics,* then the latter takes firmer hold. The two then exist side by side for awhile until ecclesiology is set aside in *Letters and Papers from Prison,* except when, in the very end, it comes back in a final vision of "being-for-others" and "sharing in the sufferings of God in the secular life." This last vision is also, in effect, a brief uniting of the two long-standing and at least semi-oppositional Christologies.

Whatever similarity this has to the treatment of Bonhoeffer's Christology above, an important difference is present. It is best seen in Phillips' conclusions for the 1933 Christology lectures. He writes:

". . . But now Bonhoeffer has moved beyond the limitations of 'Christ existing as the Church' to a conception of the person of Christ as both the centre and boundary of the individual believer. He has located the central Christological problem not in the relationship of God to Jesus nor of Jesus to the Church, but in the manner in which Jesus is in the world, for others. Revelation becomes the act in which Christ, who comes to me in Word, Sacrament and Community, the humiliated God-Man whose total existence is for me, is confessed as God. As the absolutely transcendent, he stands free from me on the boundary and at the centre of my existence; in his transcendence, I find my centre and my boundary." (*Ibid.,* p. 83.)

Phillips thus sees the 1933 lectures as evidencing a Christology of wider dimensions than the ecclesiological. This development was cut short, however, by the *Kirchenkampf,* which forced Bonhoeffer to polish ecclesiological wares for battle.

The error here is a severe neglect of the universalism in the 1933 Christology lectures, a severe neglect of the ontological dimensions of Bonhoeffer's Christology at that time. The "new" in the 1933 lectures is Christ as the center of *man, nature,* and *history,* not Christ as "the centre and boundary of the *individual believer!"* (Quoted from above, emphasis mine.) To put it differently: Phillips' tie of the Christ in the 1933 lectures to "*my* centre and *my* boundary" (quoted from above, emphasis mine) badly neglects the tie of Christ to human sociality, nature and history. Phillips fails to see the dimensions in these lectures that make *Ethics* no surprise.

There is indeed far-reaching agreement with Phillips that important changes occur in Bonhoeffer's christological thinking. But it is quite a different matter whether one argues two separable Christologies, each standing in opposition to the other, or whether one argues essentially one Christology, the development of which is a later drawing-out of long-standing, latent themes. I have argued the latter and asserted that the resistance movement (detachable for Phillips) is the major catalyst for this development.

Despite this disagreement with Phillips' *sine qua non* and his duet of Christologies, his book is most deserving of the wide reception it has received.

93

Part II
PACIFISM AND TYRANNICIDE

1
The Character of Bonhoeffer's Pacifism

Introduction

To seek Jesus Christ among new claims—"Who is Christ for us today?"—is the *cantus firmus* that winds through the polyphony of Bonhoeffer's abbreviated life. This polyphony included self-proclaimed "Christian pacifism"[1] and, seemingly at another extreme, readiness to be the assassin of Hitler, should the die so fall.[2] It is to these peculiarities of the polyphony—pacifism and conspiracy—that we now turn.

In considering the secondary motifs the reader must not let it escape him that Bonhoeffer's Christology, and not his pacifism and not his conspiracy, is the *cantus firmus*. But with this note on the arrangement of the score, the secondary themes can be entertained.

This chapter thus moves on from the previous one. The arguments, commentary, and conclusions will not be repeated; rather, they will either be assumed or reviewed with brevity.

Another delimitation will help set the parameters. Chapter Two accorded more attention to Bonhoeffer's understanding of his conspiratorial activity than to his pacifism. The latter will carry the weight of this chapter.

---

[1] Bonhoeffer wrote a girl friend of a change in his life in the early thirties. Included is: "I suddenly saw as self-evident the Christian pacifism that I had recently passionately opposed." (As cited in the *Biography*, p. 155.)

[2] *Biography*, p. 656. Bethge adds: "That was certainly a theoretical position, for Bonhoeffer knew nothing about how to handle either guns or explosives" (*ibid.*). That Bonhoeffer understood nothing about guns or explosives may be due in part to his "Christian pacifism." But it goes without saying that even such a "theoretical position" is extremely important for this study.

In the end, however, both pacifism and conspiracy must somehow flow together if Bonhoeffer meant what he said in April, 1944.

. . . Nor have I ever regretted my decision in the summer of 1939, for I am firmly convinced—however strange it may seem—that my life has followed a straight and unbroken course, at any rate in its outward conduct.[3]

It does indeed seem strange! Or is Bonhoeffer simply self-forgetful of the polar points in his own experience? Is he perhaps deceiving himself or being unmindful or unaware of the abyss between nonviolent protest and killing a head of state? Can "Christian pacifism" and approval of tyrannicide possibly lie on the same "straight and unbroken course"? If they can, did they in fact for Bonhoeffer?

Answering such questions must decipher what Bonhoeffer meant by "Christian pacifism." He himself says little of a directly definitive nature. Perhaps this is why there is no major systematic study of it.[4] Nor did Chapter Two venture a definition.

A general definition of pacifism at the outset may prove helpful. It must be general enough to let Bonhoeffer's understanding build itself without the hindrance of foregone and imposed categories.

Despite the great variety among pacifists, all share the conviction that the employment of violent coercion is an evil and war is an unallowed form of violent coercion. Some may say, as apostles of consistent nonviolence, that violent coercion must never be used. Others may allow its use in some cases, perhaps excluding categorically only the form of war. But in all cases, the employment of violent coercion is an evil. A bare-bones definition, then, is as follows: the pacifist is one who always views the use of violent coercion as an evil and who rules out war even as a necessary evil.

Occasionally "pacifism" or "Christian pacifism" will be placed in quotation marks. This refers to Bonhoeffer's understanding of that term. The reason for marking off his meaning from the above definition is my conviction that

---

[3] "11 April 1944," *LPP*, p. 135.

[4] There are a few articles that deal with the move from passive to active resistance. But they do not delineate Bonhoeffer's kind of pacifism, except in the most broad-brushed way. See: Walter Dress, *"Militia Christi*—Dietrich Bonhoeffer als Widerstandskaempfer," *Forschen und Wirken*, III (Berlin: VEB Deutscher Verlag, 1960), 709-26; Andreas Lindt, "Dietrich Bonhoeffer und der Weg vom christlichen Glauben zum politischen Handeln," *Reformatio: Evangelische Zeitschrift fuer Kultur und Politik,* XVI. Jahrgang (1967), 251-57; Winfried Maechler, "Vom Pazifisten zum Widerstandskaempfer," *Die muendige Welt,* I (Munich: Chr. Kaiser Verlag, 1955), 89-95; see also the chapter "From Pacifism to Resistance," in: William Kuhns, *In Pursuit of Dietrich Bonhoeffer* (Dayton, Ohio: Pflaum Press, 1967), pp. 221-32. There is a great deal of pertinent material and many insights in Bethge's *Biography,* but it cannot be considered a major systematic treatment of Bonhoeffer's pacifism as such.

Bonhoeffer's self-acclaimed Christian pacifism rarely meets the minimal requirements of any useful definition of pacifism.

The Literature

Because the question of war is both a critical question for pacifism and for Bonhoeffer, it will be the organizing theme for the survey of the literature. It is not the only critical question for either pacifism or Bonhoeffer, however, and the reader should not assume that conclusions about the use of violence in the form of war can be automatically transferred to conclusions about its employment in other ways—tyrannicide, for example.

The first helpful statement on war is part of the 1929 Barcelona lecture on Christian ethics. The section on war is largely unpublished, and what is published is untranslated.[5] For these reasons rather lengthy passages follow. They will serve as the base points for comparing subsequent stands.

. . . Yet there is a possibility that the commandment of love appears to be self-contradictory. The problem continually being aired to show this is that of war. . . . The full weakness and misery of Christianity, its churches and confessors, has manifest itself in the fact that it has not been possible to prevent war. Not only that, but Christians, if they really wanted to be Christians, should have resolutely opposed military service, as has been done by a number of Christian sects. They have made the duty of every single man who calls himself "Christian" in all seriousness to take the most frightful punishment upon himself rather than go to war. For it is stated clearly: "Thou shalt not kill"; "Do not resist one who is evil. But if anyone strikes you on the right cheek, turn to him the other also; and if any one would sue you and take your coat, let him have your cloak as well; and if any one forces you to one mile, go with him two miles." (Matthew 5:39-41.) "You have heard that it was said to the men of old, 'You shall love your neighbor and hate your enemy.' But I say to you, Love your enemies and pray for those who persecute you; so that you may be sons of your Father who is in heaven." (Matthew 5:43 ff.) "For what does it profit a man, if he gains the whole world and forfeits his life?" (Matthew 16:26a.) Thus it stands clear and plain in the New Testament, and all the twisting of meanings possible doesn't help: "Do not resist one who is evil"; "Thou shalt not kill." Does anyone still dare somehow or another justify war from a Christian point of view? Millions of Christian men do go to war, and not only out of constraint but because they confess the will of God. They hold services and dare draw the holy names of God and Jesus Christ into this dreadful murder. War is nothing other than murder. War is a crime. No Christian can go to war. The argument appears perfectly clear and incisive. And yet it is faulty at the most important point: it is not concrete and as a consequence does not take in the depths of Christian

---

[5] The published material is a footnote on pp. 56-57 of *Gesammelte Schriften* III. *No Rusty Swords* deleted this.

decision. It invokes the commandment not to kill and thinks it thereby has the solution in hand. But here the decisive dilemma is overlooked, the dilemma which becomes clear the instant my *Volk*[6] is attacked, [the dilemma that] for me the love commandment extends at least as much to the protection of that which is mine as it does to the prohibition against killing the enemy. It would surely be a complete perversion of ethical consciousness were I to mean that it is now my first duty to love the enemy and, in order to do that, sacrifice him who is my neighbor in a concrete sense. The possibility of loving my enemy and my *Volk* (i.e., of protecting my *Volk*) does not exist in a simple way. Rather I stand in the concrete situation of abandoning either my brother or my enemy to destruction. I am set in this dilemma in that moment when war is declared for me, i.e. in that moment when I either go to war or do not go. If out of conviction I do not go, it means nothing else than abandoning my own in the very moment of their need. And I do this by the very fact that I appeal to the Christ who says to me: "Love your neighbor as yourself." That surely means love your neighbor more than your anxious conscience. Love your neighbor as the first and only thing; what then follows is a secondary matter. Yes, but is not the enemy my neighbor as well, just as my own brother? Is it not precisely the achievement of Christianity that this external difference is leveled out by the powerful concept of universal brotherhood? Granted. But those are questions rising from theoretical reflection, not out of the concrete situation. If I suddenly stand before the dreadful decision of either exposing my own brother or my mother to the hand of the attacker or instead raising my hand against the enemy, then the immediate situation will surely tell me which of these two is and must be my neighbor, even in God's eyes. God has given me my mother, my *Volk*. What I have, I have thanks to this *Volk*. What I am, I am through my *Volk*. Thus what I have should also belong to my *Volk*. This is divine order, for God created the *Voelker*.

If I fail to act in a danger-ridden moment, the result is nothing other than the sacrifice of the neighbor.

One further matter: the Christian who goes to war will not hate his enemy because it is impossible for him to hate. Even in battle he will pray for him and his soul. When he surrenders his body up to death he will still bless him, even when he received the mortal blow from the hand of the enemy. For the enemy, too, is in the same distress as he. The enemy, too, protects his mother, his children and his *Volk*.

With that the situation appears clear to me. In such a case there remains for me no longer the choice between good and evil. The decision, as it must be made, will stain me with the world and its laws. I will raise the weapon in the awful knowledge of doing something atrocious, but being unable to do anything else. I will protect my brother, my mother, my *Volk* and nevertheless know that this can only be done through the shedding of blood. Yet love for my *Volk* will sanctify murder, will sanctify war. As a Christian I will suffer under the full horror that is war be-

---

[6] I leave "*Volk*" untranslated despite the awkward reading. The overtones of an organic entity are not sufficiently conveyed by the closest English equivalent—"people."

cause the serious responsibility weighs heavily on my soul. I will attempt to love the enemy whom I am sworn to love in death or life, as only a Christian can love his brother. And nevertheless I will do something to him which the love and gratitude to my *Volk,* in which God let me be born, commands me to do. I will finally acknowledge that only in the continuing relation to God, in which Christian decisions are made in ever-renewed submission to the divine will, can it remain certain that, even when the world violates my conscience, my decision can only be that to which God has led me in the holy hour of the encounter of my will with his, in the hour when he overcame my will.

If we look again at the argument of the other side, then we recognize as decisive the fact that its advocates make the commands of the New Testament into laws. They make themselves slaves of these laws when they should be making their decisions in freedom. They judge according to the literal meaning but not according to the spirit of the Christian. They act according to principles, not out of the extreme situation given me by God. Sparks do not spring out of empty space, but as hard stones strike one another. So, too, the Holy Spirit does not flash forth in ideas and principles but in the urgent decision of the moment.

With that the problem of war is certainly not exhausted. The question remains whether war is ethically justifiable, including the case in which one begins it himself. But that leads back to a wider problem, to the question of the leadership of history and God, of *Volk* and God, of God and the process of growth.

Voelker are like men. They are immature and need leadership. They grow to fullness of youth, to years of manhood, and they die. There is nothing in that which is of itself either good or evil. Yet deep questions lie concealed here. For growth leads to expansion. Welling up of strength leads to pushing others aside. This is no different in the life of the individual than in the life of a *Volk.* Every *Volk* has a call of God within it to make history, a call to enter competitively into the life of *Voelker.* This call may properly be heard in growing and becoming, so that it takes place in the sight of God. God calls the *Volk* to manliness, to battle and to victory. The strength is also from God and the power and the victory, for God creates youth among men and *Volk;* and God loves youth, for God himself is eternally young and strong and triumphant. Anxiety and frailty should be overcome by courage and strength. Should not a *Volk* which has experienced the call of God in its own life, a call in its youth and strength, should not such a *Volk* be allowed to follow this call, even when it disregards the life of other *Voelker?* God is the Lord of history, and if a *Volk* bends itself in humility to the holy will of Him who guides history, then this *Volk* in its youth and strength, and with God, will overcome the weak and cowardly; then God will be with it. Of course, when this moment has come for a *Volk* can and may only be decided by men with the consciousness of utterly serious responsibility for that which they do; and they do it in the sacrifice of the will of the self to the divine will which directs world history.[7]

[7] Dietrich Bonhoeffer, "Grundfragen einer christlichen Ethik" (an address given in Barcelona, Spain, 1929). This portion was received as a typewritten copy of the original from the Rev. Christfried Berger, East Berlin. Pastor Berger obtained it from Eberhard Bethge. Further debt

One point from the published portion of the lecture must be added. Count Tolstoy's pacifism and the claim of the Christian conscientious objector are rejected because they are grounded in a legalistic exegesis of the Sermon on the Mount.[8] This is readily deducible from the above passages as well, but it is important to register what Bonhoeffer has explicitly excluded.

Eberhard Bethge writes that the twenty-two-year-old vicar "is not yet talking his own language."[9] This is certainly true for Bethge's references: Bonhoeffer's aggressive language of *"Volk"* and the picture of God as "eternally young and strong and triumphant." *"Volk"* soon turned ecclesiological and self-denying, and God became the weak Man of Sorrows of the *theologia crucis.*

Yet much of Bonhoeffer's language continues to the end. A rejection of the teachings of the Sermon on the Mount as timeless principles carries through uninterruptedly. And his ethic, however "filled,"[10] remains radically contextual, methodologically considered. Too, ethics is strictly response ethics. This persists unabated throughout Bonhoeffer's ethics, although it becomes far more christocentric than here. All these motifs have important implications for Bonhoeffer's later pacifism, as we shall see.

What does the Barcelona address yield on the specifics of pacifism and war?

Christian pacifism is rejected because it sacrifices the nearest neighbor (*naechsten Naechsten*), because it rejects God-willed history of the strong over the weak, and because it rests upon a lifeless, legalistic exegesis of Matthew 5–7 that can only make the Christian a slave of Law.

War is clearly viewed as sin, crime, murder. It is always an evil. Conscience can be violated by war. War brings the conflict within the commandment of love to its severest dilemma: love the nearest neighbor and kill the enemy, or love the enemy and sacrifice the nearest neighbor. *Ergo pecca fortiter.* Universal brotherhood is termed "a powerful concept" of Christianity, but it fails to say anything concrete for the dilemma. The love commandment and universal brotherhood do mean, however, that the Christian cannot hate the enemy even in the moment of killing him—or being killed by him. Participation in war is necessary, but it will always be agonizing for the Christian.

War can be the concrete command of God for my *Volk.* With that, war and murder are sanctified. Not only a war of defense is a moral possibility but one of aggression as well. It lies in "the consciousness of the men of serious responsibility" to determine whether this call of "the young and strong and triumphant" God has now come to my *Volk,* the call to make history by making war.[11]

---

to Pastor Berger must be acknowledged. His own unpublished thesis on Bonhoeffer's pacifism was instructive for portions of this chapter.

[8] "Grundfragen einer christlichen Ethik," *GS* III, 54. See p. 26 above, showing Bonhoeffer's rabidly anti-principle, situational ethic as presented in this lecture.

[9] *Biography,* p. 86.   [10] See pp. 26-29 above.

[11] The raging contradictions, inconsistencies, and erroneous political judgments in this lecture

Perceptible alterations are visible but a year after Barcelona.[12] The contact abroad gave flesh to the ecclesiological Christology of *The Communion of Saints*. A New York address shows this by initiating the shift of *"Volk"* from an organic, national entity to a supranational, ecclesiological one. "It must never more happen that a Christian people fights against a Christian people, brother against brother, since both have one Father." [13] Sympathy with peace movements[14] emerges in this address as well, but far too little is said to ascertain Bonhoeffer's own stand on pacifism. Clearer is the passion for peace which stamps the entire address, a robust line that weaves through all his ecumenical work.[15]

The next year Bonhoeffer and Franz Hildebrandt composed a catechism that states flatly that the Church knows nothing of a sanction for war. She prays only for peace.[16] This is in full contrast to Barcelona. Nor is it the tone of the Spanish address when Bonhoeffer and Hildebrandt emphasize the universality of mankind so strongly and flatly label "a national boast based on flesh and

---

are not the concern here. Suffice it to say that Bonhoeffer is attaching a rather conventional German Lutheran *"Schoepfungsordnung"* ethic of this time to a Barthian *Roemerbrief* stance of man before God in the naked situation. He does not see how the two cannot coalesce. Principles drawn from a crass *"Volkstheologie"* of the orders of creation are freely used at the same time Bonhoeffer asserts that only an atomistic situational ethic is possible.

[12] For reasons of economy the changes from the Barcelona stand will receive the emphasis rather than the continuities. The latter should be assumed when not stated.

[13] "Ansprache in New York," *GS* I, 72-73. The English is Bonhoeffer's. [14] *Ibid.*

[15] *Ibid.*, passim. Jean Lasserre, who so strongly influenced Bonhoeffer's pacifism (see the *Biography,* pp. 111 ff.) recalls a fact important to our subject; namely, that Bonhoeffer's ardent quest for peace preceded his turn to pacifism. Lasserre remembers especially the passion with which Bonhoeffer spoke of peace to a student group in Mexico at the end of the year at Union. (Interview with Jean Lasserre, West Berlin, November 16, 1968.) Bonhoeffer's friend and brother-in-law has written that if one wants to locate a single controlling political motive throughout all the years of passive and active resistance, it must be the quest for national and international peace. This preceded his pacifism, and it is clear throughout his conspiratorial work. (Walter Dress, *"Militia Christi:* Dietrich Bonhoeffer als Widerstandskaempfer," *Forschen und Wirken,* pp. 718 ff). Another close friend, Otto Dudzus, writes: "This passionate call [Fanø] to a world Church which feels itself responsible for peace was for Bonhoeffer not an isolated affair which was broken off because it obviously found no echo. He stuck to this responsibility throughout all the complications and confusions, including his personal 'change' from a pacifist to an active resistance fighter. Even the Bonhoeffer of the conspiracy who saw clearly how far he had removed himself from his direct charge within the Church, and who at least sometimes, asked whether this did not make him unfit for the service of the proclamation, even he can only be grasped within this ecumenical responsibility for peace." (Otto Dudzus, "Arresting the Wheel," *I Knew DB,* p. 90.) Bonhoeffer's last message is consistent with the interpretations of Dress and Dudzus. Payne Best was to pass along the following words to Bishop Bell: "Tell him that for me this is the end but also the beginning—with him I believe in the principle of our Universal [sic] Christian brotherhood which rises above all national interests, and that our victory is certain." (G. K. A. Bell, "The Church and the Resistance Movement," *I Knew DB,* pp. 209-10.)

[16] Bonhoeffer and Franz Hildebrandt, "Glaubst Du, so hast Du," *GS* III, 252. It is a sign of Bonhoeffer's "unorthodoxy" that this was the first German Lutheran catechism to handle the war, peace, and ecumenical themes. (*Biography,* p. 144.)

blood" as "a sin against the Spirit." [17] Participation of the Christian in war is not ruled out, however,[18] and the issue of conscientious objection is not raised.[19]

In a 1932 address Bonhoeffer writes that two modes of self-assertion have developed in modern times—passive resistance as exemplified in Gandhi's movement, and war and technology as developed in the West.[20] The speaker exhibits deep sympathy for Gandhi's ways and in the process draws a fully romanticized picture of India.[21] Yet he still hesitantly allows the possibility that war, despite the massive destruction brought on by technological "progress," might occasionally be justifiable, although for one reason only—preparation for community. Where this rare case arises, the sacrifice of the individual is rightly required.[22]

Through this 1932 address, then, it must be concluded that Bonhoeffer was not a pacifist. He has certainly said that war is always evil. But he has not ruled it out as an occasionally necessary evil. On the contrary, the literature from 1929 through 1931 and into 1932 has rendered the justification of war and particpation in it possible for the Christian. It is significant, however, that both are less and less possible. Bonhoeffer's attraction to pacifism has been growing; his ecclesiastical, christological universalism has been broadening; and his campaign for peace as an act of the Ecumenical Church has been gathering momentum.

The 1932 ecumenical addresses have not yet been considered. They both exemplify and strengthen these bold shifts away from the Barcelona picture. In these addresses a prime task of the Ecumenical Church is to excommunicate War.[23] "War today and therefore the next war" is so utterly destructive of both body and soul that it "must be utterly rejected by the Church." [24] As a consequence, "we should not shy from using the word 'pacifism'." [25]

With this positive use of the term "pacifism" the question becomes: what kind of pacifism is meant by Bonhoeffer?

Strong clues are provided but no definition as such. This "pacifism" is clearly provisional, however. "Therefore the Church must not preach timeless principles however valid, but only commands which are valid today. To us God

---

[17] *Ibid.*   [18] *Ibid.*, p. 253.

[19] In this chapter "conscientious objection" never refers to legal status. Such did not exist in Germany at this time. Rather, conscientious objection is used in a general way meaning the individual's opposition to participation in military service because such participation violates his conscience.

[20] "Das Recht auf Selbstbehauptung," *GS* III, 261-69.

[21] *Ibid.*, pp. 261-62.   [22] *Ibid.*, p. 267.

[23] "Ansprache in Gland," *GS* I, 168 ff. and "A Theological Basis for the World Alliance?" *NRS*, pp. 157 ff.

[24] "A Theological Basis for the World Alliance?" *NRS*, p. 170. Trans. corrected.

[25] *Ibid.* Trans. corrected.

is 'always' *God 'today.'* "[26] Thus, "[the Church] should be able to say quite definitely: 'Engage in this war' or 'Do not engage in this war.' " [27]

We have already probed the structure of Bonhoeffer's contextual ethics.[28] This can only mean Bonhoeffer's "pacifism" must "always" be provisional (assuming he is faithful to his own emphatic assertions on methodology). Respecting Christ's full sovereignty and seeking his commands in all claims, Bonhoeffer must allow war and participation in war as possible commands, however exceptional. If pacifism is now the concrete shape of obedience to Christ's command, it is the shape *now*. Bonhoeffer's methodology dictates that pacifism be provisional. The Church is to say: "Engage in this war" or "Do not engage in this war." This is no more and no less than Bonhoeffer's lifelong assault on *"Prinzipien,"* now applied to absolute pacifism on the one hand and unquestioning obedience to the war-involved State on the other.[29] In different words, to affirm a pacifism on principle (or obedience to the State on principle) would fall into the timeless and placeless moral discourse that Bonhoeffer repudiates with his radical contextualism. Any pacifism must, in Bonhoeffer's scheme, consistently search out whether it remains Christ's concrete command as the historical context changes. It cannot be an abiding pacifism that knows no exception to its course (absolute pacifism or pacifism on principle). It must be God's command valid *today* and thus a provisional or conditional pacifism (although certainly a renewable one "tomorrow").

Bonhoeffer's "pacifism" is also militant pacifism. Struggle *(Kampf)*[30] is commended. Indeed the command of Christ "can demand the most radical destruction of orders of preservation for the sake of Him Who builds up."[31] Yet there is one means of struggle not allowed among the various means of radical destruction—war *(Krieg)*. "Today [it] stands under God's prohibition."[32] *Kampf,* even radical destruction, but not *Krieg today*—such is Bonhoeffer's "pacifism" in the 1932 ecumenical addresses: provisional and militant.

Today there must be no more war—the cross will not have it. We must make a distinction: nothing happens without struggle in the world fallen from God, but there must be no more war.[33]

"The cross will not have it." Bonhoeffer began his love affair with the Sermon on the Mount at this time, and he interpreted it in accord with his *theologia*

---

[26] *Ibid.,* p. 162. Trans. corrected. [27] *Ibid.,* p. 163. [28] See pp. 24-26 ff. above.
[29] *"Prinzip"* in German carries a more negative connotation than "principle" in English. It is a stiff, bloodless formula quite unbendable in the face of history's unpredictable onslaughts. History must be formed with it, not vice versa. This is important to note because Bonhoeffer rightly sees no contradiction between his attack on *"Prinzipien"* and his assertion about the binding nature of Christ's concrete commands.
[30] *"Kampf"* is a strong word. It is struggle as combat, battle, engagement, conflict.
[31] "A Theological Basis for the World Alliance?" *NRS,* p. 167. Trans. corrected.
[32] *Ibid.,* p. 171. [33] "Ansprache in Gland," *GS* I, 168.

crucis. If his was a genuine pacifism, it was genuinely one of the cross, a pacifism of the *theologia crucis,* as even a hurried reading of *The Cost of Discipleship* verifies.[34]

The *theologia crucis* means considerable for Bonhoeffer's "pacifism." He distinguished sharply between a pacifism of suffering love and the "humanist" or "secular" pacifism rather prominent between the World Wars. The latter was, in his mind, a naïve, optimistic strategy confident it could bring about a new international order without tragic conflict. Herbert Jehle, who probably discussed pacifism with Bonhoeffer more than anyone in the years 1931-1935, recalls that Bonhoeffer again and again distinguished his "pacifism" from that of liberal humanism.

. . . The times he made exceptions to pacifism were times he rejected the purely secular pacifism which intended to bring a beautiful order in the world smoothly, without recognizing the basic terrible conflicts in life, without realizing that the forces of evil are great and grotesque. . . . Gerhard Jacobi distorts matters somewhat when he says Bonhoeffer's interest in India is primarily out of his attraction to *"Leiden"* [suffering].[35] Bonhoeffer was not looking for the occasion to prove faith by suffering. Rather he looked at the political life of nations, in particular Germany, and concluded that obedience to the Sermon on the Mount would inevitably bring *"Leiden"* and sacrifice. His pacifism was not grim in the face of this fact because he understood the cross as victory, not defeat; but he could not share the smooth optimism of much of the Anglo-Saxon pacifism of those days because it did not understand the depths of evil and the consequence that Christians would really literally suffer.[36]

Bonhoeffer's pen gives evidence of the same distinction Jehle recalls as important. The theses for discussion at the 1934 meeting of the Universal Christian Council for Life and Work in Fanø, Denmark, cut a wide swathe between an ecclesiological pacifism of the cross and what Bonhoeffer labels simply "secular pacifism." [37]

The Fanø statement is Bonhoeffer's most unqualifiedly pacifist one. He is very close to absolute pacifism. It is more militant and courageous than ever

[34] See pp. 15-24 above for the place of the *theologia crucis* in Bonhoeffer's thought and pp. 156 ff. of *The Cost of Discipleship* for the consequential nonviolence and nonresistance. *The Cost of Discipleship* was pieced together over the years 1932-1937.

[35] The reference is to Gerhard Jacobi, "Drawn to Suffering," *I Knew DB,* pp. 71-74.

[36] Interview with Dr. Herbert Jehle, Charlottesville, Virginia, March 1, 1968. Other close friends recall the identical distinction made by Bonhoeffer during the years he espoused pacifism. Interviews: Franz Hildebrandt, Edinburgh, Scotland, September 17, 1968; Gerhard Jacobi, Oldenburg, West Germany, September 23, 1968; Winfried Maechler, West Berlin, February 22, 1969; Julius Rieger, West Berlin, February 21, 1969; Albrecht Schoenherr, East Berlin, February 24, 1969.

[37] "The Church and the World of Nations," *GS* I, 444-46.

and wholly single-minded; it is a desperate plea for bold "unconditional, blind obedience of action." [38]

To be sure, the goal is not pacifism but peace. Peace must be dared. It is the opposite of security. It is a battle on the way of the cross. It means sheer witness and pure suffering. But it must be ventured because Christ so commands.[39] The question of consequences is the question of the Serpent. Simply obey and obey simply. This is surely the militancy and the witness-without-reservation of *The Cost of Discipleship* and, it might be added, of formal or vocational pacifism. Precisely this kind of pacifism is the great, desperate venture needed to achieve peace "today."

Fanø is also pacifism of an ecclesiological, christological genre. The Ecumenical Church is to speak out as an authentic Council to prevent her sons from taking up arms against one another. For if they do, they "take up arms against Christ himself!" [40] (A more fundamental basis for Christian pacifism is not possible for one so christocentric and church-centered as Bonhoeffer at this time.)

The questions of Barcelona surface again. But now they are castigated as forms of the Serpent's question, "Yea, hath God said. . . ?" "Did God say you should not protect your own people? Did God say you should leave your own a prey to the enemy? No, God did not say all that. What he has said is that there shall be peace among men—that we shall obey Him without further question." [41] Barcelona is reversed. Not only is the just war denied but the nearest neighbor is apparently not sufficient reason for justifying participation in a war of defense.

Is Bonhoeffer's "pacifism" now absolute? That is, is he saying "never war and in the case of war never military service"? The language as such would confirm such a judgment. Yet friends at Fanø reply in the negative. Winfried Maechler remembers the protracted discussions with Bonhoeffer about the rapidly degenerating international situation. Bonhoeffer, who believed from 1933 on that Hitler meant war if allowed his course,[42] was markedly distressed over Germany's withdrawal from the Disarmament Conference in Geneva and from the League of Nations, Hitler's amalgamation of the posts of *"Fuehrer"* and *"Reichskanzler,"* the so-called "Roehm revolt," and the murder of Austrian statesman Dollfuss by the Nazis. In light of the swiftly worsening conditions and the breakdown of the potential international peace organs, the *militia Christi* who wrote that "some things are worth an uncompromising stand and it seems to me that peace and social justice, *or actually Christ,* are just such" [43] now felt it a matter of utmost necessity to issue a resounding ap-

---

[38] "The Church and the People of the World," *GS* I, 447.

[39] *Ibid.,* p. 448.   [40] *Ibid.*   [41] *Ibid.,* p. 447.

[42] *Biography,* p. 191.   [43] "Brief an Karl-Friedrich Bonhoeffer," *GS* III, 25. Emphasis mine.

peal for radical action by some international body to create peace. And Bonhoeffer at this time was emphatic that *the* body to make the great venture was the Body of Christ in the form of the Ecumenical Church. In short, Maechler, himself as absolute pacifist, understands his friend's pacifism at Fanø as a rallying of forces "now" to create peace in a precarious moment.[44] "Who is Christ for us today?" is the question, as ever, and "today" Christ is the commander of brave pacifist action for the sake of peace in our time. Bonhoeffer's "pacifism" thus appears to remain provisional. That is, there is no indication Bonhoeffer's contextualism has been altered—indeed, the use of the word "today" in the Fanø sermon and in the address at Gland underlines Bonhoeffer's continuing conviction about the concrete *now* of Christ's command. Further, and closely related, the testimony of friends at least points to the particular historical context as influential for Bonhoeffer's stand.[45]

Even pacifism must not move front and center: "It is not pacifism that is the victory which overcomes the world (I John 5:4) but faith, which expects everything from God and hopes in the coming of Christ and His Kingdom." [46]

Otto Dudzus, also at Fanø, agrees with Maechler's account and adds the important point that Bonhoeffer's language, lacking "ifs," "whens," "hows," and other qualifiers of absolute pacifism, was the language of proclamation and demand, of grace and its claims. There is a very good reason, for the Fanø address was a sermon.[47] The attainment of peace is not up for discussion; it is simply the command of Christ which must be obeyed. Serious ethical deliberation might have sounded different, perhaps with the more guarded tones of a memorandum six months later.

. . . I am in favour of an international youth conference and I should be glad if the question of conscientious objection would be one of the subjects under discussion. I feel that one of the weaknesses of our cause is the lack of a common and definite

[44] Interview with Winfried Maechler, West Berlin, February 22, 1969. It is Maechler who, in another place, records Bonhoeffer's answer at Fanø to a Swede who asked what Bonhoeffer would do in case of war. Bonhoeffer replied he would pray to God to give him strength not to take up arms. (Maechler, "Vom Pazifisten zum Widerstandskaempfer," *Die muendige Welt,* I, 92.) For a like account that the German course in 1934 meant war in Bonhoeffer's judgment, see: Julius Rieger, *Bonhoeffer in England* (Berlin: Lettner-Verlag, 1966), p. 12. Reiger and Bonhoeffer were pastors in London at this time.

[45] Further confirmation is found in a recently discovered letter to Th. de Fèlice. Referring to his Fanø address Bonhoeffer writes that he has "altered the content in accordance with the present state of affairs." (Dietrich Bonhoeffer, "Brief an Th. de Fèlice, 12.8.1934," *Dokumente zur Bonhoeffer Forschung,* ed. Jørgen Glenthøj [Munich: Chr. Kaiser Verlag, 1969], p. 228.) Because Bonhoeffer does not indicate in what way the content was changed, the letter cannot be used to demonstrate the nature of Bonhoeffer's "pacifism" except to point up Bonhoeffer's sensitivity to "the present state of affairs" as influential upon content. (See also the *Biography,* pp. 300 and 310-13.)

[46] "The Church and the World of Nations," *GS* I, 446.

[47] Interview with Otto Dudzus, Cologne, West Germany, October 11, 1968.

attitude in this very crucial question. We should march on whatever the older people think and do. . . . One of the special topics I should like to propose for the youth conference is: the use of coercion, its right and its limitations. Before this fundamental question is given an answer to, the theoretical basis of pacifism is very weak.[48]

Finally, the pacifism that reached its peak at Fanø, if absolute, is qualifiedly so because, like almost all Bonhoeffer's appeals in these years, it is directed almost wholly to the Church. Bonhoeffer placed great hope in the Ecumenical Church and there made his pacifist pleas. To my knowledge, there is, in fact, only one instance of evidence that Bonhoeffer's pacifism may have envisioned a broader constituency than the ecclesiastical one. He speculates: "Which of us can say he knows what it might mean for the world if one nation should meet the aggressor, not with weapons in hand, but praying, defenceless, and for that very reason protected by 'a bulwark never failing'?" [49]

Yet this is a question, a conjecture, a hope, and Bonhoeffer's typical stance during these years is that of *The Cost of Discipleship*. Here nonviolence and even nonresistance are required of disciples, but Bonhoeffer is emphatic that this cannot be made a principle for secular life. The world will not follow Jesus' way of nonviolence and nonresistance; to transpose his way into a strategy for public order would thus be to wear "the blinkers of perfectionism" and to indulge "in idealistic dreams." [50] But there is a "gracious order for the preservation of the world," [51] an order Christians acknowledge as God's, an order that is manifest when the State wards off chaos through the exercise of hard coercion.[52] Bonhoeffer even says that to seek to make nonviolence and nonresistance principles for secular life is "to deny God" [53] because this would flaunt God's gracious provisions for preservation through the maintenance of public order. Yet *Christians* and the Church are to traverse the way of Jesus without deviation,[54] knowing full well the outcome is crucifixion (pacifism of the cross), and leaving the exercise of coercion to God's gracious function as Preserver.[55]

---

[48] "Memorandum an die Jugendkommission, 29.1.1935," *Dokumente zur Bonhoeffer Forschung*, p. 241. This was part of the planning for the ecumenical youth conference in Chanby in 1935.

[49] "The Churches and Peoples of the World," *GS* I, 448. In light of this classic statement of pacifism and the address as a whole it is hard to see what E. H. Robertson means when he says Bonhoeffer's sermon at Fanø "was a call to peace, but not to pacifism." (*NRS*, p. 289.)

[50] *CD*, p. 160.   [51] *Ibid.*, p. 161.   [52] *Ibid.*, p. 293.   [53] *Ibid.*, p. 161.

[54] Bonhoeffer is fully sectarian here. Nonviolence is applied *equally* to the Christian's private *and* public life. (*Ibid.*, p. 159.)

[55] This suggests that a parasiticism is part of Bonhoeffer's pacifism. Physical, often violent, force must be carried out by someone in obedience to God's will for public order and justice. But disciples cannot be the agents of the necessary coercion. Yet they live from its benefits. This might also hint of asceticism in Bonhoeffer's pacifism if the disciple's abstention from using

The distinction may not be minor. It mirrors a version of the two-spheres doctrine Bonhoeffer held at this time. Perhaps the two-spheres demarcations explain why the Bonhoeffer writing *The Cost of Discipleship* was angry when England and France failed to intervene militarily as Hitler took the Rhineland.[56] Hitler meant national chaos and international war. The coercion of intervention must meet his violence. Yet it must not be undertaken by disciples.

There are other plausible reasons why Bonhoeffer could evince seemingly ambivalent behavior at this juncture. One is simply his own indecision about these matters. In the drafts for another catechism (1936) Bonhoeffer first wrote: "May a Christian take part in war?" Then he crossed this out and substituted: "What does God say to war?"[57] This too was struck, and the final draft reads:

How should the Christian conduct himself in war? . . . Here there is no clear command of God. The Church can never bless war and weapons. The Christian can never take part in an unjust war. If the Christian takes up the sword he will call to God daily for forgiveness of the sin and for peace.[58]

Bonhoeffer apparently is riding the border between "agonized participation"[59] and conscientious objection. It may be the latter, as Bethge suggests,[60] but it is clearly not an absolute pacifism. A just war is assumed possible. Since the entire Bonhoeffer family felt Hitler meant war, a war against Hitler might represent such a state of affairs. In any case, Bonhoeffer's indecision about the questions and answers around pacifism, conscientious objection, and agonized participation is made evident in these drafts. The certainty about the disciple's way in *The Cost of Discipleship* is absent.

Another plausible reason might be drawn to explain the reaction to the reclaiming of the Rhineland. For most of the thirties Bonhoeffer's Christian "pacifism"—provisional, militant, ecclesiological, and grounded in the *theologia crucis*—may well have been much closer to selective conscientious objection

---

coercion is based upon his refusal to be the agent of a necessary evil. Both parasiticism and asceticism will be discussed later.

[56] Interview with Otto Dudzus, Cologne, West Germany, October 11, 1968. With the possible exception of the Fanø question cited above, there is not the slightest evidence that Bonhoeffer ever wanted any state to be "pacifist" over against Hitler. The evidence is to the contrary. Dr. Hanfried Mueller believes Bonhoeffer would have approved use of violence in every case where he was convinced of the rightness of the political goal and where all indications were that nonviolent means would not suffice. Violence then is *ultima ratio* means—hardly the exclusive property of pacifism and rejected by consistent pacifists. (Interview with Hanfried Mueller, East Berlin, February 24, 1969.)

[57] *Biography*, p. 144.   [58] "Zweiter Kathechismus-Versuch," *GS* III, 342-43.

[59] The term is borrowed from Edward LeRoy Long, Jr., *War and Conscience in America* (Philadelphia: Westminster Press, 1968), p. 41.

[60] *Biography*, p. 144.

than to any Christian pacifism of a vocational sort.[61] It is probably accurate to call Bonhoeffer at least a conditional pacifist from 1932 to 1934 and mean by that no war in this epoch because its massive destruction rules it out as even an exceptional command of Christ; and if war, then no military service for the Christian. The evidence is cumulative and sound for such a designation. But this is a short time and not the decisive one.

It is not the decisive one because the pacifist's test comes with the war. It comes, as Bonhoeffer said in Barcelona, "in that moment when war is declared for me, in that moment when I either go to war or do not go." [62] A different kind of test comes when the pacifist plans the society's structures for the post-war order, i.e., when he must answer the question of turning the cheeks of millions. In the light of both tests, Bonhoeffer sounds more the selective conscientious objector as the war approaches, as well as during its course. And selective conscientious objection is not identical with conditional pacifism, much less with formal pacifism.[63]

In March, 1939, he wrote Bishop Bell:

The second point is of an *entirely personal character* and I am not certain if I may bother you with it. Please, do take it quite apart from the first point.[64] I am thinking of leaving Germany sometime.[65] The main reason is the compulsory military service to which the men of my age (1906) will be called up this year. It seems to me *conscientiously impossible* to join in a war *under the present circumstances.* On the other hand, the Confessional Church as such has not taken any definite attitude in this respect and probably cannot take it as things are. So I should cause a tremendous damage to my brethren if I would make a stand on this point which could be regarded by the regime as typical of the hostility of our Church towards the State. Perhaps the worst thing of all is the military oath which I should have to swear. So I am rather puzzled in this situation, and perhaps even more because I feel it is really only on Christian grounds that I find it difficult to do military service *under the present conditions,* and yet there are only very few friends who would approve of my attitude. In spite of much reading and thinking concerning this matter *I have not yet made up my mind what I would do under*

[61] "Vocational" or "formal" pacifism in this chapter is a synonym for "absolute" pacifism, i.e., the creed of "never war and in the case of war never military service."

[62] Quoted from p. 97 above.

[63] The selective conscientious objector would not base his refusal to serve on the obsolescence of war as such in this epoch, as Bonhoeffer did as a qualified pacifist, but he would oppose fighting for his nation in a particular war judged unjust. Bonhoeffer's case would be constructed thus: he viewed the launching of war against Hitler as the launching of a just war, and he refused to serve Hitler because the justice lay with victory by the "enemy." This is far different, viewed ethically, from the pacifist position outlined for the 1932-1934 period.

[64] The first was about the Confessing Church's representation in the ecumenical councils.

[65] The second trip to the United States was the outcome. For the importance of this see pp. 58-63 above.

different circumstances. But actually *as things are* I should have to do violence to my Christian conviction, if I would take up arms "here and now.". . .

My Lord Bishop, I am very sorry to add to your trouble. But I thought, I might speak freely to you and might ask your advice. You know the Confessional Church and you know me a bit. It was with regard to this matter that I wanted to see Visser 't Hooft too.[66]

Here, where it turns "very personal," [67] Bonhoeffer's stand sounds very much like that of the selective conscientious objector: "It seems to me conscientiously impossible to join in a war under the present conditions . . . I have not yet made up my mind what I would do under different circumstances. . . ." The Sermon on the Mount, the commandment against killing, the concrete command against war in this epoch issued at Fanø, all go unmentioned. They may well be included in the "Christian grounds" that prohibit Bonhoeffer from serving now. But if so their directives are highly subject to "conditions" and "circumstances."

"Perhaps the worst thing of all is the military oath which I should have to swear." Here is Bonhoeffer battling the *"Fuehrerprinzip"* and the new Nazi *Ersatzreligion.* He was always in the front ranks of that campaign, but, until the words turned "entirely personal," it was not always so clear that what he saw symbolized in the military oath (which swore personal fidelity to Adolf Hitler, not simply to Germany) evidently affected deeply his own stand on war, "pacifism," and conscientious objection. This is not the place to trace Bonhoeffer's stand on the oath itself. Is it only to show that it and not, for example, the inviolability of the principle of nonviolence for Christians, was given as a main reason for wishing to avoid conscription. This letter makes it extremely doubtful that Bonhoeffer can be called anything but a selective conscientious objector at this time. It cannot be ruled out that opposition to military service here is an appendage of a conditional pacifism, but the sentence, "I have not yet made up my mind what I would do under different circumstances," gives no hint of the reason Bonhoeffer gave for such pacifism earlier, namely, that the massive destruction of modern war eliminates it as even an exceptional command of Christ today. Rather, "under different circumstances" seems much more closely bound to the fact of being a German in the Third Reich who is fully opposed to Hitler's course. In any case the tone of this letter is at considerable distance from any programmatic pacifism, even if a doubtful conditional pacifism is permitted. It is of course possible that, in accord with his testimony to Lehmann,[68] Bonhoeffer's general *bearing* is pacifist, if by that is meant a strong opposition to war and if by that is indicated that nonparticipa-

---

[66] "Brief an G. K. A. Bell, Bischof von Chichester," *GS* I, 281-82. The English is Bonhoeffer's; emphasis mine.

[67] *Ibid.,* p. 280.   [68] See pp. 58-59 above.

tion is the *starting point,* placing the burden of proof upon participation in the event of war.

Perhaps Bonhoeffer's position can be clarified with a refinement of terms. If one correlates the content of the letter to Bell with his contemporaneous remarks to Lehmann and Visser 't Hooft, then perhaps the term "selective conscientious objection" is not the most precise. If Bonhoeffer's bearing is pacifist any case for joining in war must be made as *an exception to nonparticipation.* That is, the starting point is a disposition of unwillingness to participate in any war, and the burden of proof for any exception to this basic stance of nonparticipation rests with making the case *for participation.* Such a stand is probably more accurately termed "selective conscientious *participation"* than "selective conscientious *objection."* "Selective conscientious objection," by way of contrast, is the expression of a disposition given to beginning with a willingness to participate, and the burden of proof for any exception to this basic stance rests with making the case *for nonparticipation.* In short, for selective conscientious participation the bearing is that of pacifism, and the burden of proof is laid upon making the exception from nonparticipation; for selective conscientious objection the bearing is that of agonized participation, and the burden of proof is laid upon making the exception from participation.

The subtleties in such a distinction may throw light upon a possible movement in Bonhoeffer's stands from the near absolute pacifism of Fanø to a just war position in *Ethics* (as we shall see). In this movement the late thirties would seem to expose a vacillation between the above refined positions. However, the written and spoken accounts simply do not allow more than surmise here. For this reason I have used "selective conscientious objection" in a general way in this chapter, a way that covers what *may* be a vacillation between two subtle although separable stands.

But how far Bonhoeffer was from programmatic pacifism, provisional pacifism, and even from selective conscientious objection as a binding principle for all Christians in this situation, is clear in the case of Martin Niemoeller. In the autumn of 1939 Bonhoeffer unhesitatingly supported the suggestion that Niemoeller volunteer to take up his old post as captain of a U-boat.[69] Niemoeller was in Dachau, and Bonhoeffer felt the wartime economy might have insufferable consequences for the inmates of the concentration camps.[70] Just this reason shows how Bonhoeffer's contextual ethic prevented even conscientious objection "under the present conditions" from becoming a *Prinzip.*

Ethics, begun at this time, handles the pertinent questions as minor themes in three separate sections. This is an ethic written for the building of a postwar order and as such probably says more about Bonhoeffer's overall position than do his stands in the fitful moments of personal decision in the Third Reich. Here a future society is being outlined, its foundations being laid, its structures

[69] *Biography,* p. 569. [70] *Ibid.*

sketched, the rights of its citizens being discussed. By its nature such a theological/ethical roughing out of a social order is far less subject to those "present conditions" and "circumstances" that carved out the alternatives and stands Bonhoeffer saw and took from 1930 through the very years of writing *Ethics*.

What does Bonhoeffer say on the questions around pacifism and the postwar order?

One section has already been handled at some length above—the discussion of "The Structure of Responsible Life."[71] The abnormal times of *necessità* confront men with the question of *ultima ratio* and appeal to "the free responsibility of the agent, a responsibility that is bound by no law."[72] "In the political field this *ultima ratio* is *war,* but it can also be deception and the breaking of treaties for the sake of one's own vital needs."[73]

This relation of free responsibility to the *ultima ratio* was shown to be Bonhoeffer's rationale for conspiratorial breaking of law. Times do arise which demand violence as *ultima ratio* action, but the employment of this violence must never be made normative for other times. The use of violence must never be made *prima ratio*. "Baldwin was right when he said that there was only one greater evil than violence and that this was violence as a principle, as a law and a standard."[74]

War is also among the examples of the *ultima ratio* case. In short, Bonhoeffer conceptualizes conspiracy and war in the same way![75] War is violence, and violence is allowed as *ultima ratio*. War obviously can never be a normal policy for a state's conduct of its international affairs. Is is only a matter of the last of the last resorts, of "extraordinary and abnormal necessity."[76] In this situation, appeal cannot be made to some law, for the arrival of *necessità* is only on the other side of legal norms. Appeal can only be made to the free responsibility of responsible men for the necessary action—and to God for the necessary mercy. This is precisely the conclusion in the Barcelona address[77] although it must not be overlooked that war in *Ethics* is much more clearly *ultima ratio* action.

[71] See pp. 36-63 above.   [72] *E,* pp. 238-39.
[73] *Ibid.*, p. 239. Emphasis mine.   [74] *Ibid.*
[75] There is an important qualification of this even though it does not alter the relation here of war and conspiracy to violence, to *ultima ratio* action. It was shown in Chapter Two that the acceptance of guilt was decisive to Bonhoeffer's entry into conspiracy and that appeal to forgiveness of sins and justification by faith were important to Bonhoeffer's willingness to join the plot on Hitler's life. Tyrannicide is clearly a sin of enormous magnitude. But in the second section in *Ethics,* to be treated shortly, participation in war is not viewed with the same hesitation as participation in conspiracy. It is considerably less problematic, ethically considered. So the like conceptualization of the two as *ultima ratio* does not hold all the way. Nothing could better show Bonhoeffer as a child of his time and of his theological and cultural heritage than this, that killing Hitler, who was the full embodiment of tyranny for Bonhoeffer, was ethically more problematical than joining Hitler's armies against the foes Bonhoeffer prayed would win.
[76] *E,* p. 239.   [77] See p. 98 above.

The test for the justice of the *ultima ratio* action is not in the deed itself but in the end it serves and in the acknowledgment of the guilt incurred in attaining that end. It must be the breaking of law for the sole purpose of restoring the Rule of Law. "Whether an action arises from responsibility or from cynicism is shown only by whether or not the objective guilt of the violation of the law is recognized and acknowledged, and by whether or not, precisely in this violation, the law is hallowed." [78] "In war, for example, there is killing, lying and expropriation solely in order that the authority of life, truth and property may be restored." [79] Bonhoeffer has said much the same before; war is sin; it must never be blessed; yet in some rare instances it may be allowed, even commanded as a *necessary* evil, if the end is preparation for community. [80]

This section lacks the desired precision because Bonhoeffer does not set out the crucial criteria that measure *necessità*. But it does tell us something important—war is allowed as *ultima ratio*. This hardly puts Bonhoeffer in a pacifist camp. What Christian ethicist does not *always* consider war as *ultima ratio* in the struggles for justice and peace? Reinhold Niebuhr, for example, said just that in the same writings in which he was unrelentingly setting out the case *against* pacifism. [81] (And he was equally sincere about both.) When Eberhard Bethge says Hanfried Mueller has not taken Bonhoeffer's pacifism seriously enough because Mueller does not strongly underline the *ultima ratio* character of Bonhoeffer's approval of violence, [82] then Bethge makes the same mistake of virtually every close friend of Bonhoeffer's: Bonhoeffer was extremely hesitant about approving the use of violence, *ergo* he was a pacifist. Anyone who knows the absence of discussion on pacifism in German Lutheran circles, and who further knows how "pacifist" the reticence about employing violence appeared in the Third Reich, readily understands why Bonhoeffer was thus judged by others, *and by himself,* to be a pacifist. Bonhoeffer may have been a pacifist earlier, but not at this time and above all not because he felt war justifiable solely as *ultima ratio!* This does not match even the minimal definition of pacifism.

In the section on "The Right to Bodily Life," Bonhoeffer talks of arbitrary killing as unlawful because it is a violation of a basic human right. [83] Arbitrary killing is defined as deliberate destruction of the innocent, and an innocent life is in turn denoted as one "which does not engage in a conscious attack upon the life of another and which cannot be convicted of any criminal deed that is

---

[78] *E*, p. 262.   [79] *Ibid.,* p. 261.

[80] The 1932 address on self-assertion formulated it this way. See p. 101 above.

[81] For example, see: Reinhold Niebuhr, *Reinhold Niebuhr on Politics,* eds. Harry R. Davis and Robert C. Good (New York: Scribner's, 1960), p. 151.

[82] Eberhard Bethge, "Besprechung: Hanfried Mueller, *Von der Kirche zur Welt," Die muendige Welt,* IV (Munich: Chr. Kaiser Verlag, 1963), 173.

[83] *E*, p. 159.

worthy of death." [84] Bonhoeffer goes on: "This means that the killing of the enemy in war is not arbitrarily killing. For even if he is not personally guilty, he is nevertheless consciously participating in the attack of his people[85] against the life of my people and he must share in bearing the consequences of the collective guilt." [86] This is not all. There is nothing arbitrary about "the killing of civilians in war, so long as it is not directly intended but is only an unfortunate consequence of a measure which is necessary on military grounds." [87]

In short, once war as *ultima ratio* has begun, killing of the enemy and of civilians is justified, provided the latter is the unintended outcome of necessary military action. That this is not a pacifist position is clear beyond cavil. It belongs instead to the adherent of "just war" theory, a position in rather sharp contrast with pacifism. Incidentally, we shall meet adaptations of just war criteria in the discussion on tyrannicide, and it may be related to the fact Bonhoeffer conceptualizes war and active resistance in similar ways.

The last section germane to the questions of this chapter is the draft for postwar church/state relations. Discussed amid other items are the claims of government upon its citizens. First the normal bearing of the Christian is drawn: "His duty of obedience is binding until government directly compels him to offend against the divine commandment, that is to say, until government denies its divine commission and thereby forfeits its claim. In cases of doubt obedience is required." [88] This *could* be a pacifist's position if the commandment against killing were interpreted literally and without exception. But we have seen Bonhoeffer's qualification—the *arbitrary* killing of innocent life. Next, disobedience "can never be anything but a concrete decision in a single case." [89] This rule presumably extends to all the government's normal political functions. Two of these for Bonhoeffer are "the acceptance of loyalty oaths and military service." [90] Further, the individualistic nature of disobedience and Bonhoeffer's hesitation about using violence presumably stand behind the statement that Scripture knows "no right to revolution," [91] clearly meaning it is not permitted the Christian.[92]

Bonhoeffer does not entertain the complex variables in the State's administration of the military service it rightfully requires. It is difficult to see, however, that much room for refusal to serve is allowed until the point is reached that the

---

[84] *Ibid.* [85] The German is *"Volk."* [86] *E*, p. 159.
[87] *Ibid.*, p. 160. [88] *Ibid.*, pp. 342-43. [89] *Ibid.*, p. 343. [90] *Ibid.* [91] *Ibid.*, p. 351.
[92] Eberhard Bethge commented: "I've always maintained that Bonhoeffer was never a good democrat—except in perhaps a theological sense with the talk of 'the world come of age' and its praise of men's achievements. If he had lived I suspect he would have joined the CDU [the more conservative of Germany's major parties] and would have been rather pacifist—the rearmament question, for example." (Interview, Rengsdorf, West Germany, October 11, 1968.) Bethge speaks of Bonhoeffer's "inherent [political] conservatism" in the *Biography*, p. 355.

State commands disobedience to a divine commandment; until, for example, the State commands the intentional destruction of innocent life—such as the Nazi State did. In any case, Bonhoeffer's German State of the postwar order rightfully obliges the Christian to military service as part of his obedience to government, i.e., as part of his obedience to God's provisions for order. If legal provisions for conscientious objectors, selective or otherwise, are to be a part of the law of the land, nothing is intimated in this direction.

The last mention of military service appears in a letter from prison.

. . . I wonder whether, if I am not condemned, but released and called up, it might be arranged for me to join your regiment.[93] That would be fine! Anyway, if I should be condemned (one never knows), don't worry about me. It really does not worry me at all, except that in that case I shall probably be kept here for a few more months longer "on probation," [94] and that is really not pleasant.[95]

Being "called up" upon release was not one possibility among others. It was standard procedure for men such as Bonhoeffer; that is, for agents of the Military Counter-Espionage Service who were removed from their posts, as Bonhoeffer would have been even if not convicted of the charges before him. To *then* refuse military service would have violated a law carrying the death penalty.[96] Thus choice was virtually nonexistent. Just as important, for the sake of the conspiracy Bonhoeffer did not wish to undertake an action that would initiate further investigation. Yet it is worth pointing out that the man who seriously considered taking a stand for conscientious objection in 1939 now was willing to join Hitler's troops.[97] In the face of possible death, "willing" is a word too easily used. What can be said with assurance, however, is that Bonhoeffer does not regard conscientious objection as a *"Prinzip"* for himself in the midst of war, just as he did not for Niemoeller at its beginning.

[93] Meaning Bethge's in Italy.

[94] Bethge adds that this is "a veiled expression of hope that Hitler would soon be overthrown." (*LPP*, footnote, p. 71.)

[95] "18 November 1943," *LPP*, p. 71.

[96] Hermann Stoehr, an acquaintance whom Bonhoeffer invited to Finkenwalde to discuss pacifism, was hanged in 1940 for refusal to do military service.

[97] There may be an important difference. It is not one of the law, for conscientious objection was also punishable by death in 1939. But the reason for refusing to serve at that time and accepting service in 1943 may be related to altered situations. We know that Bonhoeffer, already in late 1941, felt the Russian campaign was the beginning of the end for Germany. (Visser 't Hooft, *Das Zeugnis eines Boten*, p. 7.) By 1943 he could hardly have been convinced otherwise about Germany's eventual defeat. Joining the Army in 1943 would not, therefore, have been what it was in 1939—maintaining and expanding the rule of Nazism. By 1943 the defeat of Germany, for which Bonhoeffer prayed, was in the making, and he would have had the strange consolation of joining an Army on its way under. The difficulty of this explanation, however, is that it does not handle a major reason given by Bonhoeffer for considering refusal to serve in 1939—the military oath.

Summary and Conclusions from the Literature

It would not be amiss to accept Bonhoeffer's self-designation as a Christian pacifist for at least the years 1932-1934. He saw the use of violent coercion as an evil, and modern warfare as an unallowed form of struggle.

This pacifism can be more closely identified for these years. Despite the absolutist language of his pacifism in the Fanø sermon, Bonhoeffer's was in all likelihood a provisional pacifism because of his unswerving fidelity to elements in his ethical method (contextualism) begun in Barcelona and carried through in the prison letters, methodological elements that persist despite an increasingly "filled" ethic. His was a militant pacifism, commending struggle and even radical destruction of any orders that close out formation by Christ. This was also a churchly pacifism. It could hardly be otherwise when Bonhoeffer was theologically centered in an ecclesiological Christology, vocationally totally committed to the struggle of the Confessing Church, and politically placing great hope in the Ecumenical Church as *the* supranational agent for helping effect international peace. But the deepest roots of this pacifism were embedded in the *theologia crucis*. From there it drew nourishment for the way of the non-violent cross. Suffering love, self-denial, endurance, the power of powerlessness, nonviolence, and nonresistance—here were the marks of disciples passing the stations of the cross as they strove after the One who said simply "Follow me" and never hedged about consequences. Here were also the themes of Bon-hoeffer's pacifism at this time.

Beyond 1934 it is difficult to know where the border falls between a qualified pacifism and one form or another of selective conscientious objection. Perhaps it rises, falls, and even moves about, as the 1936 catechism, the reaction to the Rhineland takeover, and the writing of *The Cost of Discipleship* would seem to indicate. By 1939, however, Bonhoeffer's own stand in all probability is that of a kind of selective conscientious objection, as documented in the intimacy of the letter to Bishop Bell.

Throughout this period and beyond, Bonhoeffer was extremely wary about the employment of violence. When used it must be *ultima ratio* use. In different words: Bonhoeffer apparently regarded the use of violent force as an evil, although often a necessary one, and when necessary, then a sign of God's gracious rule as Preserver. This may be sufficient warrant to call Bonhoeffer's basic attitude "pacifistic"; but if so, the mistake should not be made of calling him a pacifist and thereby badly obscuring the significant alterations throughout the years 1929 to 1945. *Ethics* especially exposes the distance of Bonhoeffer's stand from that of any pacifist and marks it as in fact belonging to the just war tradition. And in *Letters and Papers from Prison* selective conscientious objection to serving in Hitler's war machine can be sacrificed in the face of the risk that death at the gallows is likelier than death at the front.

In all cases war is an unmitigated evil. It is crime. It is murder. It is always sin. When Bonhoeffer allows war as a necessary evil he never varies from the Barcelona conviction that "I will raise the weapon in the terrible knowledge of doing something atrocious, but also being able to do nothing else." [98] (Parenthetically, this is precisely his conviction about raising the weapon against the tyrant; this parallels the conceptualization of war and tyrannicide alike as *ultima ratio* for the purpose of re-establishing the Rule of Law.) The striking omission in *Ethics,* however, is the earlier argument (1932-1934) that war in this epoch is so massively destructive as to be ruled out even as *ultima ratio.* This is all the more striking because Bonhoeffer wrote *Ethics* amidst the most destructive war of world history.[99] In any case, given the possible justification of war, Bonhoeffer's deep-seated certainty of the *pecca fortiter* nature of war means that his could only be an "agonized participation."

The conclusion from the literature and from the testimony of close friends must be this: Bonhoeffer held to positions that can be termed "provisional pacifism" (1932-1934 minimally, with possible advocacy on and off to 1939), "selective conscientious objection" (once Bonhoeffer's age group was ripe for induction and the war appeared impending; possibly his actual, half-formed, vacillating position well before this), and "agonized participation" (Barcelona, *Ethics, Letters and Papers from Prison,* and perhaps scattered throughout these years, as the 1936 catechism suggests). The whole, except for highly "un-Bonhoefferian" tones in the Barcelona address,[100] shows a man of peace in quest for national and international peace but working within a theological and cultural heritage solely lacking the resources for peace. This was a violence-abhorring man whose ecclesiastical superior intended double damnation when he wrote: "Because the reproach can be raised against him that *he is a pacifist and an enemy of the State,* it might be advisable for the Provincial Church Committee to disassociate itself from him and take measures to ensure that German theologians no longer be trained by him." [101]

---

[98] See p. 97 above.

[99] Is the reason Bonhoeffer's knowledge that a "peace" of Nazism would be worse than the war and so the "necessity" of a just war must be kept open, despite massive destruction, for such extraordinary cases as Hitler?

[100] "Yet love for my *Volk* will sanctify murder, will sanctify war."

[101] "Bischof D. Heckel an den Landeskirchenausschuss," *Dokumente zur Bonhoeffer Forschung,* p. 184. Emphasis mine. The writer is Bishop Heckel, Bonhoeffer's superior when Bonhoeffer was a pastor in London. Heckel, then and at the time of this letter (March, 1936), was chief of the Protestant Church's External Affairs Office, which was responsible for German congregations abroad and for participation in the ecumenical movement. He was never a Nazi and never a *"Deutscher Christ."* Neither was he a pacifist or an enemy of the State! His letter reflects the opinion, widespread in church circles, that pacifism was a heresy and submission to the State an unquestionable virtue. Even the Confessing Church did not take a stand for legal provision for conscientious objection. Among Bonhoeffer's students, too, his pacifism was an oddity of the first order. Two-thirds of the Finkenwalde students died as soldiers.

A Straight Line?

Commentators' praise of Bonhoeffer as a pacifist, and his condemnation for the same reason, have both been "well-meant" but neither has been helpful. The same can be said for his praise and condemnation as a conspirator. Precision of terms has been lacking. The result has been the failure to see how highly qualified was his Christian "pacifism" and how extremely hesitant his approval of tyrannicide. When these qualifications and this hesitation are taken into account, then Bonhoeffer's contention that a straight and unbroken course marks his conduct as a whole takes on tenability. Then Christian "pacifism" and conspiracy/tyrannicide may lie not on two separate paths but on the same one.

If we allow this as a possibility, how would such an unbroken course be explained?

A warning must be issued at the outset. Thus far Bonhoeffer's "pacifism" has been analyzed largely in light of the question of war. Now the attention turns to his "pacifism" and conspiracy, his "pacifism" and the secret "war" against Hitler. The conclusions about violence on the issue of war are not necessarily transferable to the issue of resistance against the head of state, even though we have noted that Bonhoeffer views violence in both instances as *ultima ratio.* For example, participation in a just war has often been allowed by the same Christian ethicist who denied the citizen's use of destructive force against his own government. Or, to turn matters around, one might conceivably justify tyrannicide while ruling out war as *ultima ratio,* because the latter is so massively destructive in a technological age. Alterations within Bonhoeffer's Christian "pacifism" on the question of war are, theoretically at least, not automatically alterations of his Christian "pacifism" on the question of active resistance and tyrannicide.

One theory of a straight line can be stated very simply. "Christian pacifism" was so broadly understood by Bonhoeffer that violence as *ultima ratio* action was actually a part of it. With the kind of rule by the dictator in the 1940s, the time of *necessità* had arrived; thus the "Christian pacifist" reached the terrible, highly unlikely, but very real point of approving the death of the tyrant by violent means. This is the theory held by some of Bonhoeffer's friends, reflected in the comment of one of them: "To understand the extremes to which pacifism went in Nazi Germany, you have to understand the degrees of hell in that land." [102]

This picture of a straight line rests upon an understanding of "Christian pacifism" which means nothing more precise than a strong aversion to the use

[102] Herbert Jehle, Interview, March 1, 1968, Charlottesville, Virginia.

of violence by Christians as Christians.[103] That seems to have been Bonhoeffer's meaning at times, and I have tried to show this obfuscates what are
three separable positions on the question of war, two of which are not the
property of even minimally defined pacifism. Now the issue is conspiracy and
tyrannicide and not war, but this broad understanding of "Christian pacifism"
bridges both. If Bonhoeffer occasionally used "Chrisitan pacifism" *in this way,*
then tyrannicide is allowed *on this same path* as a case of the extremely exceptional but necessary use of violence by men undertaking the illegal venture
of free responsibility.

Such a straight-line theory can muster materials from Bonhoeffer's writings
and conversations. This testimony is not conclusive, but it does show Bonhoeffer advocating active resistance against the State at the same time he called
himself a pacifist. For example, the 1932 address that asked that Christians not
shy from using the term "pacifism" also asserts: *"Any order—however ancient
and sacred it may be—can be shattered,* and must be shattered if it turns in
upon itself, grows rigid and no longer permits the proclamation of revelation." [104] In 1933 he stated that the Church should engage in "direct political
action" and "fall between the spokes" of the State's wheel when the State ceases
to be the State, i.e., when it fails "in its function of creating law and order." [105]
As late as 1939 Bonhoeffer still called himself a pacifist.[106] This was at a time
he knew of the conspiracy and fully approved of a Putsch, although most of
the planners did not yet consider tyrannicide necessary as the way to rid themselves of Hitler.[107]

What means are required and legitimized for toppling Hitler's regime by
Putsch, for "falling between the spokes" to grind the State's apparatus to a stop,
and for "shattering" an ingrown order of preservation (the State being one such
order), is not discussed by Bonhoeffer. But it is difficult to infer that only nonviolent means are permissible for such disruptive designs. There can be no
doubt that war as a means of struggle was ruled out by Bonhoeffer for a portion
of this decade, but perhaps violence as *ultima ratio* means for disposing of Hitler's iron hand and criminal course was allowed, even while Bonhoeffer called
himself a "Christian pacifist." When "Christian pacifism" means no more than

---

[103] As I have tried to make clear earlier I do not regard this as defining any kind of pacifism.
But because this is Bonhoeffer's understanding at times, I have put "pacifism" in quotation
marks. In my judgment, the issue for conspiracy and tyrannicide is a question *not* of pacifism
as such, which must necessarily include a stand on war, but of violence and nonviolence. Nonviolence as the only legitimate means of protest against one's own government can be espoused
by one who is not a pacifist. For Bonhoeffer, too, I hope to show the issue was violence
and nonviolence.

[104] "Zur theologischen Begruendung der Weltarbeit," *GS* I, 151. Emphasis Bonhoeffer's.

[105] "Die Kirche vor der Judenfrage," *GS* II, 48.

[106] Paul Lehmann, interview, New York City, March 13, 1968. See p. 58 above; also Visser 't
Hooft, *Das Zeugnis eines Boten,* p. 6.

[107] *Biography,* pp. 532-33.

abhorrence of violence, but allows its use as the great exception, then "Christian pacifism" and tyrannicide *can* lie on the same path.

Another theory is possible for a straight line from Bonhoeffer's pacifism to his approval of tyrannicide. It does not rest on the understanding of "Christian pacifism" which means abhorrence of violence in general but permits its use in specific rare cases. Rather, this view sees Bonhoeffer's pacifism as registering *only* his hesitation to participate in *war*. (Qualified pacifism, selective conscientious objection, even agonized participation could all be included.) In this case, Bonhoeffer's pacifism is wholly a matter of a stand on war; it is *not* a part of his resistance against the Nazi State. The following formulation is then possible: tyrannicide is to be committed precisely to prevent war; or, if war is underway, to bring it to an end. War in this epoch is so destructive of men and materials that the leader embarking upon a course of war must be stopped by whatever means necessary. If nonviolent means are ineffectual, then violent ones must be utilized.

The outcome of this theory is the same as the first: tyrannicide is allowed at many points along the way (at least theoretically) by the same man who terms himself a "Christian pacifist." The difference between the two views is one of understanding Bonhoeffer's "pacifism." Did he mean it so broadly (aversion to violence applied to both war and resistance and the rare permission for its use in both events) that tyrannicide was allowed within the notion of "pacifism"? Or did he clearly separate a broad understanding of pacifism on the question of war from a stand on the matter of resistance against the State, and so allow tyrannicide while yet calling himself a "Christian pacifist" because that term only signified his opposition to war?

The second theory is plausible, but it faces serious obstacles. One is Bonhoeffer's attraction to Gandhi.[108] The other is that he found tyrannicide ethically more problematical than participation in war during the 1940s.[109] Both these difficulties are discussed elsewhere. The reader is directed to those discussions.

Decisive, however, is that both formulations run aground on the seriousness with which Bonhoeffer teaches that nonviolence and nonresistance in both private and public life are marks of the disciple's way of death.[110] This suggests that some modifications had to be made in order to move from the categorical nonviolence of *The Cost of Discipleship* to violence as *ultima ratio* in *Ethics*. To these we now turn. The effort is still that of explaining the relation of Bonhoeffer's "pacifism" to his conspiracy.

[108] See Appendix A, "Bonhoeffer, Gandhi, and Resistance."
[109] See note 75 p. 111 above.
[110] See especially Chapter Twelve, pp. 156 ff., of *The Cost of Discipleship*.

Theological Modifications, Pacifism, and Conspiracy

The nonviolence and nonresistance taught in *The Cost of Discipleship* fit poorly with any contention that Bonhoeffer, as simultaneously a "pacifist" and a conspirator, always made allowance for violence as *ultima ratio* means. A rebuttal can be quickly launched to the effect that even *The Cost of Discipleship* values coercion as a means of God's preservation of order in a sinful world. Yet this bypasses the crucial issue, for in *The Cost of Discipleship* violence is never allowed the *disciple* while in *Ethics* precisely *he* is called upon to make the illegal venture of free responsibility, meaning, in Bonhoeffer's case, the use of violence for felling the head of state. All the twisting possible cannot make the author of *The Cost of Discipleship* a volunteer for assassinating even Adolf Hitler. Somewhere some modifications have taken place. Two follow here, both theologically traceable.

The first and most important theological element has already been discussed —the deputy's taking on the guilt of his nation as the responsible act of the free man. Chapter Two traced this theologically and biographically; it need not be replayed here.[111] Suffice it to say that, *in that situation,* finding the guilt-bearing, freely responsible Jesus amidst the new claims of resistance effected the end of the asceticism that surfaced as "pacifism," specifically as nonviolence and nonresistance in *The Cost of Discipleship*. It is this asceticism which Bonhoeffer later criticized in the most revealing of all the prison letters, the one written the day after the failure to assassinate Hitler.[112]

The issue of asceticism in Bonhoeffer's ethics is a subtle one. The asceticism of *The Cost of Discipleship* is not in the slightest an avoidance of the onslaughts of evil. On the contrary! Costly grace means unflinchingly facing the powers of evil, knowing this is the way of crucifixion, and knowing crucifixion is the way evil is overcome. Discipleship is a pacifism of the nonviolent *cross*. It is deputyship *in* the world *for* the world by taking the world's anger unto itself in vicarious suffering. It is not the least bit world-escapist in its four-square confrontation with the powers that be. It is innermost concentration for outward-directed service whether that service meets sympathy or wrath.

If this Christian life together is not at all the cloister turned in upon itself, what then is the asceticism and perfectionism claimed here? *It is shunning those entanglements with the powers of evil which could only lead to sinful compromise in the political arena.* Precisely these entanglements are Bonhoeffer's in conspiracy. He exchanged the clean vest of this asceticism for the vest of Nazism in order to battle the latter, in the process unavoidably exercising "the arts of equivocation and pretense" and being "drenched by many

---

[111] See pp. 51-58 above. The references to Chapter Two are extremely important to the argument here. The reader is urged to review them.

[112] See pp. 76-80 above.

storms."[113] The form of protest of *The Cost of Discipleship* is indubitable public condemnation of the Nazi State by one who will have no traffic with the vocabulary, symbols, arts, and weapons of Nazism. The end of that road is Paul Schneider's testimony and fate.[114] The *ultima ratio* doctrine in *Ethics* of "deception in the political field" is quite another path of resistance. It is not possible with the theology of *The Cost of Discipleship* if it remains unaltered.

In brief, deep-running streams in Bonhoeffer's own theology sweep away his momentary fascination with saintliness when he searches for Jesus Christ among the new claims of seditious resistance. The Christology of being-for-others, responsibility, deputyship, and the acceptance of guilt means the abandonment of the asceticism of *The Cost of Discipleship*. Categorical nonviolence for the Christian then opens up to the possibility of violence as *ultima ratio*. For Bonhoeffer this is the opening that led to the approval of tyrannicide in the 1940s. The change was subtle and the way narrow, but the move was made.

The abandonment of asceticism is related to another theological modification —the overcoming of "thinking in terms of two spheres."

Two-sphere thinking meant a certain parasiticism in Bonhoeffer's social ethics. One sphere could survive only through the existence of the other. When this two-sphere thinking is modified by Bonhoeffer, the parasiticism is dropped. But what does this mean for the question of pacifism, violence, and conspiracy?

Nonviolence in Bonhoeffer's ethics is parasitic in that he acknowledged the necessary use of violent coercion by some as obedience to Christ's command while denying it as a possibility for disciples. In *The Cost of Discipleship* this parasitic dependence is stark. Power, coercion, self-assertion, violence are all necessities for any facsimile of community in a sinful world. Not only does Bonhoeffer not deny this; in these he recognizes God-in-Christ's own gracious rule with the left hand. But the disciple, in both his private and public life, can have no traffic with such means. His fidelity to Christ prescribes powerless-ness, self-denial, suffering love, nonviolence, and nonresistance. He lives in and off the institutions of society that necessarily exercise physical force, but he can-not exercise that coercion himself.

This is two-sphere thinking. Sometimes it takes the form of a rather common Lutheran two-kingdoms doctrine of that time.[115] Sometimes it is fully sec-

---

[113] "After Ten Years," *LPP*, p. 17.

[114] Paul Schneider was a German pastor who was tortured to death in Buchenwald Concentration Camp in 1939 for his refusal to use Nazi slogans and symbols.

[115] One example is from the 1933 address on the Jewish question.

"Without doubt, the Church of the Reformation has no right to address the state directly in its specifically political actions. It has neither to praise nor to censure the laws of the state, but must rather affirm the state to be God's order of preservation in a godless world; it has to recognize the state's ordinances, good or bad as they appear from a humanitarian point of view, and to understand that they are based on the sustaining will of God amidst the

tarian.[116] In all cases it places the highly ambiguous instances of the rawer uses of power beyond the domain of the disciple's expressions of his deputyship.

When Bonhoeffer abandons this parasiticism he also leaves behind his insistence upon nonviolence and nonresistance, i.e., he leaves behind elements of the "Christian pacifism" of *The Cost of Discipleship.*

A chapter of *Ethics* is entitled "Thinking in Two Spheres." The spheres portrayed there are not those ascribed to Bonhoeffer here. Yet the base point for his critique of two-sphere thinking in that essay is also the one that overcomes his own two-sphere thinking: "Sharing in Christ we stand at once in both the reality of God and the reality of the world. The reality of Christ comprises the reality of the world within itself." [117]

Taking seriously "the reality of the world" as the only place where Christ *is* Christ leads Bonhoeffer to include, as important components of the *Gestalt Christi,* such phenomena as power, self-assertion, and coercion. Politics is no longer a sphere foreign to Christian action. With this dissolution of two spheres Bonhoeffer relinquishes the necessarily parasitic dependence of his own ecclesiological pacifism in *The Cost of Discipleship.* He also opens the way to legitimizing the use of violence by the disciple.

The abandonment of asceticism and parasiticism were both necessary for the move from nonviolence to violence as approved means. Bonhoeffer abandoned both for christological reasons. The expansion of his Christology as described in Chapter Two[118] dissolved the two-sphere thinking; the "deepening" of his Christology swept away the strain of asceticism. ("Deepening" means the discovery of the guilt-bearing Jesus who is found in full this-worldliness, in the midst of life's "duties, problems, successes and failures, experiences and perplexities.")[119]

Letting go of the asceticism and parasiticism is nicely illustrated by the change in Bonhoeffer's exegesis of the Sermon on the Mount[120] once he entered the military/political conspiracy with its "agonized participation" in the silent war against Hitler.

The source is the neglected first draft of the chapter in *Ethics* on "History and Good."[121] The second draft, published in *Ethics,* shows plans for a section on "Politics and the Sermon on the Mount,"[122] but unfortunately it was never

---

chaotic godlessness of the world. . . . [The Church] recognises the absolute necessity of the use of force in this world and also the "moral" injustice of certain concrete acts of the state which are necessarily bound up with the use of force." ("The Church and the Jewish Question," *NRS,* pp. 222-23.)

[116] *CD,* p. 159.   [117] *E,* p. 197.   [118] See pp. 32-36 above.

[119] "21 July 1944," *LPP,* p. 193. Biographically, both the expansion and deepening are in no small part results of accepting the claims of resistance as explicated in Part I.

[120] The Sermon on the Mount was always Bonhoeffer's chief scriptural basis for his "pacifism."

[121] This first draft is published in *GS* III, 455 ff.   [122] *E,* p. 262, editor's note.

begun. Thus the first draft is all the more important because it is the single source that makes clear the contrast with the Sermon on the Mount of Bonhoeffer's Christian "pacifism."

No longer does obedience to the Sermon include obedience to the literal interpretation of Christ's commands, as is the case in *The Cost of Discipleship*.[123] The words now are interpreted as christologically as ever, to be sure; they reveal *the character of Christ's existence*.[124] This shows men the heart of "reality"; its secrets are unlocked, and men are thereby placed before genuine Christian responsibility.[125]

The Sermon is an "exposition of that reality in which history comes to its fulfillment in the Incarnation of God, in the reconciliation of the world with God." [126] Bonhoeffer's insistence on the Sermon's propelling men into "genuine worldliness" and responsible action in history is striking. The words of Matthew 5–7 are

divine commands for action in history by virtue of being the commands of historical reality fulfilled in Christ. They are words buried in history in and through Jesus Christ. They are its secret, simply the revealed life of Christ. So they are not valid only as an abstract ethic—they are hardly valid there at all!—but rather in the reality of history.[127]

One could further cite Bonhoeffer's rejection of the Sermon as a "group ethic" that sets the "worldly defined on principle" in opposition to the "Christian defined on principle." [128] But the above suffices to show the dissolution of the Church/world borders in *The Cost of Discipleship* and to discern quite another tone than the perfectionist strains of the latter chapters of that book.

Bonhoeffer continues, and the contrast grows. The conclusion of the manuscript relates the Sermon to political life. The words are few, but the effort is extremely significant because it is fully the opposite of *The Cost of Discipleship*. In *The Cost of Discipleship* the most "political" chapter demands nonresistance of disciples, but rejects it, however, as a possible political policy for the world [129] and removes the Church "from the sphere of politics and law." [130] The Church is to be "a community of believers without political or national ties." [131]

In the draft for *Ethics* Bonhoeffer chooses *precisely* "the political sphere" [132] to answer the question "about the validity of the Sermon on the Mount for the

---

[123] *CD*, p. 93. [124] "Die Geschichte und das Gute," *GS* III, 470. [125] *Ibid.*, pp. 475-76.

[126] *Ibid.*, p. 470. The reference to the Incarnation should not be bypassed too quickly. In *Ethics* it is *the* doctrine for the this-worldliness of faith. It is partially responsible for overcoming Bonhoeffer's asceticism and parasiticism. The comparison of this doctrine in *The Cost of Discipleship* and *Ethics* would yield the same conclusions that the comparison of the Sermon on the Mount does. The latter was chosen because it is so closely tied to Bonhoeffer's "pacifism."

[127] *Ibid.* [128] *Ibid.*, pp. 470-71. [129] *CD*, pp. 160-61.

[130] *Ibid.*, p. 157. [131] *Ibid.* [132] "Die Geschichte und das Gute," *GS* III, 477.

action of men in history." [133] Specifically the question is about "the validity of the word about self-denial and love of enemy for one engaged in political action." [134]

It belongs to the abstractions of pseudo-realistic thinking to label self-assertion the lone law of the political sphere and self-denial as the lone law of Christian action and so to see in both mutually exclusive opposition, a double morality. Then it is a matter of an understanding of the worldly and of the Christian defined on principle, an understanding which bypasses the reality of the Incarnation of God and therefore comprehends neither the worldly nor the Christian. That the love of God also includes political action, *that the worldly gestalt of Christian love therefore can also embrace the gestalt of those struggling for self-assertion, power, success, security, can only be comprehended there where the Incarnation of the love of God is taken seriously....*
Political action means to perceive responsibility. It cannot happen without power. Power enters the service of responsibility.[135]

Unfortunately the manuscript breaks off before the Sermon's specific directives for political life are drawn. But that the political sphere was chosen at all is irrefutable evidence of the influence of the military/political resistance on Bonhoeffer's conception of reality. That those "struggling for self-assertion, power, success, security" are also embraced by the *Gestalt* of Christian love is a vision rather late in Bonhoeffer's life. It is wholly out of tune with *The Cost of Discipleship*. It is wholly in accord with the experience of conspiracy.

The ascetic and parasitic strains of *The Cost of Discipleship* had to be abandoned when Bonhoeffer took seriously those struggling for "power, self-assertion, success, security" in the military/political resistance. These strains are absent in the last, regrettably abbreviated consideration of the Sermon on the Mount. The theological reasons are thoroughly christological, the biographical ones those of the resistance experience, as Bonhoeffer sought Jesus Christ among new claims.

Summary and Conclusions of the Chapter

When Bonhoeffer sounded pacifist themes he did so almost wholly alone, even in the Confessing Church. Indeed, he did so *against* the Confessing

---

[133] *Ibid.*   [134] *Ibid.*

[135] *Ibid.* Emphasis mine. Among the scraps of papers for *Ethics* is one with the sentence: "Absence of power can be sin. Power, too, is an ethical qualification." (Microfilm No. 395, Frame No. 27.) In all periods Bonhoeffer emphasizes the power of powerlessness which rests at the heart of the *theologia crucis.* But it is not until after he enters the military/political conspiracy that he writes sentences like these. Even then they are few. Theologically viewed, it is not until after the rejection of all two-sphere thinking.

Church. The same was of course true for his serious consideration of taking a stand for conscientious objection. When he joined in clandestine resistance as a clergyman he was even more alone.

What was this lonely "pacifism" on the question of war and in the light of conspiracy?

We have followed Bonhoeffer through literature and conversations to discover the varying positions of provisional pacifism, selective conscientious objection, and agonized participation. The continuity throughout all these is a strong aversion to the use of violence by Christians, even as a means of last resort. This aversion, rooted in the *theologia crucis* for Bonhoeffer, is what he and his friends (occasionally his foes as well) called "Christian pacifism," whether the issue was war and participation in war or the broader one of the use of all forms of violent force. The term is thus very imprecise[136]—understandably so, considering the ethos of the Third Reich and the absence of discussion of pacifism in the German theological and cultural heritage.[137]

The relation of this "pacifism" to conspiracy focuses on the question of approving violent means or rejecting all such means for the Christian's conduct. While some of the literature of the 1930s seems to infer occasional legitimate use of violence against the State, the student of Bonhoeffer must nevertheless come to terms with the categorical nonviolence taught in *The Cost of Discipleship*. On that count, two modifications in Bonhoeffer's theology were necessary, the abandoning of strains of asceticism and parasiticism. Biographically traced, these are left behind when Bonhoeffer analyzes the structure of responsible life (especially the acceptance of guilt) and when he overcomes two-sphere thinking. Theologically, the basis for these modifications is christological. Politically, the result is that violence is legitimized as *ultima ratio*. This opening for the exception made possible Bonhoeffer's approval of tyrannicide.

The relation of Bonhoeffer's "pacifism" to tyrannicide can be described roughly in the same terms as the views on pacifism and war.[138] "Provisional

[136] This is not to say that "Christian pacifism" is not used with more precision than this *at times*. But just as an inclusive definition of pacifism was given at the beginning of the chapter, I have tried to find one that includes all Bonhoeffer's references to his own pacifism. The result is "pacifism" as strong aversion to using violence. Because "pacifism" apparently meant no more than this in some instances does not mean it meant no more than this in all. This definition is the common denominator of all Bonhoeffer's uses.

[137] The considerable variety within pacifism has not been delineated in this study, although I have attempted to specify the character of Bonhoeffer's "pacifism" with as many distinctions as I feel the evidence will support. A general discussion of the kinds of pacifism has been omitted because of two factors: (1) there is little documentable indication Bonhoeffer himself made distinctions beyond those discussed above; (2) the German theological and cultural heritage was noteworthy for the absence of a discussion of pacifism, except to condemn it in all its forms. (Thus Bonhoeffer's own stand was not one that gained sophistication by exchanges with numerous schools of pacifist thought.) These two reasons render difficult further description of the character of Bonhoeffer's pacifism and his cognizance of other kinds.

[138] This does not assume the analogy holds at every point; it does not assume, for example,

pacifism" would mean the times of categorical nonviolence, such as reflected in *The Cost of Discipleship*. "Selective conscientious objection" designates Bonhoeffer's approval of conspiracy by others but his own reticence to join because he was a Christian and a clergyman, a period from no later than early 1938 through 1939. "Agonized participation" characterizes the years he was active in the military/political resistance, thus 1940 following. The continuity here, too, is the strong hesitation to approve the use of violent means.

This chapter has said little about the ethics of tyrannicide as such, except to trace the modifications of Bonhoeffer's pacifism which made affirmation of tyrannicide at least a possibility. Little more has been said because that topic is the concern of the following chapter.

The effort here has been to make sense of pacifism, war, and conspiracy in light of Bonhoeffer's own sparse testimony on these issues and in view of his statement that his life was without any great fractures and discontinuities.

The continuities *are* strong. Theologically, the *cantus firmus* of Christology carries on robustly through all the concerns of pacifism, war, and resistance. There are modifications, but they must be termed *as* modifications and not as new Christologies. Politically, resistance against Hitler and the quest for "peace and social justice, or actually Christ" [139] continues unabated throughout the thirties and forties. Seen in line with its broad theological and political contours, Bonhoeffer's was indeed an unbroken course.

Even the lesser contours can bear up the contention of a single road. Or, more guardedly stated, at least Bonhoeffer is not vaulting any abyss in moving from a highly qualified militant pacifism to a highly exceptional approval of violence in the form of war and conspiratorial acts. He treats both war and violent resistance as the last of last resorts, and his "pacifism" on the question of war and his teaching of absolute nonviolence for resistance by Christians are positions traceable for only short periods of time. Throughout the issue of violence both in the form of war and in the form of active resistance runs the same reticence about its use at all, a reticence that is the common denominator of his various "pacifist" positions. There are modifications, as we have seen, and they are significant; but the search for Jesus Christ among new claims can still be said to show continuities strong enough so as to merit the judgment that his life had been without major breaks.

---

that changes in Bonhoeffer's stand on war paralleled changes in his stand on violence and nonviolence in resistance.

[139] "Brief an Karl-Friedrich Bonhoeffer," *GS* III, 25.

2
The Measuring of Tyrannicide

Background

Guilt. I hear a trembling and quaking,
a murmur, a lamentation outbreaking,
hear anger within men's spirits rending.
In myriad voices mazily blending
a dumb choir
assails God's ear:
We, hunted by men and abused,
made defenceless and then accused,
unbearably burdened and losers
of all, we are yet the accusers.

We accuse all those who forced us to sinning,
who let us share in their guilty winning.
Into witnessing of injustice surprised us,
and then as partners in guilt despised us.
Our eyes upon outrage had to gaze
until we were lost in guilt's dark maze;
then they locked our mouths up fast,
dumb as dogs we became at last.

We too had learned to lie before long,
and adapted ourselves to public wrong
and when the defenceless were felled by force,
we took it all as a matter of course.
And what within our hearts still flamed
remained unspoken and unnamed;

127

we checked our blood's insurgent flow,
and trampled out the inward glow.

What sacredly had united men
was torn to tatters again and again;
friendship and loyalty were betrayed,
of tears and regrets a jest was made.
We, sons of many a sacred name
in the annals of Justice and Truth, became
despisers of God and of man as well,
and around us all was the laughter of Hell.

But now, with both freedom and honour denied,
before men we can hold up our heads in pride,
And if we are brought into evil fame,
we ourselves before men can clear our name.
Man against man, our ground we choose,
and we the accused will in turn accuse.

Before Thee only, all Being's-Beginner,
Thee only, is each one of us a sinner.
With pain avoided, with deeds declined,
we have betrayed Thee before mankind.
We saw the Lie uplift its head,
and did not honour Truth instead.
By brothers oppressed we were greatly needed,
but danger of death was all we heeded.

As men we come before Thee,
to pardon our sins we implore Thee.
Lord, after these days of fermentation,
grant us days of confirmation.
After so much going astray,
let us see the break of day.
Let us, far as eyes can see,
build ourselves a road to Thee.
Till our guilt through Thee shall cease,
keep us patiently at peace.

We in silence still prepare
till Thou call to days more fair,
till the storm and flood Thou still,
working wonders through Thy will.

Brother, till the night shall flee,
pray for me.[1]

---

[1] Dietrich Bonhoeffer, "Prison," *Union Seminary Quarterly Review*, March, 1946, pp. 6-8.

It is the military/political resistance, and not the *Kirchenkampf,* that looms large behind these lines of trepidation. It is clandestine passive and active resistance, not public passive resistance and open protest, that led to being "lost in guilt's dark maze." Learning "the arts of equivocation and pretence," [2] learning to lie and adapting to public wrong, cultivating relationships with convinced Nazis and practicing Nazi speech and ways, doing the clearly evil to prevent the even more so—all this and more was the repugnant way of those who sought to battle "the Lie" from within the web of its own weaving.

This was not Bonhoeffer's manner of opposition for most of a decade. For years the author of *The Cost of Discipleship* did not check his "Blood's insurgent flow and trample out the inward glow." What flamed his heart did not remain "unspoken and unnamed." He accused—but not as a member of "a *dumb* choir." Rather, his resistance was purposely public. Costly grace had to be plain in deed. There was nothing whatsoever clandestine about the disciple's contest with evil. In fact, aboveboard, outspoken, and uncompromising witness was a test of Christian character for Bonhoeffer.[3] So the witness in resistance was uncamouflaged and resonant. What the French resister later wrote could as easily have been penned by the German one in *The Cost of Discipleship:*

. . . What the world expects of Christians is that Christians speak out loud and clear, and that they should voice their condemnation in such a way that never a doubt, never the slightest doubt, could rise in the heart of the simplest man. That they should get away from abstraction and confront the blood-stained face history has taken on today. The grouping we need is a grouping of men resolved to speak out clearly and pay up personally.[4]

Bonhoeffer did voice his condemnation loudly and clearly—and reaped Gestapo-directed prohibitions against public addresses,[5] publishing,[6] teaching,[7] and traveling to Berlin for any visits except those to his parents.[8] His manner of public protest during this period included election flyers and others,[9] verbal

---

Trans. J. B. Leishman. Bonhoeffer composed this poem in Tegel Prison in the early summer of 1944. Only a portion is quoted above.

[2] "After Ten Years," *LPP,* p. 17.   [3] *Biography,* p. 532.

[4] Albert Camus, *Resistance, Rebellion and Death,* trans. Justin O'Brien (New York: Knopf, 1961), p. 71.

[5] *Biography,* p. 602. The reason given was Bonhoeffer's "activity demoralizing to the German *Volk.*" (Cited from the Gestapo document quoted by Bethge, whose source is Dusseldorf police files.)

[6] *Ibid.,* p. 634.   [7] *Ibid.,* p. 426.

[8] *Ibid.,* p. 502. This restriction hardly impeded clandestine activity because the Bonhoeffer family residence was a crossing point of lines running to many different resistance cells.

[9] *Ibid.,* p. 226. The high bourgeois and aristocratic profile of much of the German resistance

and written communiqués protesting euthanasia and persecution of the Jews,[10] memoranda to convince high-placed officials, even Hitler, to alter course,[11] resolutions read from the pulpit,[12] formulation of confessions of faith with clear political import,[13] calls for an interdict on burials,[14] protest exits from meetings,[15] etc.[16]

Yet all this is not the resistance mirrored in the poem, for it is not "sharing in the guilty winning" of those "who forced us to sinning." Such sharing came when Bonhoeffer joined the conspiracy as a confidential informant or "V-man" (*Vertrauens-Mann*), an intelligence agent in the Military Counter-Espionage Service.

To be sure, even the methods of waging opposition listed above could not be adopted without rubbing raw delicate portions of time-honored German and Lutheran tradition. A theologically motivated model for *any* direct political activity was simply lacking. In German Lutheran circles the age-old question of the relation of faith to politics had been answered in ways that either neglected the issues of resistance against governing authority or else negated the answers of those who called for civil disobedience. Yet if resistance were allowed at all, then the ethical legitimation of passive resistance in its public and legal forms was not seriously contested. And for Bonhoeffer personally, passive resistance in public and *illegal* forms was morally sanctioned with certainty as well, provided the disciple willingly bore the suffering meted him.[17]

All this is only to say that the ethical problematic in Bonhoeffer's opposition to Nazism did not seriously arise for him until he moved underground. Entering the conspiracy was a moral, as well as biographical, turn. The sinful compromises with Nazism in the political arena, unthinkable for the disciple in *The Cost of Discipleship,* were the necessary entanglements that led to being "lost in guilt's dark maze." *Clandestine* and *seditious* passive and active resistance, carried out *within* the Nazi war machinery, is what churns the pathos in this poem. Doing lesser evils to prevent greater ones involved Bonhoeffer in a movement that he experienced as one soaked with guilt. It is here, in the military/political conspiracy, that the problematic of the moral life of the disciple gathers dimensions it did not in the *Kirchenkampf.* "No Ground under our Feet," "Who stands fast?" "Contempt for Humanity?" "Are we still of any use?"[18]—these headings from sections of Bonhoeffer's account of resistance

---

is rather amusingly captured in the picture of Bonhoeffer now and again delivering flyers with the help of his father's car and chauffeur!

[10] *Ibid.,* pp. 235, 649-50.   [11] *Ibid.,* pp. 440-42, 594.   [12] *Ibid.,* p. 445.

[13] *Ibid.,* p. 232-33.   [14] *Ibid.,* p. 224.   [15] *Ibid.,* p. 279.

[16] This list of references to Bonhoeffer's forms of public resistance is only meant as indicative of his activity for most of the thirties. No claim is made for an exhaustive list.

[17] This is the view of *The Cost of Discipleship,* as we have noted often elsewhere.

[18] "After Ten Years," *LPP,* pp. 1 ff. This account was written in late 1942, a time of considerable optimism on the part of the resistance movement.

are not really echoes of deep despair; rather, they are expressions of utter candor about the genuine moral discomposure brought on by cultivating Nazi relationships and learning and exercising Nazi arts.

A certain severity in this problematic came when the question of tyrannicide was raised and the decision to plot it was made. The severity was especially sharp for those, such as Bonhoeffer, who drank deeply from a German Lutheran reverence for *"Obrigkeit."*

This chapter will focus upon the nest of issues around this decision to plot Hitler's death. The issues and guidelines of Bonhoeffer's approval of active resistance in general will be plain as well. The organization, however, will center on the question of tyrannicide, one with which the men of the conspiracy never really came to moral rest.[19]

There is no question that Bonhoeffer approved of the assassination of Hitler and even volunteered for the task.[20] A troublesome decision for any morally sensitive German, it is all the more intriguing in light of Bonhoeffer's earlier self-designation as a "Christian pacifist." For one as basically nonviolent and reflective as he, there could only have been extensive wrestling with the issues of tyrannicide.

Documentary evidence is rather sparse, however. The entire written account is even sparser than the limited commentary on pacifism. The testimony of a close friend involved in much the same way in the same conspiracy, such as Bethge, is thus all the more indispensable. Yet even then the whole remains an unfinished mosaic. Perhaps this is in the nature of any abortive conspiracy whenever the survivors are few. The reason for Bonhoeffer's lack of extended commentary is also obvious to anyone who understands the dangers of the written word to an underground movement in a totalitarian state. Despite the fragmentary witness, however, a study of Bonhoeffer's resistance cannot bypass this active approval of tyrannicide. And it ought to illumine this from the standpoint of ethics, and not only biography and history. Such is the task of this chapter.

---

[19] *Biography,* p. 656.

[20] *Ibid.* Bonhoeffer's own assignments in resistance were chiefly those of informing church circles abroad and, through them, the Allies, of the resistance movement's plans and preparations. This was done in the hope of active approval and assistance at the time of the coup and in the hope of laying ground for post-coup peace negotiations. That is to say, his personal participation involved no violent acts even in working as a "Nazi" agent in the Nazi war machine. He did, however, belong to the group plotting the revolt, approved of its action, and worked as a part of it. I mention this only to prevent the possible implication from the above that Bonhoeffer himself actively sought to be the assassin of Hitler. This biographical note does not change the case for moral reflection by Bonhoeffer on tyrannicide, since he approved and even volunteered. But it nevertheless seemed important to mention the actual setting, viewed biographically.

The Operative Guidelines

What were Bonhoeffer's operative guidelines for this extreme form of active resistance? What were the ethical criteria of this man, as one of those who were "hunted by men and abused, made defenceless and then accused," bore unbearable burdens and lost all, yet were "the accusers"? In short, how did Bonhoeffer measure tyrannicide?

Karl Barth writes:

> . . . The life of a national community may be threatened from within as well as from without, particularly by an evil individual thrust or thrusting himself into the limelight under the pretence and pretext of being an instrument of lawful government. This man may perhaps have climbed to the top and gained control over the means of power in the state illegitimately, or he may have done so legitimately, only to make illegitimate, corrupt and perhaps even criminal use of these means. And his action is calculated not only to curtail and suppress the rights of many or perhaps even all the subjects of the state—which might in itself be tolerable and is not the real point at issue—but to do possibly irreparable harm to the state as a whole and all its members. Now let us suppose that there are no constitutional or legal means to put an end to his evil work, or to remove him from a position in which he has now become a universal danger. Let us suppose that all power is now tyrannically concentrated in the hands of this one man, and he perpetually causes might to triumph over right. Let us suppose that the next highest or nearest responsible authorities which can and should take the initiative in restoring law and order as now broken at the highest level are unable and unwilling to do so. May not someone from the lower ranks of the political hierarchy, or even from outside it, take up the obviously abandoned cause of the state on his own responsibility for the salvation of the whole, and, since all other ways are barred, proceed at the risk of his own life to the elimination, i.e., the killing of this publicly dangerous person? Is this really murder, or is it an act of loyalty commanded *in extremis,* and therefore not murder? Might it not be that on occasion certain men not only may but must undertake it? [21]

This is Barth's reconstruction of Bonhoeffer's real case, the case for that portion of the German Resistance which plotted Hitler's death. To be sure, Barth is not mirroring only the German conspirators' setting; he intends a general outline of the case for tyrannicide. Yet, knowledge of the German conspiracy and his own first hand run-in with Hitler's tyranny is the prime material informing these otherwise seemingly hypothetical sentences.[22] (Among his sources was Bonhoeffer, who divulged the resistance plans to him in 1941.[23])

---

[21] Barth, *Church Dogmatics,* III/4; authorized English translation (Edinburgh: T. & T. Clark, 1961), pp. 448-49.

[22] *Ibid.*

[23] Jørgen Glenthøj, "Dietrich Bonhoeffer und die Oekumene," *Die muendige Welt,* ed. Eberhard

But most important for us, Barth's reconstruction is faithful to the way Bonhoeffer in fact viewed the arrival of *necessità* and the need for plotting tyrannicide. Thus it provides a helpful frame for analyzing his resolution of the weighty ethical issues involved here.

The life of the national community was indeed threatened, from within as well as without, by an evil individual and his underlings who had gained control by legal means only to make illegitimate, corrupt, and criminal uses of the powers secured. There was, in other words, clear evidence of grandiose abuse of the powers of state.

Bonhoeffer was convinced of this early on. Already in 1934 he wrote Reinhold Niebuhr that the Roehm affair and other events of that year showed beyond a doubt where Germany was headed.[24] The Roehm affair was a classic case of widespread political murder carried out on the pretext of a plot against the head of state. With the help of malicious propaganda and an elaborate frame-up Hitler managed the liquidation of hundreds of actual and potential opponents and thereby secured a hold on his rather reluctantly loyal Army. Bonhoeffer knew the true story, however, because his brother-in-law passed information he had gathered in the Ministry of Justice.[25]

This was hardly the only reason Bonhoeffer very early judged that Hitler's rule was stamped with the marks of tyranny. The same brother-in-law, Hans von Dohnanyi, now transferred from the Ministry of Justice to a high post in the Military Counter-Espionage Service, tabulated a "Chronicle of Scandal," a record of Hitler's crimes. Its purposes were multiple. One was to convince wavering dissidents of the demonries of Hitler's rule and win these dissidents to the cause of the resistance movement. Another was to have the evidence on hand for combating another "stab-in-the-back legend" once the resistance movement succeeded in dislodging Hitler. From Dohnanyi's materials Bonhoeffer learned of much closed to the public ear, deafened as it was by the shrill organs of propaganda. The various programs, and later pogroms, against the Jews, the treatment of concentration camp inmates and prisoners-of-war, the purges by political murder, and the mass cruelties committed in the occupied countries— instances of all these and other crimes were known to Bonhoeffer.[26] Here is the material that hangs as the backdrop to Bonhoeffer's understanding of his resistance in terms of guilt and repentance.[27] But the point is that Bonhoeffer earlier than most had no doubts that the rule of Hitler and his under-tyrants was gross misrule.[28]

Bethge, II (Munich: Chr. Kaiser Verlag, 1956), 185.

[24] From the unpublished letter to Reinhold Niebuhr of 13 July 1934, included as Appendix B.

[25] *Biography*, p. 299.

[26] See the testimony of Christine von Dohnanyi, Bonhoeffer's sister, printed as Appendix F in the *Biographie*, pp. 1096 ff.

[27] See pp. 54-58 above.

[28] Concerning misrule, Bonhoeffer's friend, Otto Dudzus, writes: "The smallest offence

The evil perpetrated went beyond curtailing and suppressing the rights of the citizenry. It threatened what Barth calls "possibly irreparable harm" [29] to the state and all its members.

For Bonhoeffer, too, the real issue was not the infringement of rights as such, [30] but rather the "possibly irreparable harm" threatening the citizenry of Germany and, it must be added, the international community. Hitler's

---

against order shocked him. For the sake of the order which had been destroyed on a grand scale, he became a revolutionary." (Dudzus, "Arresting the Wheel," *I Knew DB*, p. 82.) Paul Lehmann's note on Bonhoeffer's pacifism was quoted earlier (p. 58 above): "His pacifism may have been rooted in an inbred Lutheran disquiet about the anarchy to which revolutionary social change is prone." Here is the intriguing suggestion that both Bonhoeffer's "pacifist" activity and his "revolutionary" activity are related to the absence of order. The nonviolent modes of combating Nazism were preferable to revolutionary violence in part because the latter meant anarchy. (See the discussion of Rauschning, p. 59 above.) Yet the exceptional approval of the use of violence against Hitler by Bonhoeffer, which Dudzus judges to make Bonhoeffer "a revolutionary," came about as the response to the massive misrule of the Nazis, i.e., the massive organization of arbitrary rule by the Nazis; in Dudzus' words, order had been "destroyed on a grand scale." (And for Bonhoeffer regimentation as such is not order. See the lengthy footnote, 30, below.) The suggestive item then is that both Bonhoeffer's "pacifist" activity and "revolutionary" activity may be responses rooted in Bonhoeffer's sensitivity to order. Parenthetically this chapter will, I hope, show how highly qualified the designation "revolutionary" must be if applied to Bonhoeffer, just as the last chapter did so for the designation "pacifist."

[29] From the paragraph quoted on p. 132 above.

[30] Bonhoeffer clearly did not approve of this curtailment and suppression of rights. It was grounds for "direct political action" against the state. But it was not, of itself, sufficient warrant for the extreme direct action of tyrannicide. (See "Die Kirche vor der Judenfrage," *GS* II, 47-48, for a limited statement on rights and resistance.) Perhaps this is the place to call attention to the fact that dictatorship and tyranny are by no means necessarily synonymous. Many dictators have based their rule upon the conviction that they are agents of the common good and, decisively, they have respected time-honored traditions and basic human rights as grounded in common law, natural law, or religious premises. This is to say that even when dictatorships abuse the power of state temporarily to bring order out of anarchy (as one example), they are not, for that reason, tyrannies. The tyrant is a totalitarian dictator whose aim is the regimentation of all manifestations of human expression in the exclusive interest of the state, the final determination of such interest resting with him. This aim amounts to a permanently intended annihilation of all individual and group-consciousness which does not exclusively serve the interests of the state. This regimentation and annihilation distinguishes those dictatorships which are tyrannical from those which are not. When Barth says that curtailment and suppression of rights as such is not the real issue, but rather possible irreparable harm to all members of the state, he is making a distinction applicable to differences between nontyrannical and tyrannical dictatorships. Certainly for Bonhoeffer it was not highly authoritarian rule from above downward *as such* that measured the arrival of *necessità*, but this rule turned fully totalitarian. He was inclined to give authoritarian rule considerable latitude to create order, even by coercive means, but he was likewise insistent that government, as one of the mandates, must respect the limiting of it by the other mandates. It must not regiment marriage, labor, culture, and church to serve its exclusive interest. If it does, it ceases to be God's mandate. In different words: when a state turns totalitarian it ceases *to be* a state, in Bonhoeffer's view. "Whenever the state becomes the executor of all the vital and cultural activities of man, it forfeits its own proper dignity, its specific authority as government" (*E*, pp. 334-35). "Necessity of state" then calls upon men to reestablish a genuine state. But the point here is that Bonhoeffer's opposition is to totalitarian dictatorship, and not to highly authoritarian government as such. (See, for example, *E*, pp. 207 ff., 287 ff., and 332 ff.)

134

Weltanschauung was permeated with a depraved moral cynicism and a fixation upon destruction;[31] it was indeed a revolution of nihilism that threatened possibly irremediable harm the moment the Nazis obtained the means to conform those men who would mold and eliminate those who would not. Such a pervasive moral corruption combined with totalitarian power could only end in widespread criminality. This was harm far beyond curtailment and suppression of rights. It was tyranny.

Bonhoeffer's portrait of Hitler captures the menace of the irremediable harm he saw in "the tyrannical despiser of men." [32] We have quoted this passage before,[33] but it bears close reading again in order to underscore the point that Bonhoeffer saw in Hitler's cynicism and contempt for mankind a degradation that ultimately would destroy civilized society itself; he saw a world view whose triumph would threaten every even minimally decent life with the same corruption that rotted the rulers.

. . . Fear he calls responsibility. Desire he calls keenness. Irresolution becomes solidarity. Brutality becomes masterfulness. Human weaknesses are played upon with unchaste seductiveness, so that meanness and baseness are reproduced and multiplied ever anew. The vilest contempt for mankind goes about its sinister business with the holiest of protestations of devotion to the human cause. And, as the base man grows baser, he becomes an ever more willing and adaptable tool in the hand of the tyrant. The small band of the upright are reviled. Their bravery is called insubordination; their self-control is called pharisaism; their independence arbitrariness and their masterfulness arrogance. For the tyrannical despiser of men popularity is the token of the highest love of mankind. His secret profound mistrust for all human beings he conceals behind words stolen from a true community. In the presence of the crowd he professes to be one of their number, and at the same time he sings his own praises with the most revolting vanity and scorns the rights of every individual. He thinks people stupid, and they become stupid. He thinks them weak, and they become weak. He thinks them criminal, and they become criminal. His most sacred earnestness is a frivolous game. His hearty and worthy solicitude is the most impudent cynicism. In his profound contempt for his fellow-men he seeks the favour of those whom he despises, and the more he does so the more certainly he promotes the deification of his own person by the mob. Contempt for man and idolization of man are close neighbours.[34]

This implies that tyrannicide for Bonhoeffer was seen as the effort to end the reign of Nazi cynicism and nihilism, together with its criminal consequences, and to liberate the genuine moral energies that yet existed in Germany but which had been effectively muzzled by the totalitarian regimentation of all life.

[31] See the letter quoted on p. 147 below. The reader is also reminded of Bonhoeffer's analysis of "The Idolization of Death" as discussed in Chapter Two.
[32] *E*, p. 72.   [33] Pp. 70-71 above.   [34] *E*, p. 73.

Tyrannicide was seen as the effort to stop the irremediable harm trailing in the wake of the Nazi *Weltanschauung*.

Barth continues and the case is still Bonhoeffer's. There were no constitutional or legal means to remove Hitler from the position in which he had become a universal danger. Or, more precisely, the few plausibly legal procedures available were either inaccessible or were known in advance to be futile undertakings.

Such legal tacts were discussed. One was a proposed arrest and trial of Hitler in 1938. Karl Bonhoeffer, father of Dietrich and probably Germany's most respected psychiatrist, was to present the psychological evidence that proved Hitler's mental health made him fully incapable of ruling a nation. The plan would have been, at least in the trial process, a legal way of disposing of Hitler. But it required much cooperation by men close to Hitler. This was not forthcoming, and the plan was abandoned.[35]

In this connection it is important to record that Bonhoeffer was not in favor of conspiracy and active resistance until the forms of legal and nonviolent resistance had either been tried or were known to be unavailing.[36] This comes as no surprise, to be sure, for the "Christian pacifist" and author of *The Cost of Discipleship* continues to place great emphasis upon the sanctity of law in precisely those sections of *Ethics* where the rationale for conspiratorial breaking of law is given.[37] Yet a scale from legal to illegal and nonviolent to violent means is crucial to the ethics of resistance and tyrannicide; so it is important that Bonhoeffer's measurement be cited.

Barth's paragraph continues. Totalitarian power did come to concentrate in Hitler's hands, and he used it in accord with his criterion of brute success as divine sanction.

A tyrannical person with his depraved outlook, early Bonhoeffer's assessment of Hitler, does not make a tyranny. He must acquire sufficient power to be a totalitarian dictator.[38] Hitler had acquired that power. Thus, says Bethge, the hour for conspiracy came for Bonhoeffer when the tyrant had the means effectively to threaten virtually every neighbor.[39]

Next, the high-placed authorities near Hitler, who could have and should have taken the initiative in halting the blatant abuse of the power of state, either were unable to do so (in some cases) or unwilling (in others). So, asks Barth, "may not someone from the lower ranks of the political hierarchy, or even from outside it, take up the obviously abandoned cause of the state on his own responsibility for the salvation of the whole, and, since all other ways are barred, proceed at the risk of his own life to the elimination, i.e., the killing of this publicly dangerous person?"[40]

---

[35] *Biography*, p. 535.   [36] *Ibid.*, p. 699.   [37] See pp. 45-49 above.
[38] See footnote 30, p. 134.   [39] *Biography*, p. 699.   [40] From the passage quoted p. 132 above.

When Bonhoeffer volunteered to be this "someone" he did so as one outside even "the lower ranks of the political hierarchy." But he did so at the end of the sequence Barth outlines. That is, Bonhoeffer felt the responsibility for straightening the course of the Ship of State lay first of all with those in high public office.[41] When these civilians and their offices had been effectively silenced Bonhoeffer saw the responsibility fall to the military; it was the appropriate agent for a police action to end a rule by criminals.[42] In the face of the generals' repeated hesitation to act, Bonhoeffer then saw civilians in the lower ranks of the political hierarchy and outside it as the men who must take on responsibility not ordinarily their own.[43]

A glimpse of the way Bonhoeffer understood the distribution of political responsibility is given in the draft for postwar church/state relations. Resistance as such is not mentioned, but the reader can easily perceive that Bonhoeffer's willingness to assassinate Hitler could only come at the end of the scale of political authority described above.

Is there a political responsibility on the part of individual Christians? Certainly the individual Christian cannot be made responsible for the action of government, and he must not make himself responsible for it; but because of his faith and his charity he is responsible for his own calling and for the sphere of his own personal life, however large or however small it may be. If this responsibility is fulfilled in faith, it is effectual for the whole of the *polis*. According to Holy Scripture, there is no right to revolution; but there is a responsibility of every individual for preserving the purity of his office and mission in the *polis*.[44]

[41] *Biography,* p. 699.

[42] Interviews with Franz Hildebrandt, Edinburgh, Scotland, September 17, 1968; Eberhard Bethge, Rengsdorf, West Germany, October 10, 1968; Winfried Maechler, West Berlin, February 22, 1969.

[43] Interviews (see previous note). There are other reasons why Bonhoeffer entered the conspiracy when he did. But they are highly personal ones, so I add them here rather than above. The concern above is with constructing the ethics of tyrannicide as I think Bonhoeffer saw it; as such, biographical elements are secondary (to the ethics, not to Bonhoeffer!). The further step in the sequence for Bonhoeffer was that he entered the conspiracy only after his appeals for strong action by the Confessing Church and the Ecumenical Church had failed, and after he had tried to resolve his dilemma with conscription and vocation in ways that either did not work or that he found unacceptable (such as remaining in the United States in 1939). Employment in the Military Counter-Espionage Service came as an answer in three ways: (1) it was a way of avoiding service in Hitler's army or taking the extremely dangerous stand of conscientious objection (dangerous to himself, the resistance of family and friends, and to the Confessing Church); (2) it provided an opportunity to continue resistance to Hitler, to which he had long been committed; (3) it was employment after Finkenwalde had been closed on Himmler's orders and Bonhoeffer was without the work he said was the most fulfilling of his life. There was the additional pressure of the sheer need of men for the underground resistance. But all these are not the kind of factors that belong to the sequence of responsibility that attempts to say when someone such as Bonhoeffer might justifiably take on the responsibility for waylaying the tyrant.

[44] *E,* pp. 350-51.

The times assumed are normal ones, when something like life is complementary and limiting mandates is possible. But in the extraordinary times of a totalitarian system the case is another. In a totalitarian state all offices and missions are incorporated into the system and share in the injustice and guilt of that system. A "purity" of offices and missions is not possible. Nothing is nonpolitical in a totalitarian state. So the moment can arrive when a clergyman who wishes to be nothing other than a clergyman must bear responsibility and venture the extraordinarily exceptional deed for no other reason than to make possible the return to the order where he can perform normal clerical duties. The moment can arrive when the illegal venture of free responsibility must be undertaken for no other reason than to return to the normal functioning of the offices and missions of the *polis,* to return to the proper distribution of political responsibility. For Bonhoeffer, too, that time came. Yet it came only when those whose offices and missions more directly responsible for the course of State were either occupied with Nazis or with opponents of Hitler whose actions were stymied or who simply lacked the civil courage Bonhoeffer so missed among Germans in general.[45]

Given all these qualifications—clear evidence of gross misrule by an evil individual whose power had taken on totalitarian dimensions, the failure of the "first resorts" of nonviolent and legal efforts to alter the state's course, and the inability or unwillingness to strike down the tyranny by those to whom the guardianship of state was entrusted above all—may it not indeed be that on occasion even men outside the ranks of the political hierarchy "not only may but must undertake [tyrannicide]"? [46]

Whether it "may" or "must" requires still more consideration, at least in Bonhoeffer's case. Accordingly, the appropriate question is whether there are yet other criteria deducible from his words and deeds. That is, are there further guidelines that illumine his answer to the question of "may" or "must"?

Another can be stated with certainty: there must be reasonable assurance that tyrannicide can be successfully carried out.

This is not the platitude it sounds upon first hearing. For Bonhoeffer, what is involved in creating the conditions that reasonably assure success greatly restricts when and by whom tyrannicide might be attempted with ethical justification.

The goal, after all, was not the end of Hitler as such but of his totalitarian system. Nothing would have been gained if Hitler were slain but the organs of dictatorship remained intact. And in a vast bureaucratic, totalitarian dictatorship such as the Nazis', that was wholly possible. This was the main reason for the conviction of the military/political resistance that the time of assassination

---

[45] "After Ten Years," *LPP*, pp. 4-5.
[46] From Barth's paragraph as quoted p. 132 above.

must coincide with a widespread takeover of key positions, both civil and military. The danger of moving from intolerable tyranny to equally intolerable anarchy, civil war, or a bloodbath by Hitler's under-tyrants still occupying the organs of dictatorship, had to be minimized as far as possible. In short, preponderantly probable success was to be measured not by Hitler's death but by the diminishing of evil.

Such success meant a double qualification of the decision to commit tyrannicide. This decision must rest with men who could survey the real situation; and these men must be a part of, or have close contact with, an organization of resistance capable of moving into key posts at the time of the strike against the *"Fuehrer."*

The criterion of success thus leads to a version of "estates' theory" in Bonhoeffer's considerations about tyrannicide. That is, an individual is not in a position to judge with any accuracy the complexity of the consequences of his act against the tyrant. He must rather be a part of a group, or at least coordinate his plan with a group already in such positions as to be able to survey and plan prior to the assassination strike, and already in such positions as to be able to remain in and/or move into positions of power at the time of the strike. The slayer of the tyrant must act in accord with a group in such positions as to reasonably assure that tyrannicide will lead to the diminishing of evil. In a modern totalitarian system the death of one tyrant by no means guarantees this. The system itself must be subjugated.

A crucial implication is clear, one that highly qualifies the case for ethically legitimated tyrannicide. Tyrannicide must not be the work of individuals acting virtually alone, or of groups with very limited resources by which to measure the probable outcome of their action. Too, purity of motive, including willingness to risk one's own life for the welfare of others, is not sufficient justification for venturing tyrannicide. The criterion of reasonably assured success rules out these justifications even when the other three extracted from Barth's paragraph and Bonhoeffer's testimony have been met. "Responsibility" as Bonhoeffer's continuous theme while he participated in conspiracy means the most careful concern for consequences. One could say that "The Structure of Responsible Life" forms this criterion of success when Bonhoeffer deliberates about tyrannicide.

This criterion is what was at work when Bonhoeffer insisted that conspiracy include well-calculated plans for government takeover and well-considered proposals for the post-Putsch order.[47] (As part of his own contributions Bon-

[47] Eberhard Bethge, "Adam von Trott und der deutsche Widerstand," *Viertaljahrshefte fuer Zeitgeschichte,* 11 Jahrgang (1963) 221-22. In this piece Bethge does not list the men, beyond von Trott, who saw the planning as essential to an ethics of tyrannicide. But in the *Biography,* p. 697, he uses an abbreviated version of the same scheme and says it was Bonhoeffer's as well. (In all likelihood, Bethge actually applied a scheme built on his and Bonhoeffer's

hoeffer worked on church/state relations[48] and drew up a statement to be read from the pulpits after the success of the revolt.)[49] This criterion is at work in Bonhoeffer's Christmas essay for his co-conspirators:

. . . The ultimate question for a responsible man to ask is not how he is to extricate himself heroically from the affair, but how the coming generation is to live.[50]

The clearest and most dramatic evidence of Bonhoeffer's measuring tyrannicide by the criterion of success is related by a long-time friend, Wolf-Dieter Zimmermann. In November, 1942, Zimmermann invited a group of friends to his home for the evening. Among them were Werner von Haeften, staff lieutenant in the Army High Command, and Bonhoeffer, at that time employed as a V-man in the *Abwehr*. From childhood Bonhoeffer knew the older brother of Werner von Haeften, Hans Bernd von Haeften, and now met him again in resistance work. He knew Werner less well. But Zimmermann knew the sentiments of all his guests, and the conversation soon turned to matters of resistance.

Zimmermann recalls the abrupt interruption by von Haeften. He (von Haeften) had access to the military conferences held by Hitler. Furthermore, it was possible for him to enter armed with a pistol. He asked Bonhoeffer: "Shall I shoot? May I shoot?"

To Zimmermann's recollection the discussion of tyrannicide lasted into the early morning hours. The exchange took place chiefly between Bonhoeffer and von Haeften. The specifics of the intense debate can no longer be recorded with certainty, but Zimmermann is certain about the points Bonhoeffer made over and again.

Bonhoeffer told von Haeften that, from the point of view of confession and absolution, he "may." But this was not the real question. The real question was whether he "should."

Zimmermann recalls that it took some time to draw this distinction clearly, for understandable reasons. Von Haeften sought from Bonhoeffer, the pastor and theologian, the pronouncement that divine permission could be accorded him for killing Hitler. Von Haeften, comments Zimmerman, was speaking from a Christian conscience outraged at Hitler's crimes and from a patriotism despondent over Germany's future. He was also speaking as one of the few enemies of Hitler who had access to him and who thus felt a special sense of

---

thoughts and actions to von Trott's resistance, not the reverse. This is not to imply that it was not equally von Trott's view.)

[48] Part of this is published in *Ethics*, pp. 332 ff.

[49] An English translation of this draft is printed in: Dietrich Bonhoeffer, *I Loved This People*, ed. and trans. Keith R. Crim (Richmond: John Knox Press, 1966), pp. 45-48.

[50] "After Ten Years," *LPP*, p. 6.

responsibility to act for others who had no such access, even a special sense of responsibility to act for the salvation of the entire nation. But Bonhoeffer gave an answer that must have been bewildering to the Christian military careerman. The first question is not whether God allows this act of free responsibility, but whether it has political relevance. When the questions of consequences are answered, then the question of the more ultimate ethical justification according to the canons of divine law should be asked.

Zimmermann remembers two points Bonhoeffer reiterated again and again, both setting the "should" question before the "may" one. The following is his paraphrase of Bonhoeffer's argument.

1) The issue is not between you and Hitler and his death and/or yours. Nor is it even between your conscience, our consciences, and Hitler's crimes. The issue is between this demonic system and the future. Nothing is changed if Hitler is liquidated and Nazism remains in office. Things could even become worse. They well might in an even greater paranoia about the enemies of our *"Volk"* within and without. It is not a question of conscience. It is a question of outcome. You must not think that by having divine permission for this deed, you have the solution in hand. The real question is: What is responsible toward the future?

2) Hitler's machinery is incredibly complex. I cannot tell you whether you should kill him. That must be done by men in better positions to calculate the results. Nothing must be left to chance. All must be coordinated. If you do decide you can and should shoot, then we must all move together, but after the yet unforeseen complications have been discovered and measures have been taken to solve the tactical problems of the revolt.

Bonhoeffer and von Haeften never did come to a decision about the "should" question, even though Bonhoeffer said the "may" question was "answered" in confession and absolution by God. Von Haeften later did answer the "should" question as well. On the night of July 20, 1944, he was executed in the courtyard of the Army High Command in the Bendlerstrasse, Berlin, because of his part in the abortive assassination attempt of that day on Hitler's life.[51] That morning he took communion in St. Ann's Church where Martin Niemoeller had confirmed him, knowing his friend and colleague Stauffenberg was on his way with the bomb.[52]

The qualification, "reasonably assured," must always be used when referring to the criterion of success so emphasized by Bonhoeffer in this exchange with von Haeften. Especially in a totalitarian state the opaqueness of human acts is ever present, all the more so for those directed against the regime in a precarious

[51] Interview with Wolf-Dieter Zimmermann, May 5, 1969, West Berlin, Germany. A shorter account of the Bonhoeffer/von Haeften conversation is published in *I Knew DB,* pp. 190 ff.
[52] Interview with Susanne Dress-Bonhoeffer, February 2, 1969, West Berlin.

moment. Risk is unavoidable, and the stakes could hardly be higher. Among Bonhoeffer's materials for *Ethics* is a scrap that puts it succinctly: "The incalculable aspect of responsibility, therefore risk." [53] So only a "reasonable" assurance of success is possible, if any at all. But if none at all, then tyrannicide must not be risked.

An aside is appropriate here. When Bonhoeffer spoke of the "unbearably burdened" who were forced to sinning and who shared in the "guilty winning" of the Nazis, he was speaking of a phenomenon directly related to the operative guideline of success for active resistance. Reasonably assuring success meant obtaining a platform from which an effective takeover of the organs of dictatorship was probable. This meant, by and large, the necessity of having men of the conspiracy placed high within these organs themselves. (Such was the case in the Military Counter-Espionage Service and the Army High Command.) This is the aspect of "estates' theory" in Bonhoeffer's measuring of tyrannicide.

Yet remaining in high office, or attaining the same, carried an immense moral burden—it meant a greater sharing in the operation of Hitler's criminal machinery. The scale was roughly this: the higher the office, the greater the power at the disposal of the resistance movement and therefore the greater the chance for the success of the Putsch being reasonably assured; at the same time, the higher the office, the greater the degree of service to the totalitarian state and thus the heavier the moral burden. Bonhoeffer's poem seethes with the moral distress of this battling the system from within. Yet this was necessary if a successful revolt were to be assured, i.e., if one were to act responsibly "for the sake of the coming generation." [54]

> We, sons of many a sacred name
> in the annals of Justice and Truth, became
> despisers of God and of man as well,
> and around us all was the laughter of Hell.[55]

Bonhoeffer's extreme hesitation about approving the use of violence even in seditious resistance, discussed above,[56] indicates still another guideline operating in his considerations of active resistance and tyrannicide: the use of only so much force and violence as is necessary to abolish the abuses of tyrannical rule is morally allowed.

Neither is this the platitude it sounds upon first hearing. Any effective jamming of the apparatus of such a massive totalitarian system as Hitler's could not take place without major interferences with that apparatus. The possibilities were great that a soon uncontrollable chain of violence would be unleashed. Thus public order must be disturbed as little as possible. The effort to end the

---

[53] Microfilm No. 395, Frame No. 27.   [54] "After Ten Years," *LPP*, p. 15.
[55] From the poem quoted p. 128 above.   [56] See pp. 45-49 and 136 above.

rule of rampant injustice should not itself be characterized by excesses. Revenge is not an act of justice for Bonhoeffer. Violence must be minimal. "Baldwin was right when he said that there was only one greater evil than violence and that this was violence as a principle, as a law and a standard." [57]

Pressure for the criterion of minimal force is fully understandable in light of the conspirators' goals. These men were fighting for a morality and a politics the opposite of Hitler's. Hitler's political method was hard coercion, and his morality was that right rested in might and success. Force was the *prima ratio* of his methods, not the *ultima ratio*. This was true whether exercised internally as threat, tirade, and terror or internationally as threat, terror, and war. Blood and battle were Nazi gods, and men who worshiped them were proclaimed heroes. War was not just or unjust. It was just won or lost.

The conspirators became conspirators in large part because they were shocked and repulsed by Nazi "morality." They hardly wished to copy it. They wanted to manage renewal with hands as unbloodied as possible. It is indicative of virtually the whole conspiracy that the twentieth of July Putsch was to be revolt without bloodshed except for the bomb in Hitler's conference room and that the last paragraph of the conspirators' order to the Armed Forces read as follows:

The executive power must tolerate no arbitrary or revengeful acts in the exercise of its authority. The people must be made aware of the difference from the wanton methods of their former rulers.[58]

Here a far-reaching fact explaining the failure of the German resistance is exposed: all the scruples regarding the use of violence were lodged on the side of the conspirators, and none was present on the side in power. The failure is not the discussion here, however; rather, the concern is to point out that a criterion for the ethics of tyrannicide is exposed here as well: only the minimal amount of force and violence necessary to halt Nazi rule should be applied. Bonhoeffer's lines about the employment of violence and his whole moral posture certify this as a criterion for him, too, although no clear-cut formulation of this operative guideline can be quoted from his writings.

The last guideline is that tyrannicide must be the most exceptional of all acts. This was implied in saying all other means must be exhausted first. But it deserves special stress because of Bonhoeffer's own emphasis. Tyrannicide is, for Bonhoeffer, a violation of divine law, and the man who commits this violation stands under the judgment of that law.[59] Tyrannicide is an act justi-

---

[57] *E*, p. 239.
[58] "General Order to the Armed Forces of the State," translated and published as Appendix 2 in: Constantine FitzGibbon, *20 July* (New York: Berkley Publishing Corporation, 1956), pp. 281-82.
[59] *E*, p. 240.

fied by *no* law, even when the purpose is to hallow the law by doing what is necessary to return to the Rule of Law. Such a venture, as we discussed at greater length above,[60] is the venture of free responsibility acting in the extraordinary situation of "necessity of state." [61] Such *necessità* cannot itself appeal to legal norms for justification, even the norms of divine law, and so Bonhoeffer throws this last of last resorts up to God for judgment.

> . . . Violence as *ultima ratio* or as principle? The eternal law—which is last, an eternal law or the free responsibility before God? *An irresolvable dilemma!* Remains open! Also the doer of the deed must remain open for the indictment! Forgiveness! Grace! Justification! [62]

It is true, and important, that a penultimate justification for tyrannicide exists in Bonhoeffer's designation of *necessità*—in this case, "necessity of state."

The notion of *necessità* belongs to the understanding of the state itself for Bonhoeffer. If the present state ceases *to be* the state, the time of "necessity of state" has arrived and measures must be taken to reestablish a true state. For Bonhoeffer, Hitler's state ceased *to be* a true state. This condition does not immediately allow tyrannicide, of course, for we have seen Bonhoeffer's scales of moral measurement: (1) from legal to illegal and nonviolent to violent means; (2) from political responsibility lodging with those men and offices most directly concerned with matters of state down to citizens much less directly involved. But given the movement along these scales, there is a relative justification for tyrannicide cited in "necessity of state," albeit one that can appeal to no legal institution set up for this emergency, one that can actually appeal to no legal justification at all.

". . . Before other men the man of free responsibility is justified by necessity; before himself he is acquitted by his conscience; but before God he hopes only for mercy." [63] "Mercy" is the "justification" Bonhoeffer cites as the final one for the assassin of the tyrant. It is clearly not an ethical justification at all, but a confident hope that God's grace also extends to those who violate divine law. Jesus Christ creates a liberty for a man to break, as the extraordinary exception, even divine law—of this Bonhoeffer is certain. But the man who acts in that liberty is wholly "dependent on grace" [64]—of this he is equally certain.

The conclusion is this: whether from the point of view of Bonhoeffer's penultimate justification of tyrannicide as an act of "necessity of state" (an act, however, with no appeal to legality), or whether from the point of view of tyrannicide as an act violating divine law (an act that can only fall upon God's

---

[60] See pp. 45-49 above. The reader is urged to review this section because I have not repeated the argument here. The theological grounding for the content of this chapter is clear there and omitted here.

[61] *E*, p. 238.

[62] From the notes for *Ethics*, Microfilm No. 395, Frame No. 19. Emphasis Bonhoeffer's.

[63] *E*, p. 248.   [64] *Ibid*.

mercy for "justification" by grace), the outcome is the same for the establishment of an operative guideline: such an act must be the most exceptional of all acts, the last of the last resorts, the ultimate of the deeds allowed as *ultima ratio*.

A summary of Bonhoeffer's operative guidelines for the case of tyrannicide is as follows.

1) There must be clear evidence of gross misrule, showing possibly irreparable harm to the citizenry.

2) Active resistance and tyrannicide must respect the scale of political responsibility. The man in the lower ranks of the political hierarchy or outside it can take on heavy political responsibility only after it has been abdicated by those placed higher, or when these have been muzzled.

3) There must be reasonable assurance that tyrannicide can be successfully executed. The important corollary is that the act of assassination must be coordinated with the plans of a group capable of quickly occupying, or remaining in, the key organs of the totalitarian dictatorship.

4) Only such force and violence as is necessary to abolish the abuses of misrule is permissible.

5) Active resistance in general and tyrannicide in particular can be turned to only as the very last resort, after nonviolent and legal means have been exhausted. The exceptional character of tyrannicide must be emphasized (for Bonhoeffer) because a violation of the divine law is involved and appeal to legal justification of any kind is not possible.

This is but a skeleton of the possible criteria for the ethics of tyrannicide. Yet, in my judgment, further criteria cannot be extracted from Bonhoeffer's witness with any certainty that he himself used them. These could be fleshed out and other commentary on conspiracy brought forward to illumine them. But it is doubtful that additional ones could be added. For example, Bonhoeffer's well-known verbal picture denotes the case of *necessità* and says something about a cleric's responsibility, too, to use force. But it adds nothing to the summary just compiled. "He stated that, as a pastor, it was his duty, not only to comfort the victims of the man who drove in a busy street like a maniac, but also to try to stop him." [65]

What more can be said about Bonhoeffer's understanding of conspiracy and tyrannicide on the basis of his own testimony? Perhaps not a substantial amount if we recall that this chapter is not an isolated one, but builds upon the major chapter on Bonhoeffer's theology and ethics. The two must be read together, just as the section on pacifism was not divisible from the chapter preceding it. When the total is kept in view, it is hoped that the fragmentary wit-

[65] Letter of Professor Gaetano Latmiral to Dr. Gerhard Leibholz, as cited in the *Biography*, p. 755.

ness of Bonhoeffer on active resistance has been treated as comprehensively and fairly as his necessarily limited testimony allows.

One additional consideration should be appended, however.

Whatever the guidelines by which Bonhoeffer measured the moment for active resistance and tyrannicide, he nevertheless responded more in terms of duty than right, more in terms of "must" than "may," to recall Barth's paragraph. The criteria that I have tried to show were actually operative in Bonhoeffer's resistance *could* be easily transposed into a case for the right to active resistance. They are in fact criteria paralleling those of the just war tradition (factors of justifying cause, just intentions, just means, proper authority, reasonable hope of victory, due proportion, war as the last resort), criteria transposed by other men in other traditions into an articulated right to resistance and sometimes revolution and tyrannicide. Yet the reader cannot help noticing how strongly Bonhoeffer emphasized the lack of appeal to any right, the full absence of any formal authorization, the extreme extraordinariness of employing violence with moral certainty, the non-generalizable character of the *ultima ratio* deed (meaning that it must never be made a principle). Even more telling is that *any* disobedience to government is so unprogrammatic, so individual in nature, so tied to the specifics of a concrete situation, and so weighted on the side of the rights of the governing,[66] that active resistance and tyrannicide have virtually no room to be conceived of in terms of rights—this despite the fact that Bonhoeffer used guidelines easily stated as components of the case for a right of resistance.

So long as Bonhoeffer operates with the resources of the Lutheran and Prussian heritage, such an outcome is predictable. The weight must fall on the duty of resistance, rather than the right, for a simple reason: the latter did not exist. So long as Bonhoeffer draws from his own inheritance, the argument for active resistance has to hinge upon the extraordinariness of the situation; the time must be seen as one when accepted norms do not hold. When these norms were thus to be suspended momentarily, appeal by a Lutheran and Prussian Christian could not be to the "right" of using extreme forms of active resistance but only to the "duty" to do so—in order to create a situation where the suspended norms would again be operative. When Bonhoeffer writes, "The *ultima ratio* lies beyond the laws of reason, it is irrational action,"[67] he is giving voice to a heritage that understands *necessità* as a time of the temporary, virtual suspension of rights. This *ratio* is *irratio*nal! The German designation is: "*Ausnahmezustand*," translated most often as the "state of emergency." But a literal translation better expresses the heritage Bonhoeffer drew upon: the "condition of exception" or the "exceptional state of affairs." So long as Bonhoeffer knowingly or unknowingly brings this heritage to expression in his

[66] *E*, p. 343. [67] *Ibid.*, p. 239.

fragmented commentary on resistance (and he does so to the end), he responds more in terms of "must" than "may" in the push to oppose Hitler. He does this even while he employs criteria used by others in other traditions as expressive of the right to resistance, including tyrannicide.

Discussion related to this and other matters of this chapter will occupy part of the upcoming critique. It seemed important, however, to finish a chapter that could have been interpreted as Bonhoeffer's right of resistance with the note that he did not see matters quite that way.

Postscript

Portions of letters from an Italian resistance fighter to Bonhoeffer's twin sister and brother-in-law form a fitting close to the treatment of Bonhoeffer's own commentary on his resistance activity and the theology and ethics that lie behind and run through it with formative force. That precisely these recollections are most vivid to a fellow inmate who had known Dietrich Bonhoeffer only a very short while may well be an index of their importance to Bonhoeffer himself.

... When we had our walk together, half an hour or longer every day, we talked of political, religious and scientific problems. . . . He explained to me the meaning of many passages in the Gospel and told me that he was writing a poem on the death of Moses, when Moses climbed Mount Nebo and God showed him, before he died, the land that would one day belong to his people, but that he would never enter. He loved this theme. . . . He also spoke of the tragic fate of the German people, whose qualities and shortcomings he knew. He told me that it was very difficult for him to desire its defeat, but that it was necessary. He said he had little hope that a German government could save Germany from the worst consequences of defeat by making a sensible capitulation. The Nazis had a fanatically tragic will to involve everyone in the catastrophe. He observed that Wagner's music was, for him, an expression of this barbarous pagan psychology. He stated that, as a pastor, it was his duty, not only to comfort the victims of the man who drove in a busy street like a maniac, but also to try to stop him. The leading German families had in part expiated their guilt by trying to remove Hitler, though far too late. He said that he was not sure that he would see the end, for he feared that he would then be taken to a concentration camp, where he would be killed along with other political prisoners. In that case he hoped that he would be able to accept death without fear, in the belief that it was in a just cause. . . . He was always so interesting and good-humoured. He was the best and most gifted man I have ever met.[68]

> But now, with both freedom and honour denied,
> before men we can hold up our heads in pride,

[68] Excerpts from the letters of March 6 and April 2, 1946, to Dr. and Mrs. Gerhard Leibholz from Professor Gaetano Latmiral as quoted from the *Biography*, pp. 754-55.

And if we are brought into evil fame,
we ourselves before men can clear our name.
Man against man, our ground we choose,
and we the accused will in turn accuse.

Brother, till after the long night
our dawn arises,
let us withstand.[69]

---

[69] From "Prison," quoted earlier, pp. 127-28.
The discussions of this chapter and the preceding one have not involved the subject of torture. There have been instances in which Christians have legitimized the use of torture in order to extract information needed to protect themselves and others. But the moral dilemmas here were not actual for Bonhoeffer, and thus the topic has not been given special attention above. Bonhoeffer does write a paragraph on torture in a section on "The Freedom of Bodily Life" in *Ethics* (p. 185). But it says nothing that indicates whether he would view any use of torture by the resisters as morally permissible. A letter from Bethge gives some help, however. It is a statement that parallels exactly the question above about the "justification" of tyrannicide.
". . . Now to your question [about torture]. The question itself nearly startled me and and I can tell you with certainty that we [Bethge and Bonhoeffer] never had a conversation in which any kind of justification of torture could have arisen. I admit that there were probably many matters we did not think through. But if situations could have been conceived in which one did it [tortured], then he surely would not want to justify it afterward; rather he would take upon himself full responsibility for what he had done—in any case he would take on full responsibility if he were a Christian. To draw up a teaching for the possible justification of torture is really hardly possible in Bonhoeffer's understanding. In any case I cannot remember any conversation whatsoever in which these things were mentioned." (Letter from Eberhard Bethge to the writer, 24 September 1969, Rengsdorf, West Germany.)

Part III
CRITIQUE

1
Critique of Methodology

Introduction

The life and death of Dietrich Bonhoeffer generate the deepest respect because in them he enacted his own Christology with extraordinary power. His life bore with unquestionable integrity the very conformation to Christ which he set at the center of his ethics. If a paradigm of "religionless Christianity" is sought, Bonhoeffer's own "participation in the sufferings of God in the secular life" is there.

For these reasons and others, a critique of Bonhoeffer's thought and action is often difficult for those instructed and fascinated by him. His message, so embodied in his life, bears a power that his admirers genuinely fear will be abated by a growing Bonhoeffer "scholasticism." Furthermore, dissecting the interior of any martyr's witness in order to expose the shortcomings smacks of something slightly perverse. It is glee only for the polemicist.

Yet the discipline of ethics must deal rather cold-bloodedly with a man's creed and deeds if it is to be truly helpful. Pros and cons should be argued critically and without respect to persons. *Ad hominem* extractions are not in

149

order, whether in malediction or benediction of the man. And in any case, charity in ethics is measured not by the gentleness of the analysis but by its verity. The martyr's message cannot be exempted from this kind of scrutiny, whatever the respect held by the ethicist for the man—and his message.

The scope of this chapter is a rather modest one. It is to evaluate Bonhoeffer's methodology in ethics, especially as this is tested in his political engagement. The chapter following attempts a critique of his resistance activity as such, via a moral profile of the military/political conspiracy.

It need only be mentioned that critical remarks rather than expository ones are the prime concern now. The following arguments will therefore assume, rather than restate, the descriptions and demonstrations of the previous chapters. There are some few instances, however, when complementary exposition is required for the task of criticism.

One final item belongs to these introductory comments. Since a major contention of this chapter is that Bonhoeffer's methodology is an inadequate one, cognizance must be taken of the fact that such an inadequacy *may* be due to the shortness of his life. Even *Ethics* was not written by Bonhoeffer in its present form. It is an edited collection of largely unfinished essays. Any critique of Bonhoeffer must therefore be exceedingly cautious, seeking at every point to avoid doing violence to the thoughts of a man who never had the opportunity to complete them.

Yet the effort here will be to show that the most fundamental and most continuous elements in Bonhoeffer's methodology are responsible for the inadequacies. In other words, the criticism builds less upon what he failed to say than upon what he said most emphatically. Certain absences in his ethics are less the result of inadvertent omissions than they are the necessary consequences of his own understanding of ethics. At least this is the contention. The procedural clue is adapted from Bonhoeffer himself: "It is not the sins of weakness, but the sins of strength, which matter here." [1]

The Question

The question posed is whether Bonhoeffer's methodology, even his understanding of ethics, is an adequate one. The contention is that it is not,[2] despite

[1] "1 July 1944," *LPP*, p. 183.

[2] The bluntness of this contention should not obscure the fact that the writer believes Bonhoeffer's deliberations in ethics constitute "ethics" in a number of meaningful ways. Bonhoeffer is profound in elucidating the meaning of reality for morality. We have seen, for example, his critique of Nazi morality with insights drawn from the "real" dynamics of Incarnation, Crucifixion, and Resurrection and his understanding of resistance under the christologically permeated rubrics of "The Structure of Responsible Life." The *Gestalt Christi* is deeply a matter of morality for Bonhoeffer, and he demonstrates discernment and originality in drawing behavioral consequences from it. In the illumination of morality by expounding what he under-

the fact his is a brilliant statement of Christian ethics done in the relational mode. The attempt of this chapter will be to show that from many angles there is a convergence at the same point, namely, Bonhoeffer's methodological inability to handle the hard question of Christian ethics: how am I, as a Christian, to assess different claims to Christian action, *all* of which assert that they bring to expression the will of God? Without providing, or at least working to provide, such adjudication, ethics is a truncated discipline. If the methodology in ethics neglects or works against raising and seeking to answer this question, it is doubtful whether the understanding of Christian ethics is adequate.

The Grenzfall

The extreme case of tyrannicide (the *Grenzfall*) provides a case study by which to probe Bonhoeffer's ethics. This deed of free responsibility is understood as the exceptional, concrete command of God-in-Christ. As we have seen above, it is without doubt regarded *as* exceptional; such an *ultima ratio* action can never be transposed into a normative guide. And if the sections in *Ethics* on the command of God, method in ethics, and the warrant for moral discourse, written during these years of active resistance, are to be taken as seriously as Bonhoeffer states them, then this deed must also be viewed as the will of God *in concreto* "here and now." If Bonhoeffer's own methodological claims and assertions are to be treated seriously, tyrannicide was the exceptional command that, by virtue of being the command of God, was "clear, definite and concrete to the last detail." [3]

This raises the question of measuring the exceptional command; or, viewed historically, of ascertaining that the time is truly that of *necessità*.

From a methodological perspective, how is the exceptional command to be

stands as reality, Bonhoeffer's ethics can surely be understood as ethics proper, which is to say ethics in the broad sense of systematic reflection upon the base lines of the Christian life, ethics in the sense of the disciplined drawing out of the implications of Christian dogma for Christian action. Bonhoeffer's ethics also concerns itself with elements that belong to an ethical theory and structure of decision-making. However briefly, he clearly seeks to contrast his conception of Christian ethics with other versions, among them the ethics of the good, of duty or principles, of virtue and of conscience. He subjected these standards to testing in the resistance and found them wanting, as documented in *Ethics* and "After Ten Years." Too, the distinction of his motif of relationship from explicitly prescriptive and deliberative motifs in ethics is emphasized by Bonhoeffer. Furthermore, he discusses the warrant for ethical discourse and seeks to delineate the fixed time and place of the ethical. Thus, whether ethics is viewed in the broad sense of reflection upon the Christian life or in the somewhat more technical sense of an ethical theory and structure of decision-making, Bonhoeffer's deliberations are the proper subject matter of the discipline of ethics. My question is not whether Bonhoeffer says a great deal. It is whether he says enough; more specifically, whether he *can* say enough, given his basic assertions about the nature of Christian ethics.

[3] *E*, p. 278.

understood in Bonhoeffer's ethics? Several possible ways can be constructed. They lead into a discussion about measuring the exceptional command of God, and this in turn has ramifications of a rather far-reaching nature for Bonhoeffer's ethics.[4]

The Exceptional Command—Its Methodological Meanings. 1. The exceptional command is surely a way of methodologically making room for Christ's sovereign freedom. Negatively expressed, it is a way of prohibiting men from limiting Christ's sovereignty. In his sovereign freedom, he may command exceptions if he wills. The exceptional command is thus the name for marking the boundary between Christ's freedom and man's capacity to prescribe behavior. It is, in short, a methodological way of underwriting Christ's Lordship.

We should be clear. Christ is not arbitrary—there are configurations of his form, and these can be discerned by men who relate to him in faith. Further, these configurations are normative in a secondary but important way. The content may even be generalized as principles that act as guides for posting the way we ought to walk. But, *methodologically,* such principles must not be made finally determinative for uncovering the present concrete command because such would be a restriction by man of Christ's freedom. Methodologically, the will of God-in-Christ must be approached, in Bonhoeffer's words, as *"something new and different in each situation."* [5] This is Bonhoeffer's radical contextualism, and with it he makes way for the exceptional command that is not subject to secondary norms.

Yet in practical decision-making Bonhoeffer shows ambivalence and perhaps methodological irresolution here. As we have noted he experienced a great deal of guilt in executing "the deed of free responsibility," in carrying out "the exceptional command." [6] Ostensibly the reason is that law, especially divine law, remains a strong penultimate norm for Bonhoeffer, and its violation thus incurs guilt.[7] The appropriate question for method is: what is the relation of the radical contextualism to the penultimate norms, to the generalized configurations of Christ's form in a "filled" contextual ethic? If one stands by an ethic of "the concrete command" of "concrete instruction in the concrete situation," as Bonhoeffer claims a true Christain ethic is,[8] it is difficult to see why a commanded "violation" of the penultimate norms should incur guilt for him who is obedient. My criticism is *not* that a radically contextual ethic can

---

[4] A goodly portion of the discussion of the exceptional command is an adaptation and elaboration for Bonhoeffer's ethics of the suggestive analysis of John H. Yoder in *Karl Barth and Christian Pacifism,* Work Paper for the 1957 Conference, Iserlohn, Germany (Frankfurt am Main: Mennonite Central Committee, 1966), pp. 20-30. Yoder's work has since been revised and expanded and is published in *Studies in Christian Ethics* under the title *Karl Barth and the Problem of War* (Nashville: Abingdon Press, 1970).

[5] *E,* p. 38.   [6] E.g., the poem pp. 127-28 above.   [7] See pp. 45-49 above.

[8] *E.g., E,* pp. 85-86, 354.

have no place for secondary norms. It can, and the norms can be operative provided they are not regarded as finally determinative, provided they leave room to search out the will of God-in-Christ as "something new and different in each situation." [9] The argument is rather that Bonhoeffer's methodology of radical contextualism should not produce a sense of guilt in those cases of *necessità* where a violation of divine law is at the same time the (commanded) deed of free responsibility which, however "illegal," "corresponds with reality." In short it would seem that either Bonhoeffer's secondary norms are still operative when he says they have been temporarily suspended, *or* he has not taken seriously his own strong assertions of a contextual ethic of concrete instruction. Or both. I find no methodological resolution of this problem in Bonhoeffer.

But this is somewhat aside of our initial concern with the exceptional command as Bonhoeffer's way of safeguarding Christ's freedom. Even if we bypass the ambivalence in Bonhoeffer's relation of the secondary norms to the exceptional command, a critical methodological shortcoming surfaces when we test the exceptional command with the pertinent ethical question. The pertinent ethical question is: with what *measurements* can Bonhoeffer advocate any other course of action as being obedient than that which is consistent with the general lines of Christ's form? (In the extreme case of tyrannicide the crucial general lines of Christ's form are those outlined by divine law, specifically, "Thou shalt not kill.") In different words, how is the exceptional command to be tested *as* exceptional?

The exceptional command as an expression for Christ's sovereign freedom is in itself no measurement. That is, that Christ *can* command exceptions is no reason to demand they be found. An underwriting of Christ's freedom is no basis for expecting an exception to the general lines of his form, or worse, predicting one. Transposing such sovereign freedom into the principle that there must be a rejection of all principles, or into the rule there must always be exceptions to rules, would hardly be legitimate. So while the exceptional command may be a proper methodological way of maintaining an *openness* to Christ's sovereign freedom, there is no measurement as such of the exceptional command in the sheer fact of this freedom.

Because Bonhoeffer states that God-in-Christ commands permission, freedom, liberty,[10] a note must be added on *man's* freedom. Bonhoeffer's emphasis upon the exceptional command as having the shape of the deed of *free* responsibility is all the more reason to interject this note. But the matter can be handled with economy because the discussion and conclusion above can be directly transferred to this issue. That is, there is no measurement as such of the exceptional command in the sheer fact of man's commanded freedom. Such

[9] *E*, p. 38. [10] *Ibid.*, p. 281.

freedom *permits a place* for the exceptional command and obedience to it, but it does not mark its coming.

2. For Bonhoeffer the exceptional command is also a statement of the limited receptivity of principles, norms, ideals, and laws for reality. The manifold nature of reality does not conform with exactitude to the abstractions we use to answer the "ought" question (What ought or am I to do?); we must provide a way of methodologically building a space for exceptional behavior. Such a space is called the extreme case—the space for that "necessary" action which nevertheless fails to be congruent with the usual outlines of reality as we have generalized them in secondary norms.

Without further comment it should be clear that the limited receptivity of abstractions for manifold reality is no grounds or measurement of the actual arrival or presence of the exceptional command.

3. The extreme case may simply be a way of marking human finitude. That is, our formulation of the penultimate norms must always be viewed tentatively and considered binding until further notice, when new knowledge and insight reformulate them. The notion of the exceptional command may be a way of drawing our attention to the inadequacies of our apprehensions of Christ's form heretofore.

But the extreme case as a statement of human finitude is even more problematical than the common case. That is, if it is impossible to be certain about *any* formulations in ethics, it is a fortiori less sure in the case of the exception. Thus the very valid statement of human finitude in ethical decisions, and the use of the extreme case to mark this methodologically, is, in itself, no measurement for the exceptional command.

One might speculate that the extreme case is really the name Bonhoeffer gives to the situation in which he feels obliged to act in a way not accounted for in his own ethics. It may be the name for the fact that Bonhoeffer came up against historical circumstances in which he was convinced of having to act in a way not in accord with the base lines of Christ's form. *Or* he conceived of the permission character of Christ's freedom, including Christ's freedom to command permission, as simultaneously the concrete command for tyrannicide itself. In either case, the *testing* of the exceptional command *as* exceptional has not been provided. Measuring the extreme case *as* extreme is not given. The demonstration of the exception *as* exception to the general course has not been made even to those with whom Bonhoeffer agrees about the general rule; at least it has not been made on the basis of the possible understandings of the extreme case discussed here. More must be provided.

More has been provided. Thus this conjecture that the *Grenzfall* is Bonhoeffer's name for what he "knows" he must carry out, but which his ethics do not account for formally, should not go uncontested. In fact the case has already been made that Bonhoeffer did indeed have measurements of *"neces-*

sità," his appropriation of criteria reminiscent of just war teachings.[11] But just these, too, show shortcomings in his method and understanding of ethics, as we shall consider shortly.

How *does* Bonhoeffer "test the spirits" so as to distinguish between Christ's concrete command and false guidance, and between "conforming" acts and malforming ones? Several possibilities can be extracted from Bonhoeffer's writings. Investigating these will include further consideration of the *Grenzfall,* but will lead beyond it as well into elements Bonhoeffer regards as central to his understanding of Christian ethics. Whatever the range, however, our remarks are still aimed at demonstrating Bonhoeffer's methodological inability to handle the hard question of Christian ethics.[12]

Earnest Self-proving. Bonhoeffer's instruction for "proving what is the will of God"[13] must be prefaced with a few comments about his ethics as personalist-relational.[14]

"Faith in this Jesus Christ is the sole fountainhead of all good."[15]

For Bonhoeffer, communing with Christ is the key to discernment of that action which conforms to Christ's form in the world. Morality is a by-product of maturing faith. It is the outcome of increasing conformation to Christ.

---

[11] See the previous chapter.

[12] See p. 151 above. A methodological difficulty, brought to the reader's attention but left unresolved, occurs at the point of the *Church's* issuance of the concrete command. The early Bonhoeffer is clear here. The Church "should be able to say quite definitely: 'engage in this war' or 'do not engage in this war.'" (*GS* I, 146.) The Bonhoeffer of *Ethics* still says at least that "the point of departure for Christian ethics is the Body of Christ, the form of Christ in the form of the Church." (*E,* p. 84.) And ecclesiology is not absent from the prison theology, although it is certainly an open question. (See pp. 85-87 above.) But the place of the Church in Bonhoeffer's methodology is less and less clear precisely at the point of the asserted strength and uniqueness of Christian ethics, namely, concrete instruction in the concrete situation. (*E,* pp. 85-86, 354.) Surely Bonhoeffer's experience of grave disappointment in both the Confessing Church and the Ecumenical Church, and his simultaneous discovery of non-Christians doing what the Christians should have been doing, is the experience that stands behind the growing methodological uncertainty of the place of the Church. There is clearly nothing in the deliberations about tyrannicide, for example, that even hints of anything resembling the Church saying "engage in this war" or "do not engage in this war." There is the member of the Body of Christ, nourished by its resources and communing with other members, making painful decisions about this "guilty" act and that; but this can be, and is, decision-making by the Christian individual-in-community, he himself being, before God, the final forum of thought and action. That is something quite different, methodologically viewed, from Bonhoeffer's Church-decreed imperatives. So at times Bonhoeffer seems to assert that Christian ethics means a collective, public issuance of the concrete command by the Church and at other times he seems to proceed with a rather privatized hearing of the command. There is more about this above (Bonhoeffer's ethic as in the last analysis a *Gesinnungsethik*), but for now it can be said with assurance that Bonhoeffer's methodology suffers from lack of concrete instruction about the place of the Church in decision-making. Bethge's remarks about Bonhoeffer's discovery of a level of responsibility "necessitating [individual] action without corporate decision" are illuminating, but they in no way resolve the methodological difficulty. (*Biography,* p. 209.)

[13] *E,* p. 39. [14] The reader may wish to review p. 31 above. [15] *E,* p. 213.

Moral guidance results from relating personally to him who is the center of man, nature, and history, to him who is true Personhood, in Bonhoeffer's understanding. Even the more objective elements in Bonhoeffer's ethics are apprehensible in their fullness only through the eyes of one who has entered into communion with Christ. "The only human and natural rights are those which derive from Christ, that is to say, *from faith*.[16] *Christ* and *faith* are thus the key terms in this ethic.

. . . After Christ has appeared, ethics can have but one purpose, namely, the achievement of participation in the reality of the fulfilled will of God.[17]
. . . Participation in this reality [the divine and cosmic reality given in Christ] is the true sense and purpose of the enquiry concerning good.[18]

"Participation in reality" is stated as the purpose of ethical inquiry again and again in *Ethics*, and this participation is achieved by relating in faith to Christ. We discover how we ought to act in interaction with others as the bearers of *the* Other among us. Ethics is intensely a matter of personal relations; it is a social event.

The moral agent is thus not related to principles, programs, virtues, ideals, laws, or any other abstractions claiming guidance for the moral life. He is related to the Person who prods, leads, enables, encourages, forms, and justifies.

. . . For indeed it is not written that God became an idea, a principle, a programme, a universally valid proposition or a law, but that God became man.[19]
. . . Christ remains the only giver of forms. It is not Christian men who shape the world with their ideas, but it is Christ who shapes men in conformity with Himself.[20]

Bonhoeffer's ethics is thus clearly ethics in the relational mode; and because he finds this antithetical to all abstractions in ethics, he unrelentingly excludes any and all manner of formalism (principles, casuistry, ideals, etc.) as determinative for yielding the answer to the "ought" question.[21] Instead, relationalism is determinative for ethics, i.e., one "knows" what one must do above all from the relationship with Christ through faith and, inseparable for Bonhoeffer, from one's relationships with others.[22]

Given ethics in this mode, how does one prove "what is the will of God"? [23]

---

[16] *Ibid.,* p. 361. Emphasis mine.   [17] *Ibid.,* p. 212.
[18] *Ibid.,* p. 195.   [19] *Ibid.,* p. 85.   [20] *Ibid.,* p. 80.
[21] I have avoided excessive citation from Bonhoeffer and development of this point here, but the reader may wish to consult the argument and quotations on pp. 164-68 below.
[22] While this chapter does not borrow directly, several matters owe instruction to James Gustafson, *Christ and the Moral Life* (New York: Harper, 1968), pp. 11-60, 116-87.
[23] *E,* p. 39.

There is a "Christian self-proving,"[24] says Bonhoeffer, to ascertain whether the moral agent is in touch with the source of the good, with "the origin, essence and goal of all that is real,"[25] with the One who grants perception of the "essential nature of things."[26] Further, there is a Christian self-proving to check whether the moral agent may not be seeking his own self-justification in his action; to see if he has called upon "the whole apparatus of human powers"[27] to prove what is in fact the will of God; to determine whether he has excluded "direct inspirations"[28] as a source of guidance and taken heed to counter the inclination to identify "the voice of the heart"[29] with the will of God; to discover whether he has consulted the Scriptures, the Church's heritage, his colleagues, and the data on the situation at hand. But above all there is Christian self-proving to make certain he has participated in the indispensable "metamorphosis."[30] This is the "complete inward transmutation of one's previous form,"[31] and it is "the crucial precondition"[32] for "proving what is the will of God."[33] II Cor. 13:5 ("Examine yourselves, to see whether you are holding to your faith") is cited by Bonhoeffer as the basic step in proving the will of God. If one has done this examination with rigor and if one has rigorously examined the historical context in which he is acting, then he will "see" what he is to do.

The striking and important item here is that what Bonhoeffer describes as "proving the will of God" is actually *preparation* of the self for perceiving the concrete command. He is not providing directives for *testing* of the command itself to see if it is of God. Rather, he refers the moral agent again and again to the conditions of perception. He is thus speaking of a *preparation* of the self to *receive* the concrete command, a matter at some distance from, and prior to, a measuring of the command itself. What such "proving" cannot do—and this is the major shortcoming for ethics—is adjudicate among conflicting claims to Christian action, *all* of which assert that they are the result of such "proving." In my judgment Bonhoeffer is speaking about Christian ethos, not ethics.

. . . Intelligence, discernment, attentive observation of the given facts, all these now come into lively operation, all will be embraced and pervaded by prayer. Particular experiences will afford correction and warning. Direct inspirations must in no case be heeded or expected, for this could all too easily lead to a man's abandoning himself to self-deception. . . . there must be a lofty spirit of sober self-control. Possibilities and consequences must be carefully assessed. In other words, the whole apparatus of human powers must be set in motion when it is a matter of proving

[24] *Ibid.*, p. 41.   [25] *Ibid.*, p. 230.   [26] *Ibid.*, p. 69.
[27] *Ibid.*, p. 40.   [28] *Ibid.*   [29] *Ibid.*, p. 38.
[30] *Ibid.*   [31] *Ibid.*   [32] *Ibid.*   [33] *Ibid.*, p. 40.

what is the will of God. But in all this there will be no room for the torment of being confronted with insoluble conflicts, or for the arrogant notion that one can master every conflict, or even the enthusiastic expectation and assertion of direct inspiration. There will be the belief that *if a man asks God humbly God will give him certain knowledge of His will;* and then, *after all this earnest proving,* there will also be freedom to make a real decision, and with it the *confidence that it is not man but God Himself who, through this proving, gives effect to His will.*[34]

If doubt arises, the subject is referred to the "earnest proving" and not to any formulations of an abstract sort. Such abstract formulations (laws, norms, principles, ideals, etc.) may be of help in an intermediary way, but method-ologically they are subject to suspension if and when the *relationship* indicates something else. In the last analysis it is personal communion with Christ which "proves the will of God." If Christian ethics is not "embraced and pervaded by prayer," it is not Christian ethics.

In the end Bonhoeffer's ethic is essentially a *Gesinnungsethik* and suffers the shortcomings thereof. Such a claim would strike objection from Bonhoeffer himself, and so a careful explication of terms is necessary, as well as the claim. A *Gesinnungsethik* denotes an ethic of disposition; it claims that what really matters for ethics happens in the formation of the moral agent. An *Objektive-thik* denotes an ethic of norms or patterns of moral behavior which exist in-dependent of the agent. This ethic focuses on acts, means, and goals, whereas a *Gesinnungsethik* by contrast directs its attention to the condition of the moral subject. The propensity of an *Objektivethik* is to provide clear and definable public criteria for evaluating and testing action, whereas the propensity of a *Gesinnungsethik* is to provide the measurements for character formation. Even when the difference is only one between the *right disposition* to action (*Gesin-nungsethik*) and the disposition to *right action* (*Objektivethik*), it is an im-portant one. The claim is that Bonhoeffer's is a *Gesinnungsethik* because what counts is the formation of the self into Christ's form, formation occurring in communion with the living Christ; furthermore, and decisively, the testing of Christian action is referred to the self's preparation for receiving Christ's con-crete command. What really matters for ethics happens in character formation.

Bonhoeffer indeed points to the objective christocratic structure of reality outside the moral agent, but his methodology does not, in the final analysis, make this a controlling factor in finding the answers *at the fixed time and place of the ethical.* Whatever the amount of reflection and analysis,[35] whatever the call to attend to consequences[36] and the caution against introspection, the out-come because of the methodology is one that answers "ought" questions via guides for the formation of the self into Christ's form. Providing public criteria for evaluating and testing action may in fact be *done* by Bonhoeffer, but it is

[34] *Ibid.* Emphasis mine. [35] *Ibid.* [36] *Ibid.,* p. 192.

not a provision accounted for in his methodology. And the claim of objectivity does not meet the requirements of an *Objektivethik* if such objectivity is not assigned a significant place; nor is the constant call to assess possibilities and to consider consequences methodologically meaningful until some provision has been made for its inclusion, and for evaluating such assessing and considering. So in the end Bonhoeffer's ethic, as a *Gesinnungsethik*, does not answer the difficult question of Christian ethics: how does one judge among conflicting claims to Christian action, *all* of which assert that they discern and bring to expression Christ's form in the world? In different words, how does one *test* the validity of those differing claims by Christians who understand themselves to be carrying out the command that they have heard as a result of "earnest proving"? This question is not raised by Bonhoeffer himself; yet it is extremely difficult to see how the "answer" could be other than to refer the agent in circular fashion to the conditions of perception, to the relationship, to "faith in this Jesus Christ [who] is the sole fountainhead of all good."[37]

But we should not too quickly foreclose on Bonhoeffer's ability to yield some manner of criteria for distinguishing authentic from inauthentic Christian action. Perhaps the *Gesinnungsethik* does carry its own resources. If so, the criteria are logically sought in and from character formation.

Bonhoeffer does indeed make rather extraordinary claims for the *reconciled* man's ability to know what he ought to do. Perhaps in the impact of reconciliation on human behavior, then, we might uncover guides for identifying genuinely Christian action. Bonhoeffer claims that "simplicity" (belonging wholly to God) leads to "wisdom" when the moral agent through "metamorphosis" lets himself be conformed.[38] The moral agent then perceives the "essential nature of things"[39] and thus sees what is "necessary and right for him to grasp and do in each separate situation."[40] He is now in touch with the "real," and, with this rootedness in the cosmic reality given in Jesus Christ, he "has been set free from the problems and conflicts of ethical decisions."[41] With reconciliation, all is set upon a new basis. There is even a new knowing, one "which arises from the knowledge of Jesus Christ as the Reconciler."[42] "No longer knowing good and evil, but knowing Christ as origin and as reconciliation, man will know all."[43] With evangelistic fervor, Bonhoeffer claims this new knowledge makes "the life and activity of man . . . not at all problematic and tormented or dark" but "self-evident, joyful, sure and clear."[44]

The moral impact of reconciliation is clear: the transformed man's relation to Jesus Christ as Lord issues, not in a new set of norms, principles, or laws, but in an altered outlook and a freedom, an openness, an affirmation of life and the world, and a clarity and certainty about his activity.

[37] *Ibid.*, p. 213. [38] *Ibid.*, p. 68. [39] *Ibid.*, p. 69.
[40] *Ibid.*, p. 227. [41] *Ibid.*, p. 68. [42] *Ibid.*, p. 33.
[43] *Ibid.* [44] *Ibid.*, p. 26.

Yet even an analysis about these differences for human behavior, which might yield criteria for testing Christian action, is cut short in Bonhoeffer's version of a *Gesinnungsethik*. For despite his talk of "earnest proving," he is ill-disposed to analyze the moral agent, even the transformed one. The reason is that the subject of ethics is not man, but Jesus Christ. It is *God-in-Christ's* action in the world that counts above all, not man's—Christ is the giver of forms. For Bonhoeffer an anthropocentric treatment would give ethics an improper status, even as systematic reflection on the way the moral agent is altered by Christ's action.[45] Bonhoeffer's is a *Gesinnungsethik* with a marked aversion to introspection, a *Gesinnungsethik* with a turning away from even a description of the transformed man. It is an ethics of character formation without delineation of the character of formation.

This and other criticism in this section on "proving the will of God" does not seek to deny the power of Bonhoeffer's "doing ethics" in the relational mode with reconciliation as the starting point. His own example is sufficient testimony to the generation of freedom from legalism and formalism, to the creation of an openness to the world and for the future, to the ability to maneuver in any of several directions, and to the achieving of a deep sense of responsibility through that ultimate freedom which grows out of the relationship with God. This is to say that the relational motif is the source for the engendering of attitudes and stances that strongly affect behavior in highly desirable ways. But is this engendering a sufficient answer to the hard question of Christian ethics, namely, the adjudication of conflicting claims, all of which attribute their origin to this very real, but nonetheless rather amoeboid organism of relationship, and to this very real but nonetheless rather undepicted ethos of reconciliation? An openness to the future, for example, does not tell us how we are to act in it, even though it surely affects our behavior in the future. And freedom from formalism and for responsibility does not provide the criteria that measure which action is in fact the most responsible, even though such freedom for responsibility is surely prerequisite for such action. Or, if the suggestive and rich themes of "The Structure of Responsible Life" are again called to mind—deputyship, acceptance of guilt, conscience, free responsibility—we are still far from the concrete instruction in the concrete situation which Bonhoeffer claims for Christian ethics. The question is certainly not whether Bonhoeffer has said a great deal. He has indeed. The question is whether he has said enough for an adequate understanding of the *totality* of ethics, whether his methodology even pushes on to the truly trouble-

---

[45] "The point of departure for Christian ethics is not the reality of one's own self, or the reality of the world; nor is it the reality of standards and values. It is the reality of God as He reveals Himself in Jesus Christ. It is fair to begin by demanding assent to this proposition of anyone who wishes to concern himself with the problem of a Christian ethic." (*E*, pp. 189-90.)

some, but vital question of Christian ethics. For, if his resolution is found by casting us back full circle to the less clearly defined creativity of the reconciling relationship itself, then it must be asked bluntly whether this answer truly suffices.

Casuistry, Principles, and Pragmatism. Again the warning must be issued not to foreclose on Bonhoeffer's resources, for he *has* means of "testing the spirits," means not limited to the guides that emerge from ethics done in the relationalist mode. At least this is true in *practice* for Bonhoeffer, even if not fully accounted for in his understanding of ethics. There are numerous instances of this, some of which follow.

He sometimes employs casuistic reasoning to demonstrate that this or that is a decision and action conformative to Christ. ("Casuistic reasoning" simply means making deductions from valid ethical generalizations in order to answer the "ought" question.) Bonhoeffer does this, for example, when he uses "the right to bodily life" as the valid ethical generalization from which he reasons the conclusion of an almost unexceptionable "no" to the possibility of euthanasia.[46] Here Bonhoeffer has, in fact, moved from an objective element in his ethics (natural rights deduced from the event of the Incarnation) to conclusions he views as clear answers to the question of what ought or ought not be done. What is difficult, however, is to find the way back into casuistry once he has ruled it out in the name of the creativity and certainty of ethics done in the *relational* motif. What is difficult is to see how the ventures into using the objective elements of his ethics are not also subject to suspicion by his own blasts against deliberative and prescriptive ways of proceeding.[47] The suspicion arises that Bonhoeffer is engaging here in a way of proceeding not formally allowed by his strongest statements, but which is nonetheless necessary because the relational manner is not specific enough in its answer to the "ought" question, however genuinely creative it may be.

The suspicion is confirmed in another move by Bonhoeffer to say what the Christian is in fact to do. This comes at the point we have claimed is Bonhoeffer's weak one—the inability to adjudicate among conflicting claims. To help formulate the more concrete meaning of natural rights (which are the basic rights for Bonhoeffer because they do not originate with man, but result from the Incarnation) Bonhoeffer introduces the Roman law dictum, *suum cuique*—"to each his own." [48] Despite its limitations, it is a "principle" to be

---

[46] *E*, pp. 160-66.

[47] See *ibid.*, pp. 86, 88, 214-15, 227, 273. This discussion is taken up in more detail in the following section.

[48] *Ibid.*, p. 151.

"applied" [49] when the natural rights are in fundamental conflict with one another.

The question is: where did Bonhoeffer obtain *suum cuique,* and how does he determine its specific content in the concrete? From the ethos of reconciliation? From the "new knowledge" given by Jesus Christ as Reconciler? From the moral guidance that arises from communing with the Lord of Reality? From the Incarnation's directives for discerning Christ's form today?

It would rather appear an importing of a philosophical, rational criterion from somewhere other than Jesus Christ, a criterion arrived at in some other manner than via the operations of relational, contextual ethics. And even if not ruled out because of its source, is such an abstraction so clearly the concrete instruction that distinguishes Christ's command? Is it so clearly grounded in the configuration of Christ's form? *Suum cuique* seems first of all a rather alien body in Bonhoeffer's ethics; and second, it still yields little for testing the spirits to determine the course of action in the fixed time and place of the ethical, the time of "necessità" being one such.

Another way of "testing the spirits" is through pragmatic considerations. Here we can return to the example of tyrannicide. In the foregoing chapter it was clear that Bonhoeffer did in fact have operative guidelines. His were rules of thumb paralleling the traditional criteria for measuring just war, now applied to active resistance. And while there is no evidence Bonhoeffer borrowed from just war theory,[50] what is of significance is that there is no evidence Bonhoeffer's rules of thumb have any necessary methodological connection to his christological ethics. The distribution of political responsibility and the criterion of success, to cite but two of Bonhoeffer's guidelines, were certainly at work in determining what action should be taken, when, and by whom. They offered concrete instruction in the concrete situation. But their connection with a contextual, relational way of determining these matters is not transparent, and that is the point. Yet it should be recognized that just such a contextual approach does leave room for ethics to be pragmatic and to introduce arguments and data from many sources in presenting the "pros" and "cons" for a particular course. But exactly what methodological status such pragmatic considerations have, and especially how they test the validity of a concrete command as the command of Christ, is not clear at all. Given Bonhoeffer's most emphatic statements on methodology, one can be certain he would not allow autonomous pragmatic judgment in the potent political matter of tyrannicide as *the* way to test the exceptional command of taking life to protect life. For then the extreme case, which began minimally as a statement of Christ's sovereign freedom, would end up the statement of pragmatic considerations wholly

---

[49] *Ibid.*

[50] I suspect the just war criteria are in any case rather accessible to the common sense of morally sensitive men and do not require special revelation for their transmission!

separable from any reference to the Commander. Such a development is wholly out of phase with the discussions of method in *Ethics,* even though Bonhoeffer allows much room for the function of reason as the organ of the penultimate and with this opens up a space for pragmatic argument as one element in setting the proper course of action.

This section of the *Grenzfall* has occasionally wandered from its focus on the exceptional command to broader dimensions of Bonhoeffer's ethics, specifically his methodology. The exceptional command has been used to probe the method. Now it is appropriate to arrive at some conclusions about the exceptional command, at the same time hopefully doing justice to the broader concerns.

The exceptional command appears to be spoken of: *either* in terms that clearly relate to Bonhoeffer's ethics—such as a statement of Christ's freedom and man's, of the limited receptivity of abstractions for reality and as a way of marking human finitude—but that do not yield the criteria for testing the presence of the extreme case itself; *or* in terms of principles and pragmatic considerations that hold promise and operate as measurements, but that evidence no necessary methodological connection with the way Bonhoeffer says Christian ethics must be done. Indeed, just these procedures seem to supplement what the method does not of itself include or yield. So, faced with the challenge to show the arrival of *"necessità,"* Bonhoeffer can take two tracks. He can refer the doubter of the presence of the exceptional command to the commanding Christ and claim that the questioner will "know" what he "must" do out of the intimacy of this relation, with its resultant knowledge of "reality." The "in" group of Christans may then agree upon the proper course of action. (But if there are conflicting claims about what action is heard as the concrete command, it is difficult to see what criteria are provided to sort the conforming action from the malforming one. Much less are criteria provided for demonstrating the ethical course to whose who do *not* share the christocratic understanding of reality.) *Or* Bonhoeffer can introduce principles and arguments that yield criteria common to Christians and non-Christians, but that he does not formally include in his methodology and that thus cannot constitute ethical justification. In the end then it would seem that *either* theological convictions have transposed possibility into command *or* the method is incomplete or faulty in that Bonhoeffer has imported foreign ways of ethically accounting for the deed, i.e. ways not accounted for in his own conception of ethics. If either is true or if both are his understanding of ethics is inadequate. He cannot, on the basis of his method, adjudicate among conflicting acts, goals, and means that claim to be anchored in the same theological context; much less can he do so for acts, goals, and means anchored in differing theological or philosophical contexts, and still account for this in his method.

The Caricature of Formalism

One last point on methodology must be appended. It reinforces the conclusion above; namely, that Bonhoeffer's understanding of ethics proves inadequate.

> . . . The dogmatically correct delivery of the Christian proclamation is not enough; nor are general ethical principles; what is needed is concrete instruction in the concrete situation.[51]

The press for concreteness in Bonhoeffer's ethics excludes formally (if not in practice) proceeding with "general ethical principles" in order to arrive at "concrete instruction." It is clear that Bonhoeffer had extraordinarily good reasons to launch his frequent protest against *"Prinzipien"* and other timeless and placeless abstractions that claim to be legitimate moral discourse. Even the very resistance movement in which he often found the epitome of responsibility, acceptance of guilt, and civil courage, finally shattered because the dissident generals hung on to the timeless and placeless principles of an ethics of duty. And the Confessing Church often exhibited an equal tenacity to "general ethical principles" which prevented bold speech and courageous deeds of justice and neighbor-love "in the concrete situation."

Nor should students of Christian ethics, weary of the "principles versus context" debate, overlook the fact that Bonhoeffer made his contribution nearly three decades ago. Viewed from the perspective of time, the protest against abstractions was prophetic.

Yet whatever the contribution the question has to be asked whether Bonhoeffer's own caricatures of the abstractions in ethics (principles, laws, ideals, virtues, etc.) do not in fact hinder him from reaching his own goal, namely, "concrete instruction in the concrete situation." That is, the argument here does *not* center on principles versus context; the argument is rather that Bonhoeffer's representations of these abstractions are caricatures, and because he is serious about their deficiencies he cannot accept them as helps in providing criteria for assessing specific acts, goals, and means. Without *this* assessment, the instruction in the concrete situation is not concrete at all, but nebulous. The argument is *not* against the protests and corrections as such brought by Bonhoeffer's creative ethics in the relational mode; the argument is that his portrayals of prescriptive and deliberative modes rule out the aids with which they can supplement relational ethics. He rightly castigated the ossifications of ethical systems (prescriptive and deliberative) but he disposed of the helps along with the rigidities when he ruled out (again at least formally if not in practice) all that smacked of abstract rather than concrete instruction.

Any number of quotations show Bonhoeffer's caricatures.

[51] *E*, p. 354.

[Christ forming the real man] leads us away from any kind of abstract ethic and towards an ethic which is entirely concrete. What can and must be said is not what is good once and for all, but the way in which Christ takes form among us here and now.[52]

An "abstract ethic" is thus evidently one that says "what is good, once and for all," and that in the nature of the case cannot be concrete.

. . . The concretely Christian ethic is beyond formalism and casuistry.[53]

Ethics as formation, then, means the bold endeavor to speak about the way in which the form of Jesus Christ takes form in our world, in a manner which is neither abstract nor casuistic, neither programmatic nor purely speculative. . . . Here there are concrete commands and instructions for which obedience is demanded.[54]

But the clearest statement of Bonhoeffer's protest against abstractions and their resultant formal expulsion from his method is this:

. . . The ethical is reduced to a static basic formula which forcibly detaches man from the historicity of his existence and transposes him into the vacuum of the purely private and purely ideal. The ethical task is now . . . realization of certain definite principles, quite irrespectively of their relation to life.[55]

The understanding of "principle" is evident from another passage.

[52] *Ibid.*, p. 85.　[53] *Ibid.*, p. 86.

[54] *Ibid.*, p. 88. Trans. corrected. The skeptic would question whether the mandates' sociological relationships of superiority and inferiority inherent in the command of God (*ibid.*, p. 289) are not spoken of in rather programmatic fashion; whether the mandates, as historical but divine and essential structures of Christ's form in the world (*ibid.*, p. 288), are not rather speculative; whether Bonhoeffer's deductions from "the right of bodily life" (*ibid.*, pp. 155 ff.) are not arrived at rather casuistically; and whether there is not considerable abstraction, but which is yet determinative for human behavior, in the section on "the divine character of government," government divine in its being, task and claim (*ibid.*, pp. 339-44); or whether similar abstraction in ethics does not occur in discussions such as that of *suum cuique* (*ibid.*, pp. 151-55).

Bonhoeffer certainly allows *regulative* principles for decision-making. In the section on euthanasia, he begins:

". . . But before any particular aspects of the problem can be examined, it is necessary to state, as a principle, that the decision about the right to destroy human life can never be based upon the concurrence of a number of different contributory factors. . . . to support the rightfulness of euthanasia with a number of essentially different arguments is to put oneself in the wrong from the outset by admitting indirectly that no single absolutely cogent argument exists." (*Ibid.*, pp. 160-61.)

Here is at least a regulative principle for deciding what Christ's concrete instruction is—"a single absolutely cogent argument" must exist and not simply cumulative ones from different perspectives. Many ethicists accustomed to considerable emphasis upon rational discourse do not make the demand as exacting as this.

[55] *Ibid.*, p. 215.

. . . [The responsible man's] conduct is not established in advance, once and for all, that is to say, as a matter of principle, but it arises with the given situation. He has no principle at his disposal which possesses absolute validity and which he has to put into effect fanatically, overcoming all the resistance which is offered it by reality, but he sees in the given situation what is necessary and what is "right" for him to grasp and do.[56]

Bonhoeffer thus refuses to include such abstractions as principles, norms, ideals, virtues, etc. because they invariably presume to say what is good "once and for all" and are thereby in no way sensitive to man's historicity.

Apparently in sharpest possible contrast to such procedures, Bonhoeffer substitutes the rational motif.

. . . The ethical is not essentially a formal rational principle but a concrete relation between the giver and the receiver of commands; formal reason is not a socially constructive principle but a principle of atomization, and society consists solely in the concrete and infinitely manifold relationships of responsibility of men one for another.[57]

. . . Ethical discourse, therefore, is not a system of propositions which are correct in themselves, a system which is available for anyone to apply at any time and in any place, but it is inseparably linked with particular persons, times and places.[58]

Timeless and placeless ethical discourse lacks the concrete warrant which all authentic discourse requires.[59]

. . . Neither the limitation nor the extension of my responsibility must be based on a principle; the only possible basis for them is the concrete call of Jesus.[60]

Bonhoeffer's convictions are deeply rooted in his experience. That most suggestive essay, "What is meant by 'Telling the Truth,'" was written at the time he was camouflaging the resistance movement in the hearings conducted during his stay in Tegel Prison. As he wrote in one of the letters smuggled to Bethge:

"Speaking the truth" (on which I have written an essay) means, in my opinion, saying how something really is—that is, showing respect for secrecy, intimacy, and concealment. "Betrayal," for example, is not truth, any more than are flippancy, cynicism, etc.[61]

Bonhoeffer's essay is in part a conscious refutation of one on the same subject by Kant. Bonhoeffer was abhorrent of Kant's "timeless and placeless ethical discourse." As he noted in the margin of the essay:

[56] *Ibid.*, p. 227.   [57] *Ibid.*, p. 273.   [58] *Ibid.*, p. 271.
[59] *Ibid.*, p. 270.   [60] *Ibid.*, p. 258.   [61] "II Advent," *LPP*, p. 88.

Kant, of course, declared that he was too proud ever to utter a falsehood; indeed he unintentionally carried this principle *ad absurdum* by saying that he would feel himself obliged to give truthful information even to a criminal looking for a friend of his who had concealed himself in his house.[62]

Following Kant would have meant betrayal of the men Bonhoeffer regarded as the most moral; such "truth-telling" would have served the most immoral of men by sacrificing the most moral. What had to be recognized was how "ethical discourse . . . is inseparably linked with particular persons, times and places." [63]

This example simply illustrates that Bonhoeffer's exclusion of abstractions in favor of relational ethics is rooted in the reality of some of his most intense experiences. Yet however understandable his insistence upon the exclusion of principles, rules, norms, etc. may be, the issue remains whether such exclusion is justifiable, and whether the resolution of ethical questions need be based on mutually exclusive methodological alternatives: *either* the contextual, relational mode *or* the prescriptive and/or deliberative ones. The question is whether caricatured portrayals, even those extracted from one's intimate experiences, should be so determinative for one's methodology. The question is whether experiencing the most grotesque versions of other ways of answering "ought" questions is reason to discard these ways along with their grotesque ossifications.

Bonhoeffer's picture of principles, ideals, virtues, etc. as claiming to be formulations of the good "once and for all" which are fanatically applied without taking account of man's historicity; his picture of the general as the antonym of the concrete; his picture of absolutized criteria of a good that is good in itself; his picture of formulas that transpose a man "into the vacuum of the purely private and purely ideal"; his picture of principles possessing "absolute validity," of principles as expressions of a formal reason that is itself a "principle of atomization," of principles constituting "timeless and placeless ethical discourse" which builds systems that are available "for anyone to apply at any time and in any place"—all these are characterizations of the *worst* rigidities of prescriptive and deliberative ways of making decisions in moral matters. Bonhoeffer however turns them into standard instances of the whole. Thus even when he himself engages in some of the formalism and casuistry which Christian ethics is assertedly "beyond," [64] he does so without giving it a status and a place in his own methodology.[65]

---

[62] *E*, p. 369, note. [63] *Ibid.*, p. 271.

[64] All the quoted phrases in this paragraph are taken from passages recently cited in this section and therefore are not individually footnoted again.

[65] To hold to his exclusion of prescriptive and deliberative motifs, Bonhoeffer would have to uphold two contentions countered by representatives of these ways of proceeding: (1) that

But the chief concern here is not to show that Bonhoeffer's conceptions are caricatures; rather it is to point out the result. The result is that he is left without certain ways of proceeding in order to judge particular actions, goals, and means, and the various claims to these; or, when he does incorporate these ways of proceeding, he fails to ascribe to them methodological legitimacy. The consequence is that Bonhoeffer methodologically frustrates his own goal, for the "concrete instruction in the concrete situation" is less concrete than it could be. The polemical, exclusivist strains in his own method thwart his own claims for Christian ethics.[66]

Conclusion

The question posed was whether Bonhoeffer's methodology and understanding of ethics are adequate. The conclusion is that they are not because they work against answering the test question of Christian ethics: how am I, as a Christian, to decide among conflicting claims, all of which contend that they embody the will of God? When Bonhoeffer does in fact provide ways to answer this question, he does so with helps not included in, demanded or implied by, his methodology.

Since it was in keeping with the subject of this study, the example of tyrannicide was chosen as the illustration of the exceptional command. It was this extreme case which demonstrated the faultiness of Bonhoeffer's method, although we noted that his caricatures of formalism contributed as well. After some notes on matters of theological criticism, we shall move from the extreme case as a study for criticism of Bonhoeffer's method and understanding of ethics to criticism of the resistance movement itself and Bonhoeffer's role within it.

---

in fact they are stating what is good "once and for all" and that, if stated, this is "applied" without a sensitive account of man's historicity and his social matrix; (2) that the inability of principles or ideals to be concretely relevant in every case is any more an argument for their general invalidity than is the argument that the existence of exceptions is an argument for the invalidity of rules.

[66] This discussion about modes of "doing ethics" has its own unexpressed context, not in the debates in moral philosophy and theological ethics in German circles, but rather in the United States and Great Britain. While I have not borrowed directly, I wish to acknowledge dependence upon the following books because they have mediated these wide-ranging and occasionally esoteric debates: Richard B. Brandt, *Ethical Theory* (Englewood Cliffs, N.J.: Prentice-Hall, 1959); William K. Frankena, *Ethics* (Prentice-Hall, 1963); James M. Gustafson, "Context Versus Principles: A Misplaced Debate in Christian Ethics," in Martin A. Marty and Dean G. Peerman, eds., *New Theology No. 3* (New York: Macmillan, 1966), pp. 69-102; Edward Leroy Long, Jr., *A Survey of Christian Ethics* (London: Oxford University Press, 1967); Gene H. Outka and Paul Ramsey, *Norm and Context in Christian Ethics* (New York: Scribner's, 1968). Especially the critique of formalism and casuistry, principles and pragmatism in Bonhoeffer's ethics is indebted to background and explication provided by these sources.

Unanswered Questions

Before leaving this chapter a few remarks should be added on a substantially different topic, but not an unrelated one. To be precise, there are two different topics, each treated separately. They have to do with substantive issues in Bonhoeffer's theology rather than ethics (insofar as this is a meaningful distinction in Bonhoeffer), and they each leave unanswered questions of some magnitude.

The issues are critical ones—a basic epistomological problem and a possibly serious misunderstanding or misappropriation in Christology. Both are intimately tied into the resistance experience.

Reality and Epistomology. For Bonhoeffer, we have noted time and again, the dynamics of the Christ event are the ontological dynamics of reality in general. Bonhoeffer's Christology is thus at the same time an ontology that takes in, for him, all that is real. Too, as we have seen, the resistance experience played a catalytic role in forging the development in Bonhoeffer's thought of the ontological coherence of God's reality and the world's in Christ. Bonhoeffer's ethics thus assumes and asserts that action which conforms to Christ simultaneously corresponds to reality, and vice versa.[67] Indeed, Bonhoeffer's ethics as a whole is a working out of this Christo-universal understanding of reality for Christian life and action. This is evidenced in the concrete at every turn—the chapter on "Christological Ethics and Resistance" abounds with examples.[68]

In the resistance movement Bonhoeffer discovered that many non-Christians were doing what Christians should have been doing. He found a community whose actions "corresponded with reality" and thereby "conformed to Christ's form in the world," but whose perception, understanding, and articulation of reality was not christological. This led Bonhoeffer to write about the disturbing implications.

. . . The question how there can be a "natural piety" is at the same time the question of "unconscious Christianity," with which I am more and more concerned. Lutheran dogmatists distinguished between a *fides directa* and a *fides reflexa.* They related this to the so-called children's faith, at baptism. I wonder whether this does not raise a far-reaching problem. I hope we shall soon come back to it.[69]

[67] It is not surprising to note Bethge's high praise for three works on Bonhoeffer which make "reality" the keyword, Ott's *Wirklichkeit und Glaube,* André Dumas' *Dietrich Bonhoeffer: Theologian of Reality,* trans. by Robert McAfee Brown (New York: Macmillan, 1971), and Rainer Mayer's *Christuswirklichkeit* (Stuttgart: Calwer Verlag, 1969). The reader may find of particular interest Bethge's review of Ott in the *Union Seminary Quarterly Review,* Fall, 1967, pp. 93-97.

[68] P. 32 ff.

[69] "27 July 1944," *LPP,* p. 197. In Lutheran dogmatics *fides directa* means unconscious response to God-in-Christ; *fides reflexa,* reflective, conscious response.

An epistomological difficulty is embedded here, and if Bonhoeffer did "come back to it" we do not have the evidence.[70] But it is certain he is correct in sensing the existence of "a far-reaching problem." For if reality can be known apart from knowing Jesus Christ, or even if Jesus Christ can be known without the Church, then Bonhoeffer's stringent claims about the necessity of the christological revelation and the locus of its comprehension (the Church), are severely called into question. And if he maintains his insistence upon conscious Christology as *the* way of perceiving and understanding genuine reality, what shall he make of his discovery that non-Christian "men-for-others" lived out "religionless Christianity," albeit "unconsciously"? Might it suffice to regard them as "unconscious Christians" who live and move and have their being in some kind of "latent" Church? The difference from conscious Christians in the manifest Church would then be only one of the *consciousness* of the christological event with its indispensable clues to the nature of reality.

While such an "answer" is not without possibilities, and may be hinted at in the mention of "unconscious Christianity" and "natural piety," it is not an answer without further delimitations from within Bonhoeffer's theology itself.

There can be no solution to Bonhoeffer's epistomological problem by way of recourse to "natural religion" or "natural revelation." In the famous Barth/ Brunner debate Bonhoeffer stands unhesitatingly in agreement with Barth that revelation creates its own "contact points" (*Anknuepfungspunkte*) rather than being received by some religious a priori apparatus constitutional to human nature. So any intimations about "unconscious Christianity" and "latent Church" could not find a resolution of the epistomological problem in a Tillichian direction, for example, or any other version in the tradition of "natural revelation" and "natural religion."

Any resolution would also have to take cognizance of Bonhoeffer's continuing *christological* qualification of "being-for-others," including that of non-Christians. While Bonhoeffer does make action in correspondence with reality simultaneously action in conformity to Christ (and thereby "formation" takes place, whether one is Christian or not), he *never* dissolves his christological ethic into a humanist ethic without Christ. That is, Bonhoeffer does *not* say that *any* "being-for-others," or that "being-for-others" in and of itself, is the way reality is "realized." He says that the "being-for-others" of *Jesus,* and men's participation *in this "Sein,"* is the way the "cosmic reality given in Christ" comes to expression in the world. *"Fuer-andere-Dasein"* in and of itself is not, and cannot be, Bonhoeffer's ethic; efficacy of action is wholly dependent upon conforming to the particular *"fuer-andere-Dasein" Jesu.*[71]

---

[70] The last theological letters to Bethge were destroyed, and the drafts for the new book have never been found. ("Editor's Preface," *LPP,* p. xxi and *Biography,* p. 813.) These would have been the logical sources for any discussion of the problem.

[71] Cf. "Outline for a Book," *LPP,* p. 202. This discussion is instructed by Mayer's excellent work in *Christuswirklichkeit,* especially pp. 275-80.

This is only to say that handling the problem of epistomology cannot take a course that would set aside the christological cornerstone of Bonhoeffer's ethic. And because that cornerstone remains to the end, the problem remains. There *may be* resources for rightly understanding reality in a humanist ethic, even one that yet holds to Bonhoeffer's *language* (being-for man, nature, and history), but such an ethic and such resources cannot be Bonhoeffer's. He only asks whether *fides reflexa* may not be a way out; he does not and cannot consider a non-*fides* path.

In short, any meeting of the epistomological difficulties in Bonhoeffer's ethic, exposed as a result of the resistance experience and expressed in his mention of "unconscious Christianity," cannot take recourse either to some species of "natural religion" or some faith-free explication of "being-for-others." What he shall do, epistomologically, with the thought and action of world-come-of-age agnostics and atheists who, contrary to their own understanding, unwittingly participate in the *fuer-andere-Dasein Jesu* remains unresolved.

Bonhoeffer may have had an answer, or have been able to provide one; he was a most creative theologian, to be sure. But, as matters stand, epistomology is an unanswered question that more than portends of being "a far-reaching problem." If a risky judgment be allowed, I suspect that despite his talents, on this issue Bonhoeffer's theology ends with a sigh.[72]

A Christological Confusion? The acceptance of guilt was a theme crucial to Bonhoeffer's entry into clandestine resistance, and, as shown, this critical decision of his life was understood in christological terms.[73] But "acceptance of guilt" presents a christological difficulty apparently left suspended.

Bonhoeffer states that Jesus Christ "is guilty without sin"[74] because it is out of selfless love that he "enters into the guilt of men and takes this guilt upon himself."[75] The conclusion is that every man who seeks to act responsibly will do the same. "Through Jesus Christ it becomes an essential part of responsible action that the man who is without sin loves selflessly and for that reason incurs guilt."[76] With this understanding, Bonhoeffer saw his way clear, theologically, for participation in the conspiracy.

The difficulty in the Christology does not arise so long as Bonhoeffer means "acceptance of guilt" in one sense which he clearly ascribes to Jesus Christ; namely, taking upon himself as his own the guilt of other men. In Bonhoeffer's

---

[72] The full implications of what the epistemological problem may only be *symptomatic of* are more than can be handled within the compass of this study. The likely outcome of the problem-complex is the breakup of Bonhoeffer's ontology; this in turn has far-reaching consequences for both his theology and ethics. I hope to treat this on another occasion. The reader may be interested in the stimulating discussion along these lines in Mayer's *Christuswirklichkeit*, pp. 219-83.

[73] See pp. 58-63 above.   [74] *E*, p. 241.   [75] *Ibid*.   [76] *Ibid*.

case this pattern meant that responsible Christians take upon themselves the guilt of nation, church, and social class. To be sure, their acceptance of guilt could only show a *relative* innocence because they, too, had had a part in the conditions that brought on the guilt of nation, church, and class.[77] (By way of contrast, Bonhoeffer ascribes a full innocence to Jesus.)[78] But the point is that there is what can be termed a "forensic guilt" which Bonhoeffer attributes to Jesus and which he says all responsible men should bear. It is part of being-for-others; it is deputyship.

Is this forensic guilt truly guilt? Certainly if one means by "true guilt" that guilt incurred through violation of divine law, then this must be clearly distinguished from forensic guilt, which for Bonhoeffer is a proof of Jesus' sinlessness (because it is an act of pure love) and a proof of the relative, but real innocence of responsible men (because it is a demonstration of selfless being-for-others).[79]

But just here the difficulty arises, for Bonhoeffer appears to mix these two very different meanings of guilt (and he does not in fact make any distinctions in his writings). So Jesus becomes the *exemplum for those who incur true guilt by acts of resistance that violate divine law, instead of being only the exemplum for the forensic taking on of guilt.* In terms of the resistance, it appears that Bonhoeffer justifies christologically the guilt incurred in violation of divine law when, in fact, his argument really only supports the acceptance of guilt forensically. The conclusion must be that if *Schulduebernahme* is as crucial to Bonhoeffer's entrance into and understanding of resistance as it appears to be, and if, as is also rather evident, Bonhoeffer's *christological* understanding of this is central to his entrance into resistance, then the problem of the meaning of guilt is very severe indeed.

There is a possible "out" hinted at by Bonhoeffer. He names Jesus, too, as a breaker of the law, including the divine law.[80] Yet this transgression was "loving without sin"[81] because it was an act wholly for the other man's sake. And if the violation of divine law, which *does* incur guilt for Bonhoeffer, *is* wholly for the sake of the other, then this guilt carries with it the demonstration of its own innocence.[82]

Here Bonhoeffer may be making room for the sinless Jesus as the *exemplum* also for the violators of divine law in the conspiracy. But if so, how does this align with the strong sense of "true guilt" Bonhoeffer feels for the violation of divine law, and the need for repentance?[83] Or is there a need for repentance when one has not "sinned"? Or is one repenting for only that portion of the violation that was not selfless in its motivation?

[77] See pp. 54-58 above.   [78] *E*, p. 241.   [79] *Ibid.*
[80] *Ibid.*, p. 244.   [81] *Ibid.*   [82] *Ibid.*, pp. 244-45.
[83] See pp. 127-28 above.

Too little is said by Bonhoeffer to work carefully through this set of issues for his Christology, ethics, and understanding of resistance. But it does seem clear that one way or another the nest of issues around guilt and Christology is a very entangled one indeed. It is minimally a nest of unanswered questions and perhaps a serious christological confusion, with ramifications for Bonhoeffer's very decision to join the underground.

2
Critique of Resistance—
Bonhoeffer as a Moral Profile
of the Military/Political Conspiracy

The Term

The term "military/political conspiracy" is somewhat a misnomer in that it leaves the impression of a single organization undertaking a rather clearly defined action. Military/political conspiracies would no doubt be the more accurate designation. Numerous cell groups and configurations of these were indeed in contact with one another, but less by virtue of an overarching organization or plan of action than by an overlapping membership. Outlines for administrative coordination of activities were the subject of many meetings, but such organization never developed.[1] The first time the entire conspiracy really "got together" was in various prisons and concentration camps following the unsuccessful attempt on Hitler's life in July, 1944. So when the term "military/political conspiracy" is used in this chapter, the reference is to the maze of semi-autonomous resistance cells linked more by personal than organizational ties.

[1] Dr. Falk Harnack of the socialist/communist Schulze-Boysen-Harnack resistance cell talked with Dietrich and Klaus Bonhoeffer about this, to cite one example. The goal was the building of an organization to coordinate the work of the various resistance groups. Dr. Harnack also recounts the arrangements he had made to put the brothers Bonhoeffer in touch with the Munich university resistance group led by Hans Scholl. The day the meeting was to take place Hans Scholl did not arrive. He and his colleagues had been arrested a few days before. They were hanged only days later. (Interview with Dr. Falk Harnack, West Berlin, Germany, March 11, 1969.)

The military/political conspiracy can be further described by distinguishing it from other kinds of opposition to Hitler's rule. The conspiracy certainly could not be characterized by the open verbal and written protest and occasional public passive resistance common to the *Kirchenkampf*. It involved, on the contrary, clandestine resistance that was both passive and active. Furthermore, it involved an elaborate plot and plan to replace one regime with another; it was not only an assassination attempt upon Hitler's life. The goal of the conspiracy was not only the end of the war and of Nazism but the replacement of the Nazi State with a just state. This extensive, tedious planning for the takeover and for the future order differentiates the military/political conspiracy from most other underground endeavors in the Third Reich.

It cannot be emphasized often enough that the conspiracy drew from a wide range of social classes, occupations, political and philosophical persuasions. In this connection, one of the most heartening and also one of the most tragic aspects of the life of his group has gone largely unrecorded. The heartening aspect lay in the ability of this diversely constituted group to overcome the deeply ingrained antagonisms of previous days and to join together in a mutual exchange and influence that led to a fairly common mind in so many matters, including the cooperative building for the national future. The tragedy, on the other hand, lay first of all in the failure of the Putsch itself with the resultant dismembering of the conspiracy. Second, the wheels of the Cold War crushed the postwar influence of many surviving participants, men and women who had come together from Left and Right in the resistance but whose resultant common mind was in harmony neither with the Russians, on the one hand, nor with the Americans, English, or French, on the other, as the postwar battle lines quickly took shape. There is a hint that Bonhoeffer anticipated this in the "book review" aimed at informing the Allies of the resistance movement.

. . . The whole question is whether people in England and America would be prepared to negotiate with a regime established on this basis even if it does not appear democratic in the Anglo-Saxon sense. Such a regime could suddenly be formed. Much would then depend on whether it could count on the immediate support of the Allies.[2]

Yet in spite of the fact that the conspiracy was actually comprised of individuals from widely divergent geographical, social, and intellectual backgrounds, a disproportionate number were Prussian Christians from aristocratic and upper-middle-class circles. The list of the victims of the July 20 debacle reads like a Prussian *Who's Who*.

Finally, the designation "military/political" points to the location of the conspiracy within the structure of German society and further identifies the con-

[2] "Gedanken zu William Paton," *GS* I, 360.

spirers. Whatever the scattered nature of the resistance cells, the backbone of the conspiracy (at least for the years of our concern) was in the Military Counter-Espionage Service (*Abwehr*) and to a lesser extent in the Armed Forces High Command and the Foreign Office. To be sure, organizational ties ran beyond these central cells in the State apparatus to leaders such as Karl Goerdeler, former mayor of Leipzig; Col. General Ludwig Beck, former Chairman of the General Staff; Wilhelm Leuschner, former president of the United Trade Unions; Jacob Kaiser, Catholic Trade Union leader; and Julius Leber, a prominent figure among the Social Democrats and a labor leader. Strictly personal ties extended even further. Yet the roll call of the resisters contained a disproportionate number of military career men and others employed in some department of the military, often as civilians; and it contained strong contingents in other sections of the State Administration—thus the "military/political" conspiracy.

The military/political conspiracy can thus be profiled in broad strokes as follows. It was distinguished from non-clandestine resistance, on the one hand, and from clandestine resistance that possessed no detailed plan for an alternative regime, on the other. Its "organizational" character was a configuration of semi-autonomous cell groups tied together primarily by an overlapping membership. This membership was drawn most heavily from Prussian Christian aristocratic and upper bourgeois circles, viewed socially, and from military and political connections, viewed occupationally. Its location was chiefly, although by no means exclusively, in the Military Counter-Espionage Service, the Armed Forces High Command, and the Foreign Service, with many ties running to cells and individuals elsewhere.

When the remainder of this study uses terms such as "resistance" and "resisters," "conspiracy" and "conspirators," etc. the reference will always be to the military/political conspiracy as here described.

This chapter will critique Bonhoeffer's resistance activity by means of a profile of the military/political conspiracy. But even here it is clear from the very complex nature of the conspiracy that any single profile, while reflecting the movement generally, would be quite unable to portray it exhaustively. A discussion of Bonhoeffer's role would be no exception. It is hoped, nevertheless, that an accurate picture of the essential configurations of the movement as a whole will emerge from the discussion.

It should be clearly stated at the outset that the perspective from which the conspiracy will be viewed will center upon moral and ethical dimensions. It is a moral profile that is attempted. The contention is that a surprising consistency is seen to emerge from such an endeavor, a consistency not equally emergent in profiles cut from other vantage points, such as the philosophical, the political, or the economic.

The mosaic of the morality of these men will be pieced together by analyzing the component parts of their basic outlook, drawing special attention to the moral *posture*. This places a heavier premium upon disposition than action, upon character than methods. Yet while this emphasis on disposition and character corresponds directly to the strength of the conspiracy itself, as we shall see, the actual means of resistance cannot be ignored. Accordingly, commentary about methods will be interjected in the course of depicting the moral posture.

One last note of explanation is in order. There is sufficient new material in this chapter that the reader may wonder whether the object is criticism or exposition. Certainly this critique is not as tightly focused upon Bonhoeffer's ethics as was the preceding chapter. But I have undertaken considerable exposition for two reasons. Despite this study's asserted importance of the resistance movement for Bonhoeffer's life and thought, relatively little of the movement's actual makeup has been given thus far. And while biographical and historical details are not the overriding concern of this study, it is hoped that the inclusion of some of these here, as earlier, will serve to illumine the context of Bonhoeffer's decisions and actions. Further, to my knowledge a moral profile of the resistance movement does not exist in English, and because in the course of analyzing Bonhoeffer's resistance participation, I came across amazing congruencies of his moral profile with those of the other men, I decided to include all in the hope of contributing some original research and analysis in an area far from peripheral to the concerns of this total inquiry. Thus, while the object is first of all to provide a critique of Bonhoeffer's resistance activity, the resistance movement as a whole is also analyzed and assessed.

The Educated Elite

The conspiratorial resisters comprised an intellectual, contemplative, elitist group. Diplomats, generals, professors, journalists, lawyers, top civil servants, high men of labor, a few industrialists, a sprinkling of clergymen—such was the occupational roll call of the conspiracy.

"Intellectual" means that the men of the conspiracy were by and large well-educated and reflective men. The reference is not to professional intellectuals as such. There were professors among the conspirators, but not a great preponderance of them. In any case, "intellectual" has a broader reference.

"Elitist" is not a class designation, but is shorthand for the fact that the conspiracy drew from the *leadership* groups manifesting widely varying social origins, rather than from the rank and file.

The intellectual and elitist nature of the conspiracy is thus not a designation of professional scholarship or of aristocratic social origins but of a resistance comprised of educated leaders.

177

The ramifications of this elitist cast were extremely far-reaching. A "top-heavy" resistance movement emerged, one with an abundance of analysts, planners, and administrators—but a singular lack of technicians and troops.[3] The consequences will be drawn shortly.

This was a group of men who, by their very talents, composed a leadership complex that commanded mutual regard and exchange. The respect of each for the others' opinion and expertise generated a movement that proceeded in a "democratic" fashion. That is, decision-making was done through an exchange of mind until a common agreement or consensus was reached. This was in diametrical contrast to the system of authoritative command and unconditional obedience that clamped the Third Reich together for twelve years.

But a democratic conspiracy in a totalitarian state carried few advantages. It took an extraordinarily long while to reach decisions because of the felt need for the common clearance of plans among equals. The logistics of conspiracy reinforced these inherent delays; mail and telephone could not be used, and in the end significant communication depended upon personal contacts and/or codes. Democratic conspiracy under such conditions could not match the efficiency of the Reich's methods of command and obey. Opportunities were missed because there were too many chiefs to be consulted. In fact, the supreme irony of this conspiracy may well lie in the fact that it lacked a dynamic, charismatic *"Fuehrer"* who could direct this constellation of extraordinary talent without its collective approval of the major moves.

The erudite and contemplative character of the movement had a double consequence. One was the constant reflection upon the *grounds* for opposition, for action, and for the future order, to the near exclusion of executing particular actions themselves. In different words, the disposition of these men was to be philosophically or theologically well-based before seeking political expression of their convictions. This was as true for the generals in the resistance as it was for the professors![4] It is not surprising, given this intellectual caste, that for the great majority of these men the right to resist was not only a legal problem but also a deeply philosophical/theological one.

This contemplative character is superbly mirrored in Bonhoeffer's Christmas essay for his co-conspirators, "After Ten Years." Such a supremely reflective, non-ideological, careful and concise, but passionately existential document was fully in accord with the profile of the conspiracy in general. Furthermore, it is indicative of the character of the resistance that the recipients of this essay were not chiefly professors, clergymen, and students, but members of the Military

---

[3] For details about the membership of the resistance see works such as Rudolf Pechel, *Deutscher Widerstand* (Erlenbach-Zurich: E. Rentsch, 1945) and Gerhard Ritter, *The German Resistance,* trans. R. T. Clark (London: Allen and Unwin, 1958).

[4] See the impressive documentation in an extraordinarily well researched book: Harold C. Deutsch, *The Conspiracy Against Hitler in the Twilight War* (Minneapolis: The University of Minnesota Press, 1968).

Counter-Espionage Service, including high-ranking military men and civilians at the very top. (The influence of one of these men for Bonhoeffer's *Ethics,* Colonel General Oster, was cited earlier.)[5]

Bonhoeffer's own reflection is typical of that sensitive, thoughtful nature of the conspirators which issued in a continual deliberation of the grounds and meaning of their activity. A strong case can even be made that conspiratorial conversation replaced conspiratorial action, that a feeling of powerlessness by thinking men accustomed to seeing results was compensated for by an increase of intellectual activity. However, the psychological analysis of the phenomenon, interesting as that may be, lies beyond the boundaries of this study. But there is little doubt that the disposition of this group was to reflect upon the philosophical and theological presuppositions of their activity; certainly they engaged in lengthy and elaborate discussion on these lines.[6]

More than Bonhoeffer's own reflection can be cited. Many men kept diaries. The diplomat von Hassel's is a major resistance document.[7] These diaries record not only deeds but reflection upon these deeds, not only urgings for action but thoughts about such urgings, not only wishes but also the personal interpretation of these wishes. Another source is the extraordinary collection of the last thoughts of those condemned to death by the Nazis; it is a wealth of profundity for any philosopher of life—and death.[8]

The second consequence of the inherently speculative nature of the movement was a preoccupation with careful blueprinting.[9] One of the most striking items about the conspiracy itself, and that which gave it its tragicomic character, was a virtual obsession with programs combined with an absence of physical engagement and recruitment of troops and weapons. An aside is in

[5] See pp. 68-69 above.

[6] See "Der Blick von unten," *GS* II, 441. "The View from Below" is reflection on what is to be learned by men accustomed to making history but who now find themselves suffering and without power. The piece was intended for "After Ten Years" but was not completed.

[7] Ulrich von Hassel, *Von anderen Deutschland: Tagebuecher 1938-1944* (Zurich: Atlantis Verlag, 1946).

[8] Helmut Gollwitzer, Kaethe Kuhn, and Reinhold Schneider (eds.), *Dying We Live,* trans. Reinhard C. Kuhn (New York: Pantheon Books, © 1956). Kurt Huber, a member of the Munich university resistance group, spoke for all these people when he closed his statement before the Nazi tribunal with the words of Fichte:

> "And you must act as though
> On you and on your deeds alone
> The fate of German history hung,
> And the responsibility—your own."
>
> (Quoted from p. 161 of this volume.)

[9] To cite an example from Bonhoeffer: The criterion of reasonably assured success used to measure tyrannicide was a criterion wholly indicative of the resisters' outlook. It is indicative even when the measurement was not for tyrannicide. There was a great deal of emphasis upon all planning as the key to a successful revolt, whether the particular plan included assassination or not.

order here. It is in keeping with the rest of the conspiracy that even the generals were not militarists! Rather, most were bureaucrats without tanks and troops under their command who saw their contribution to be the detailed planning of a Putsch that could be carried off by order and without bloodshed [10]—and even without physical engagement beyond making arrests and occupying offices. These military men were wholly opposed to a regime of bayonets. They were even against their own presence as state officials for more than a transitional government.[11] In different words, they were by and large not politically ambitious, but possessed a strong sense of career professionalism and were generally opposed on principle to "meddling in revolutionary action." [12] It is certainly true that, together with the other resisters they bore a strong sense of responsibility. But they were plainly not enthusiastic about conspiracy and were anything except utopian fanatics driven by a flaming vision of a new order. They regarded their resistance activity as a work of sober deputyship and, paralleling Bonhoeffer's thought on the preservation of the purity of offices and missions in the *polis*,[13] viewed the resistance movement as the means for making possible a return to the normal performance of duties.

The contemplative, meticulous character of the work of these men must be reckoned an indirect cause for the failure of the resistance. Their reticence over aganist action is not traceable simply or exclusively to lack of civil courage. It is embedded in part in an obsession with planning in such detail that opportune times for action were missed as a consequence. A frequent stumbling block to positive action was the common conviction that all was not yet fully prepared. The conclusion must be ventured that Bonhoeffer's understanding of "the incalculable aspect of responsibility, therefore risk," [14] should have been applied across the board earlier and with even more emphasis than his own.

Thus the contemplative character yielded what must be one of history's strangest military/political conspiracies; namely, one that lacked the correspond-

---

[10] The generals were hardly pacifists! But one must know that for the Prussian Army tradition (and it is from this Prussian understanding of the army and not Hitler's that the resisters came), the killing done by soldiers in war was, ethically considered, qualitatively vastly different from any violent action against one's fellow countrymen and especially against highly placed officials. While Bonhoeffer's stance was more nonviolent than theirs, the remarkable item is how noncoercive these men were and how, like Bonhoeffer, they had to move from nonviolent to violent, legal to illegal, means in opposing the head of state. Viewed ethically, war was far less problematic than active resistance, to say nothing of tyrannicide in particular.

[11] General Halder told the German historian, Gerhard Ritter, that he and von Witzleben, both military men who were to hold top posts in the post-coup regime, had pledged themselves to resign soon after the Putsch succeeded. They both felt the military way of life was endangered "by meddling in revolutionary action." Ritter adds that this observation is invaluable for understanding the nature of the military opposition. Gerhard Ritter, *The German Resistance*, p. 103, note.

[12] *Ibid*.   [13] *E*, pp. 350-51.

[14] Microfilm No. 395. Frame No. 27. See pp. 138-42 above for discussion of the criterion of reasonably assured success.

ing physical engagement even when civil courage was mustered in sufficient dosages. These men were all manner of "philosophers" who were not activists, planners who were not revolutionaries, and conspirators whose chief treasonous acts were conversational and written. Those familiar with the biographies of these men know what a comical picture emerges at the thought of this educated, contemplative, responsible, and sensitive group manning the barricades of revolution!

An astounding phenomenon is that among the entire cluster of conspirators, like Bonhoeffer, there was hardly one who was a technician with explosives, hardly one trained in sabotage, hardly one in any way educated for conspiracy or even resistance. In short, this intellectual, elitist group lacked the personnel who could make possible the *technical* success of the revolt. It programmed the Putsch, but it lacked the activist temperament and the technicians of weaponry to carry it through.[15] There was a total absence of professional revolutionaries. There were no conspirators in the grand manner present.[16] Nearly all the participants in the resistance movement would have underwritten Bonhoeffer's statement in *Ethics,* penned at the height of the conspiracy: "According to Holy Scripture, there is no right to revolution." [17]

The elitist nature of the conspiracy shaped the plans for the revolt in another important way. While these men proceeded democratically with one another, they clearly conceived of a differentiation of quality existing between

[15] When the move to resolute action did come in July, 1944, it was carried out by one of a group of men who constitute something of an exception to the characterization of the resistance movement given above. Count von Stauffenberg points up a kind of career generation gap in the military/political resistance. The first strong opponents of Hitler were by and large older men steeped in the proud traditions of the Prussian Army. They saw in Hitler a barbarization of those traditions, as well as a complete irrationalist in matters of military prognosis and foreign policy. These men formed the core of the military elite in the resistance of the thirties. At the same time, the younger officers in the thirties were caught up in Hitler's fantastic attraction of the searching, idealistic youth. The astounding military victories of the early forties hardly turned back the aspiring young officers! But with the mass crimes commanded of the Army on occasion in the forties, a number, pitifully small, turned to opposition. It was these men who were much more inclined to take action against the regime than the equally opposed older officers. But the young came late to the conspiracy. Thus while Stauffenberg, Werner von Haeften, and others represented this element, their activist orientation was not typical of the conspiracy as a whole. Their intellectual acumen was, however. Incidentally, as we have noted elsewhere, Bonhoeffer was frequently angered by the failure to act, especially by the generals. The stanza of the poem written the day after the July attempt is more indicative of the younger men, although Bonhoeffer was perhaps more inclined to diminish the risks by completing the plans than many among the younger men.

"Daring to do what is right, not what fancy may tell you, valiantly grasping occasions, not cravenly doubting—freedom comes only through deeds, not through thoughts taking wing. Faint not nor fear, but go out to the storm and the action, trusting in God whose commandment you faithfully follow; freedom, exultant, will welcome your spirit with joy."
("Stations on the Road to Freedom," *LPP,* pp. 194-95.)

[16] Margret Boveri, *Der Verrat im 20. Jahrhundert,* II (Hamburg: Rowohlt Verlag, 1957), p. 87.

[17] *E,* p. 351.

themselves and the masses. In the report on the lessons of resistance Bonhoeffer wrote:

Unless we have the courage to fight for a wholesome reserve between man and man, we shall perish in an anarchy of human values. The impudent contempt for such reserve is the mark of the rabble, just as inward uncertainty, haggling and cringing for the favour of insolent people, and lowering oneself to the level of the rabble are the way of becoming no better than the rabble itself. . . . In other times it may have been the business of Christianity to champion the equality of all men; its business today will be to defend passionately human dignity and reserve. The misinterpretation that we are acting for our own interests, and the cheap insinuation that our attitude is anti-social, we shall simply have to put up with; they are the invariable protests of the rabble against decency and order. . . . We are witnessing the levelling down of all ranks of society, and at the same time the birth of a new sense of nobility, which is binding together a circle of men from all former social classes. Nobility arises from and exists by sacrifice, courage, and a clear sense of duty to oneself and society, by expecting due regard for itself as a matter of course; and it shows an equally natural regard for others, whether they are of higher or of lower degree. We need all along the line to recover the lost sense of quality and a social order based on quality. Quality is the greatest enemy of any kind of mass-levelling.[18]

The resistance experience indeed brought about "a new sense of nobility . . . binding together a circle of men from all former social classes." Yet it was nonetheless an elitist group that felt that, as Bonhoeffer scribbled on a scrap of paper, "the masses must in the last analysis be forced to attain their own welfare."[19] Elsewhere his opinion is curt and strong: "The masses—an intoxicant."[20]

To be sure, Bonhoeffer could write of an aristocratic disdain that stood as condemned by the Incarnation as Hitler's own contempt for men.[21] And certainly the elite of the resistance did possess what Bonhoeffer termed "an equally natural regard for others, whether they are of higher or lower degree."[22] Many, probably most, shared Bonhoeffer's own compassion for all men. Yet for all this, it must also be said that a persistent and pervasive distrust of the masses to act in ways concordant with their own welfare existed among the conspirators. The resisters doubted whether the common people possessed suffi-

---

[18] "After Ten Years," *LPP*, pp. 12-13. Compare this with the statement of the German historian, Rudolf Pechel, also a member of the resistance:
 "In their *rage du nombre* the National Socialists replaced the principle of quality with that of quantity. This went so far that a high number in anything was regarded as a major Nazi achievement. We [the resisters] remained attached to the principle of quality. Any later mass movement could only be successfully released if a reliable elite were on hand." (Rudolf Pechel, *Deutscher Widerstand*, p. 45.)
[19] Microfilm No. 395, Frame No. 31. [20] *Ibid.*, Frame No. 32.
[21] *Ibid.*, Frame No. 23. [22] From the quotation above.

cient political wisdom, instinctive or otherwise, to play a part in the overthrow of Hitler and his under-tyrants.

A mammoth amount of data was on hand for such a judgment. Millions had indeed become intoxicated with their *"Fuehrer."* The emergence of a criminal rabble and untold numbers of silent accomplices was the sorry result.[23] From the standpoint of wise political calculation alone, and quite apart from any general affirmation of or disdain for "the people," the planners of the coup d'etat had the strongest case in excluding the masses as an active agent in the overthrow.

But the elitist self-consciousness is surely a factor in this exclusion, whatever political considerations yielded on other grounds. This is mirrored in the procedures for the takeover. The "parliamentary" conspiracy planned the regime change on the principle of command and obedience. The populace was not to rise up against its former oppressors but continue to obey as before. The scripts for the communiques to the German people and the Armed Forces include the following.

Germans!

For this purpose [to end Nazi rule] we have, after proving our consciences before God, taken over the power of State. Our brave Army is the guarantor for security and order. The police will fulfill its duties. . . . Every civil servant

[23] One of the characters in Bonhoeffer's unpublished and incomplete novel written in Tegel Prison is a retired officer and landed aristocrat who speaks at great length about the "little people with power" (*"kleine Gewalthaber"*) and the necessary struggle against them. The following belongs to one of his discourses.

" 'There are many oppressions, but none brings greater misery to men than the misuse of power, and that exactly at the hands of the little people. Again and again history has raised up great abusers of power; they call forth huge countermovements of power against them and almost never escape their due judgment; they are demigods who are not subject to the ordinary human standards. They rise and fall in a few years; but the little abusers of power do not die out. They live off the favor of their one-time lords, bathe themselves in it and escape every earthly court of judgment. The little abusers of power are the ones who destroy a people from within. They are like the invisible agents of a wasting disease that work unnoticed to destroy a budding young life. They are not only more dangerous but also stronger, more tenacious, harder to lay hold of, than the great abusers of power; they slip through the fingers when one tries to seize them; they are slick and cowardly; they are like a contagious disease. . . . So it goes on and on until finally everything is contaminated and the decomposition cannot be stopped.' The major paused and took a deep breath. 'Nevertheless, lads,' he continued, 'we must not let ourselves be disheartened by the seeming hopelessness of the battle. Whoever succeeds in eliminating one of these little tyrants may take pride in having saved many lives; he is a hero of humanity whether anyone else knows it or not. Many well-meaning people of our class have accustomed themselves to making light of these petty abusers of power, and consider as fools those who have declared a war to the death against them. This light-hearted treatment is as foolish and irresponsible as smiling at the diminutiveness of bacteria.' " (Excerpted from pp. 38-40 of a typewritten copy of Bonhoeffer's "Romanversuch," received from Susanne Dress-Bonhoeffer, West Berlin, Germany and used with the permission of Eberhard Bethge.)

shall obey only the law and his conscience and shall exercise his office in accord with his expertise. . . .[24]

Soldiers!

Wherever you are—on the front or in the occupied territories—I bind you to the laws of unconditional obedience, soldierly discipline and honorable, gallant, behavior. Whoever is deficient here or transgresses these laws in the future shall be called to account without leniency.[25]

The elite were to occupy the offices of the organs of dictatorship and from there exercise authority in highly centralized fashion. The assumption was that this authority would be respected without question.[26] But whatever the tactics of revolt, there is no doubt that the dominant political stance of the resisters was one that demanded essentially the substitution of a morally conscious elite for the criminal "elite" of the Nazi system. As Bonhoeffer includes in an unpublished fragment of a novel: ". . . Germany gone astray, the endangered, decaying Germany, the Germany that needs a strong hand over it to bring it back to health." [27] Thus while the conspiracy was "parliamentary" and nonauthoritarian in its plenums for Putsch-planning, it was elitist and authoritarian in its provisions for "a strong hand" over Germany "to bring it back to health." It pursued "a social order based on quality . . . the greatest enemy of any kind of mass-leveling." [28]

The effective presence of a contemplative elite at the heart of the resistance movement, given more to discussion and planning than to risky action, is mirrored in the means of resistance. It is a worthy expenditure of time and space to consider these before continuing with the profile of the resisters. Only three items are discussed here—word campaigns, strikes, and insurrections—but they illustrate well the phenomena outlined above.

Throughout the years 1938-1944 there existed what might be termed a "memoranda war" within the resistance. In fact, if the verbal and written work taken together is labeled "word campaigns," one could conclude that these campaigns were the main ones fought by the resisters.

[24] Bundeszentrale fuer Heimatdienst, "Aufrufe an das deutsche Volk," *20. Juli 1944: Dokumente und Berichte* (Freiburg: Herder-Buecherei, 1961), p. 138.

[25] "Aufrufe an die Wehrmacht," *20. Juli 1944*, p. 160.

[26] The irony of the July 20, 1944, effort was that obedience to the commands of the Putschers was not automatic. The hesitation on many fronts to follow orders endured until those commanded were certain that Hitler was actually dead. By then the revolt had shattered. In one sense, it was the *"Fuehrerprinzip"* that failed to function at the most crucial jucture. The conspirators had not sought the *agreement* of subordinates but, in accord with the *"Fuehrerprinzip,"* expected the automatic obedience of orders from superiors. This was not forthcoming, and the end was near.

[27] Dietrich Bonhoeffer, "Romanversuch," Tegel Prison, p. 46 of a typewritten copy received from Susanne Dress-Bonhoeffer, West Berlin, Germany, and used with the permission of Eberhard Bethge.

[28] Repeated from the quotation from "After Ten Years" above, p. 182.

The word campaigns had several purposes. One was to influence Hitler's course of action by subtle and evolutionary means. Memoranda were occasionally directed to highly placed advisors trusted by Hitler, but with whom the resisters also had sufficient contacts to evoke some measure of optimism about curbing Hitler's dilettantism. Great hope was never placed in such writings, but they were regarded as worth the effort, simply because so much was at stake.

The second purpose was more in line with the goal of a revolt. An almost endless stream of communiqués went out from conspirators to known or suspected dissenters from Hitler's policies in order to encourage them to become resisters. Or verbal and written campaigns were aimed at persuading the resisters themselves, especially the generals, to take decisive action. The entire period from 1938 to 1944 saw a memoranda flood for this purpose of recruiting resisters and strengthening their resolution. Many were drawn up by von Dohnanyi, Oster, Gisevius, Mueller, and others in the Military Counter-Espionage Service. Bonhoeffer was knowledgeable of them and participated in discussions about them.

Third, writings were documents of resistance. Even an archive of resistance materials was brought into being at the insistence of Beck.[29] Such documentation was intended not only for a historical recor' but also for the postwar denazification procedures, should the Putsch not succeed, or should decisive resistance be rendered impossible before the strike. For men occupying such high posts, trials by the victors posed no small threat.

Fourth, much was written to camouflage the resistance work. It was an immensely time-consuming task but vitally important, especially since the Third Reich was obsessed with forms and formalities. (A most interesting example is Bonhoeffer's backdated letter to Hans von Dohnanyi, explaining all the connections abroad which could be used to the benefit of the *Abwehr*.[30])

The paper resistance was not without its grave risks, to be sure. But it was easier and more in line with the character of these men than any acts of violent resistance. One of the conspirators in the Foreign Office, Erich Kordt, wrote after the war:

. . . Naturally the temptation was great to remain within the existing patterns and attempts to salve ourselves . . . by means of a few memoranda and warnings, although of course we knew that this would remain an ineffective gesture.[31]

[29] This archive cost many lives, including Bonhoeffer's. Certainly Bonhoeffer's involvement would have been discovered anyway. (Indeed it was.) Yet these were documents that led to the chain of events which ended in Flossenburg. Had the archive at Zossen not been kept by the resisters, it is a question whether Gestapo action would have sealed the fate of these men in time, for the end of the war was near.

[30] See Jørgen Glenthøj, ed., *Dokumente zur Bonhoeffer Forschung*, pp. 316-18.

[31] Erich Kordt, *Nicht aus den Akten* (Stuttgart: Union Dt. Verlag Gesellschaft, 1950), p. 312.

Graf Lutz Schwerin von Krosigk, another of the resisters, remarked about Col. General Beck's many memoranda: "They could quiet the conscience but they could not influence Hitler."[32]

It is not unfair to conclude that the memoranda war exemplifies the characteristics of the educated elite described above, characteristics that also find expression in their other writings. The case *is* a strong one that maintains that conspiratorial comment replaced conspiratorial action and that a feeling of powerlessness was compensated for by an increase of intellectual activity.

If word campaigns as a means were obvious by their presence, general strikes and mass insurrection were means obvious by their absence. While they were mentioned, given thought, and occasionally discussed,[33] they were rarely considered seriously and planned for by the conspiracy because of brutally stark realities. Already in the early thirties Hitler had effectively shattered the base for strikes and insurrections in both the large unions (which were declared illegal, disbanded, and replaced by the Nazi-run *"Deutsche Arbeitsfront"*) and in the political parties with large followings among the workers (the Social Democrats and the Communists). So the possibility of forming an underground organizational base for general strikes and/or insurrection was virtually nonexistent by the time it became clear that Hitler was a totalitarian dictator. Furthermore, by 1938 (perhaps before) the net of the secret police was so well woven as to prevent reorganization of the yet-remaining dissenters. And to these facts must be added the fanatic support of Hitler by the workers, a remarkable triumph of the age-old fascist glorification of the peasantry. Even if the former bases were gone and the Gestapo omnipresent, a *spontaneous* strike or insurrection by the remaining malcontents would surely have been a story of failure written in blood, for the dissenters' fellow workers would have enthusiastically shared the tasks of suppression with the police.

These are all good reasons for the resisters' exclusion of the masses as an agent in the overthrow. In different words, elementary political calculation alone ruled out general strikes and insurrection.

The conspirators' elitist disposition only reinforced this. With the exception of the leading men of labor in the ranks of resistance, the elitist suspicion and distrust of the masses was present *before* Hitler's consolidation of support. It could hardly be abated after. What the twentieth of July expected of the masses was not revolt, but a continuance of the chains of command and obedience. The July 20 strike was the perfect opposite of an instigation to mass insurrection. There were no calls to agitation (on the contrary!), no exchange of gunfire, no

---

[32] Graf Lutz Schwerin von Krosigk, *Es geschah in Deutschland* (Tübingen: Wünderlich Verlag, 1952), p. 275.

[33] *Biography*, pp. 535, 576. Bonhoeffer for one excluded action that threatened mass rebellion, just as he excluded, on the other end of the spectrum, the desperate action of an individual as a justifiable mode of resistance. (*Ibid.*, p. 699.)

186

flyers or placards. Nor were there to be. The greatest pains were taken to avoid civil war. Bonhoeffer's criterion of the minimum use of violence has strong echoes in plan after plan for the takeover, and for both *"realpolitisch"* and moral reasons.

The lack of a mass base for the resistance is a monumentally important fact. And the elitist failure to recruit members for the conspiracy among the workers appears a major mistake. The contribution of Social Democrats, Communists, or other groups holding allegiances among the workers may have meant the overcoming of scruples that plagued the gentler conspirators. It may also have contributed those men who could have made possible the *technical* success of the *coup d'etat*. Scruples and the lack of technical finesse and expertise were major causes for the failure of the revolt.

The Legal and Nonviolent Core

The core of the resistance was deeply humane, its morality antithetical to that of the Nazis at a number of crucial points. Even when many of the resisters were in agreement with some of Hitler's goals and shared some of his feelings—the rejection of the Versailles clause, a strong sense of nationalism, the approval of rearmament, the retaking of the Rhineland, and the annexation of Austria—they were repulsed by his *means*. The first paragraph of the call to the German people, intended for broadcast upon success of the revolt, reads as follows.

> Germans!
> Hitler's despotism is broken.
> The atrocious has taken place before our eyes these last years. Not called by the German people, but having come to the pinnacle of government through intrigue of the worst kind, Hitler, through demonic arts and lies, through monstrous lavishness which appeared to bring all manner of advantages but in truth plunged us into sins and shortcomings, has confused the minds and souls of our people, indeed has produced fateful delusions even outside Germany. In order to maintain himself in power he has erected a rule of terror. Once our people could pride itself in its integrity and fair play. But Hitler has mocked divine laws, vanquished justice, outlawed decency, destroyed the well-being of millions. He has deemd as nothing the honor and dignity, freedom and life of others. Countless Germans, as well as members of other peoples, have been exposed to the greatest afflictions and often subjected to terrible torture. Many have not survived. Our good name has been defiled through hideous mass murders. With blood-stained hands Hitler has treked his felonous way, leaving tears, grief and misery in his wake.[34]

[34] Bundeszentrale fuer Heimatdienst, "Aufruf an das deutsche Volk," *20. Juli 1944: Dokumente und Berichte,* p. 139.

A more impassioned expression of moral indignation can hardly be imagined. It is this moral outrage that generated opposition in the first place and then continued to propel the motor of conspiracy.

Perhaps the most unequivocal departure from reigning Nazi morality was the rejection of violence as the *prima ratio* of politics, rather than the *ultima ratio*. Political murder was wholly repugnant to the resisters. Events such as the Roehm revolt and the Commissar Order to murder Russian Army political instructors and civil servants occasioned times of recruitment for resistance. In short, abhorrence of violent means as a legitimate political tool was widespread among the resisters.

The lines must not be overdrawn, however. The picture is not that of the apostles of nonviolence standing erect over against the glorifiers of violence. While Bonhoeffer, von Moltke,[35] and a few others might in a meaningful sense be reckoned among the advocates of nonviolence, the cross section of attitudes does not record equally sharp distinctions. Yet the kind of distinctions actually made by most resisters are important, if not always sharp.

The military elite in the conspiracy were hardly apostles of nonviolence (!), *but* the use of violence and especially murder as a means for achieving domestic political goals was simply not part of the same framework of understanding as the killing done by soldiers in campaigns of war. Political murder was one category, killing in war a vastly different one. As long as tyrannicide belonged to the category of political murder, the generals would have, and did have, the greatest difficulty subscribing to it. General Halder's opinion is representative. When the question of assassination arose following the campaign that culminated in the fall of France, Halder told Stauffenberg: "Careful thought must be given to what can be reconciled with the honor of a soldier and what cannot; political murder must be rejected under all circumstances." [36] Halder was one of the generals most consistently and strongly opposed to Hitler. He sometimes carried his pistol into conferences with Hitler and shared with fellow

[35] In his farewell letter to his wife, Count von Moltke wrote: "The decisive pronouncement in the trial was: 'Count Moltke, Christianity and we National Socialists have one thing in common, and one thing only: we claim the whole man.' Did [Friesler] realize what he was saying? Just think how wondrously God prepared this unworthy vessel of his: at the very moment when there was danger of my being drawn into active preparations for the coup—Stauffenberg came to see Peter [Yorck von Wartenburg] on the evening of the nineteenth—I was taken out of it, so that I am free and remain free of any connection with the use of violence." (Gollwitzer, Kuhn and Schneider, *Dying We Live,* p. 129.) Harald Poelchau, a member of the Kreisau Circle and chaplain in Tegel Prison, reports that von Moltke's ethical disqualification of the use of violence was altered slightly at the very end when he gave approval for the assassination attempt, provided it be understood as the rarest of exceptions. (Interview with Harald Poelchau, West Berlin, Germany, April 25, 1969.) Von Moltke is a moving and articulate figure in the resistance. A comparison of his and Bonhoeffer's prison letters would be a most fruitful venture, not least on their views concerning the this-worldliness of faith. (Cf.: Helmuth James von Moltke, *Letzte Briefe aus dem Gefaengnis Tegal* [Berlin: Karl H. Henssel, 1951].)

[36] Peter Bor, *Gespraeche mit Halder* (Wiesbaden: Limes, 1950), p. 174.

resisters the remark that he was often tempted to shoot Hitler.[37] He resisted temptation.

Nor were most of the civilian elite proclaimers of nonviolence as an inviolable principle. They were sensitive, even overly so, to the preservation of order as a function of the State *as* State and they subscribed to the exceptional use of hard coercion by the proper authorities as a legitimate means to obtain and retain this necessary order. But such use of hard coercion was simply not in the same category with the political plunder and murder perpetrated for Nazi aggrandizement. In any case, whatever the differences of opinions among the conspirators on violence and nonviolence, Bonhoeffer does mirror the cross-sectional judgment *for matters of domestic politics* when he emphasizes that an abyss lies between the exceptional employment of violence and any normal use, supposedly justifiable on principle.[38] He also represents the others with the conviction that only the minimum amount of force necessary for a successful *coup d'etat* is morally allowed.[39]

The politics of brutality rubbed the moral sensitivities of these men raw in yet another way. Basic human rights were not guaranteed by Nazi law. The Rule of Law (*Rechtstaat*) was cast portside in 1933 with the declaration of the "state of emergency" (*Ausnahmezustand*), and it only returned when the Third Reich itself was gone. The resistance cells orchestrating the future order all gave special stress to the constitutional guarantee of basic human rights, and they all gave special stress to guards against suspension of these rights.[40]

Yet, paralleling the case of nonviolence and violence, it cannot be said that the resisters were simply ranged against the Nazis as the proclaimers of obedi-

---

[37] " 'Wir werden am Galgen enden!': Die Widerstandsgruppe des Generals Oster," *Der Spiegel*, May, 1969, p. 154.

[38] *Ibid.*, p. 239.   [39] Cf. pp. 142-43 above.

[40] The Kreisau Circle deserves special mention. Led by James von Moltke, it was probably the group that gave the most attention to the outline of the future order. In an August, 1943, draft, the following are a few of the principles sketched. They serve to demonstrate the point made above.

"The government of the Reich is . . . determined to fulfill the following indispenable demands, using all the means at its disposal:

1. The principle of legality, now trampled under foot, must be elevated once again to a position of supremacy over all conditions of human life. Beneath the protection of conscientious and independent judges, freed from the fear of men, this is the basis for every respect of the peaceful state of affairs which is to come.

2. Freedom of belief and freedom of conscience will be guaranteed. All laws and decrees which contravene these principles will be repealed immediately.

3. Totalitarian moral compulsion will be broken: the inalienable dignity of the human individual will be recognized as the basis for that legal and peaceful order which is the objective. Each man will work, in full responsibility, in his own field of social, political and international activities. The right to work and the right to property are under public protection regardless of race, nationality or creed." (Kreisau Circle, "Basic Principles for the New Order," Draft of 9 August 1943. Excerpted from pp. 257-58 of Appendix I in FitzGibbon, *20 July.*)

ence to law over against the apostles of arbitrariness. Nazi ideology had indeed declared as erroneous that basic human rights accrued to all men equally; and indeed this declaration was in turn denounced as erroneous by the resisters. But, quite apart from this disagreement over certain inalienable rights, the question of law-abiding takes on complexities that go to the heart of the conspiracy.

Millions of Germans not only prided themselves in obeying *orders,* they prided themselves in obeying *laws.* Nazism rewarded this pride with praise. Obedience to law was a value lauded only slightly less than self-sacrifice (to the State), and the organs of propaganda drilled it home. The Nazi terror is in fact incomprehensible apart from the pedantic correctness, bureaucratic routinization, and unswerving adherence to formalities and legalities by legions upon legions of Germans. The Third Reich was the antithesis of anarchy; its so-called "lawlessness" was actually gross *misrule by law.* Amassed injustice was organized and carried out precisely through obedience to laws and orders. The content of the laws and orders was easily altered. The formalism and functionalism remained.

To be sure, the resisters could rightly say: "The principle of legality, now trampled underfoot, must be elevated once again to a position of supremacy over all conditions of human life"; [41] for there were sufficient examples of arbitrary action. But, more importantly, it is a definite *content* in "the principle of legality" that could not be cast aside or considered exchangeable for the men of the resistance. That content had to harmonize with the basic rights guaranteed all men "regardless of race, nationality or creed." [42] Yet apart from their concern for such content, the point to be made is that the conspirators shared with virtually all Germans an obsession with legality as a highly valued measurement of the moral life. The conspirators' efforts to juristically justify a Putsch were tireless. Even the July 20 strike was conceived as a quasi-legal revolt. [43]

In short, Bonhoeffer echoes the general tone among the resisters with his use of legal to illegal and nonviolent to violent guidelines as the normative ones for determining the moral legitimacy of political means. Even when the actions present on the scales are extremely wide-ranging—conspiratorial conversation to assassination—the weight of emphasis is crucial. For the resisters, the weight

[41] Repeated from note 40, p. 189. [42] *Ibid.*

[43] See Dieter Ehlers, *Technik und Moral einer Verschwoerung* (Frankfurt am Main: Athenaeum Verlag, 1964), pp. 132-44, for documentation of a super-sensitivity to legality among the conspirators. Ehlers brings forth example after example of this and says the obsession has two bases: the need to satisfy the legality complex of the German people and the need to satisfy the conspirators' own deep-seated, sincere confession in legality as a cornerstone of the *res publica.* Ehlers also claims that it was relatively late when the resisters came to the conclusion that an illegal act could yet be a morally legitimate one.

was heavily on the legal and nonviolent sides. If anything, Bonhoeffer is among the more daring and the more emphatic in maintaining that the illegal, possibly violent, "deed of free responsibility" is a supremely *moral* deed. But Bonhoeffer also expresses the hesitation characteristic of all with the words: "Each of these men, the one who is bound by the law and the one who acts in free responsibility, must hear and bow before the accusation of the other. Neither can be the judge of the other. It is always for God to judge." [44]

What is of special note here, however, is where the inclination to nonviolent methods and the obsession with legal ones set the conspirators in relation to those they sought to unlodge. All the scruples were on the side of those who meant to storm the palace. None were on the side of those who occupied it. Too, it goes almost without saying that the concern to stay as close as possible to legality even in treasonous undertakings was a crippling impediment in a state ingenious in its conscription of legality for criminality.[45] The picture mirrored by von Hassel in his diary is an absurd one: ". . . enough generals prepared to move quickly and vigorously [against Hitler], if the command comes from above. Here lies the problem." [46] Was it such a situation that stands back of the fragment for *Ethics* which reads: "The exaggeration of thinking in legal terms, as if the world could be saved through law. The necessity of going beyond the law. The revolutionary"? [47]

The stark truth is that a vicious circle was drawn, one that virtually doomed the conspirators to failure. These men *became* conspirators in large part because of a revulsion against Nazi morality and the course it was taking Germany. The same revulsion that generated their opposition also reinforced their resolve not to adopt Nazi methods, nor in other ways mimic Nazi morality. Thus arose a "democratic" and humane conspiracy within a totalitarian state, a conspiracy disposed to use almost any means to change the course of the Ship of State except those most characteristic of Nazi excesses. But, *in this setting* could such a conspiracy topple such a regime? If *any* conspiracy would have had monumental difficulties in a state so thoroughly regimented as Hitler's by 1938, then one of moderate men moved to resistance by the negative manifestations of Nazi extremism and yet inclined to reject extreme means themselves would face virtually insurmountable difficulties. Thus the circle was drawn: Nazism prompted the most venal motives and deeds among its adherents; it purified its opponents of all but the most noble motives and

[44] *E*, p. 240.

[45] One of the stronger arguments for killing Hitler was that it would create an oath-free situation. Many of the generals in the conspiracy itself failed to take action against Hitler because of the binding force of the oath. Some of these generals argued that Hitler must die so they would be free of the necessity to obey his laws and orders.

[46] Von Hassel, *Vom anderen Deutschland: Tagebuecher 1938-1944*, p. 96.

[47] Microfilm No. 395, Frame No. 66.

prompted these men above all to active opposition; yet just these resisters were the least inclined to take up the well-practiced means of the amuck; still, without adopting such means, a successful strike against such a state was anything but reasonably assured. Around the treadmill went, and the conspiracy ended up above all and finally an insurrection of conscience.

Still the conspiracy certainly produced more than purified motives and outraged consciences. It was also the action that culminated in Stauffenberg's planting of the bomb. And the resisters *did* come very near to success. Yet precisely in the conspirators' conceptualization of this action itself are revealed the salient features portrayed thus far. For with men neither born nor educated for clandestine resistance and for men whose upbringing strongly rejected illegal and violent means for domestic political goals, the argument for Stauffenberg's action in particular, and even for underground active resistance in general, had to be built upon an ethical "condition of exception" (*Ausnahmezustand*). The widely held argument was that the acknowledged moral norms had to be momentarily suspended in the name of *necessità* precisely for the purpose of achieving a return to the normal and normative course. There was no "right" for these extremist deeds, these men felt, and no justification beyond *"necessità."* But the extreme action had to be executed if the "condition of exception" was to be overcome and legality and civility were to return as the hallmarks of the social order. This the reader will recall is precisely Bonhoeffer's statement; it is a representative and most revealing one. When Ehlers wrote the following, he was not summarizing specifically Bonhoeffer's view of the assassination, but the one held in common by the conspirators.

Whoever glorifies the history of the 20th of July sets assassination, this most spectacular of political acts, upon a pedestal to which the conspirators never laid claim. For them the attempt to kill Hitler was a sober necessity, the *ultima ratio* of opposition in the State of a personal dictatorship. Too, the decision for the strike against the State was, for them, anything but a glorious decision. There is "little honor to be won with this" Hassell believed; and Treschow prophesied after the attempt: "Now everyone will turn upon us and cover us with abuse." [48]

A philosophical and theological factor should be interjected here. It concerns a basic orientation or attitude which, although probably applicable to fewer resisters than those characteristic of the moral profile listed thus far, nevertheless marks many more of these men than one might expect in an assembly of Putschers. Among the Christians, there were a number like Bonhoeffer who

---

[48] Ehlers, *Technik und Moral einer Verschwoerung,* pp. 130-31. Ehlers' work deserves special note. To my knowledge, it is the only systematic treatment of the means considered and used by the resisters. Much of the discussion of means in this chapter is dependent upon this book, frequently by pointers to original sources but by Ehler's own presentation of the materials as well.

believed in a God who manifested his strength in weakness; and these were men who believed that the endurance of suffering was an integral part of repentance for the crimes against humanity. They possessed an ascetic inclination to do battle with intellectual and "spiritual" weapons and by disposition favored passive over active resistance. James von Moltke, the leader of a major resistance cell and a friend and colleague of Bonhoeffer's in the *Abwehr,* was such a figure. Karl Goerdeler, another recognized leader, and Admiral Wilhelm Canaris, the head of *Abwehr,* also leaned in these directions. Father Alfred Delp, as well as von Moltke, wrote letters from prison often astoundingly like Bonhoeffer's on these counts. Bonhoeffer may well have been the most theologically articulate, but he was by no means the solitary one who believed in "the God of the Bible, who wins power and space in the world by his weakness." [49]

This is not to imply that many traversed Bonhoeffer's course from a qualified "pacifism" to an even more qualified "revolutionary" activity. Bonhoeffer is often a striking figure by virtue of his standing almost alone. This is far less true in the conspiracy than in the *Kirchenkampf,* however—and that is important. Rather, what is being asserted is that especially among the civilian elite in the military/political conspiracy there was an inclination to place high value on endurance, suffering, and strength in weakness, and to regard intellectual and "spiritual" causes and means as the most worthy ones. There was an inclination to ascribe transcendental grounds to these, thus according them a measure of ontological certainty. The valuation of passive resistance was consequently very high and carried with it a concomitant reticence over against the methods employed by the Nazis.

Thus the philosophical and theological orientation of many gave support to an *acceptance* of guilt, a deepening of a *sense* of responsibility and a *posture* of repentance. This by no means resulted in passivity or inertness and certainly not acquiescence. On the other hand, neither did it engender a strong drive for active, practical political engagement directed toward achieving clearcut goals.

Again it is a worthwhile expenditure of time and space to note how particular means of resistance reflect the contours of the resisters' moral profile. The presence of a legal and nonviolent core is seen particularly well in the consideration of assassination and in the manner of sabotage used.

As stated above, the resolution to assassinate came only after the conspirers were convinced the legal and nonviolent means were exhausted or doomed to failure. Von Popitz wrote: "All attempts to be rid of this regime in a legal way are burned out. Only the dead Hitler can save us." [50]

The theory that even the dead Hitler could save Germany was not shared

---

[49] "16 July 1944," *LPP*, p. 188.
[50] Quoted from Ehlers, *Technik und Moral einer Verschwoerung*, p. 139.

by all resisters, however. A number would have no part in this deed; they agreed to methods of arrest and trial but rejected killing. The main reason for declining was surely the revulsion against conscripting Hitler's own methods, as well as a felt lack of moral justification for any tyrannicide. Karl Goerdeler, one of the acknowledged leaders of the resistance, argued that "no blessing can rest upon a revolt accomplished by murder." [51] Harald Poelchau, who discussed the question of assassination with many conspirators, summarized the feeling of those who rejected it: "He who sows the wind, reaps the whirlwind." [52]

Reasons of political calculation were present as well. Germany was in the midst of war, and war psychology reigned. Assassination might well lead to a new stab-in-the-back legend. This in turn could mean civil war.

A tactical consideration for the sake of future resistance also entered. Like Bonhoeffer many resisters already sat in prisons and concentration camps, often on charges other than treason. (The *Abwehr* arrests were for other reasons, to cite the most important case.) If assassination failed, the whole resistance apparatus might be brought down in the ensuing investigations. Thus many felt that less dramatic attempts to topple the regime should be used, ones justifiable on other grounds, such as a strike by the generals, ostensibly based on military prognosis. If assassination were used and it failed a bloodbath would result and further resistance would be extinguished. (Both did happen.) [53]

Some rejected this means because of a characteristic German notion of destiny or fate (*"Schicksal"*). The Chairman of the General Staff debunked by Hitler in 1938, General von Fritsch, gave as his reason for refusing to participate in a Putsch: "This man is Germany's destiny, in good or evil, and this destiny will see its way to the very end. If the end is the abyss, he will drag all of us along—against this nothing can be done." [54] Hans Lilje wrote just after the war: "The plan of God determined that the tyrant had to go his way in total blindness to the very end, until nothing, nothing at all was left remaining." [55] Lilje belonged to those who knew of the Putsch preparation and approved of the goal but rejected assassination as a means.

Those who did approve of assassination reacted in ways not dissimilar from Bonhoeffer's acknowledgment of violating divine law and throwing the deed up to God for its "justification." The resister Lukaschek remarked: "We all knew the place of execution awaited us and that we would have to do penance for every sin, in recognition of the eternal moral order." [56] And Ehlers is cor-

---

[51] *Ibid.,* p. 119.

[52] Harald Poelchau, Interview, West Berlin, Germany, April 25, 1969.

[53] *Ibid.*   [54] Bor, *Gespraeche mit Halder,* p. 39.

[55] Hans Lilje, *The Valley of the Shadow,* trans. Olive Wyon (Philadelphia: Muhlenberg Press, 1950), p. 62. Trans. corrected from *Im Finsteren Tal,* p. 52.

[56] Cited in Ehlers, *Technik und Moral einer Verschwoerung,* p. 124.

rect that Karl Goerdeler's "Thoughts of One Sentenced to Death" seethes with "a metapolitical guilt." [57]

Various reasons, therefore, produced the extreme hesitation about killing this tyrant. This meant the attempt would come very late. It came in fact only after a heritage had been worked through which opposed such an act from every side, and after men driven to resistance by revulsion against Nazi morality finally and painfully decided that an extraordinarily exceptional political murder was allowed, just this once and never again.

If there are criticisms to be made from a tactical point of view, it must be acknowledged that the attempt came too late and at a time inopportune for its success. Historians are of a mind that better chances existed on several occasions before the summer of 1944. And after 1938 the argument among the resisters was *not* whether Hitler really deserved to be toppled, but whether assassination was a morally permissible and politically wise path to this end.

There were other attempts on Hitler's life by these men. Yet they all reflect the belatedness traceable to factors treated above and elsewhere in this chapter.

The overriding preference for legal or quasi-legal and nonviolent means of resistance may seem strange cause for inserting an account of sabotage as one of the means employed by the conspirators. And in fact sabotage with explosives was rarely seriously considered. Such action was utterly foreign to both the disposition and skills of these men. At least for the outsider, it is a comical scene to imagine this group of high-placed office "revolutionaries" passing their evenings planting TNT beneath railroad boxcars! For Bonhoeffer, von Moltke, Goerdeler, von Dohnanyi, Bethge, and other civilians it is a rather absurd conjecture. But for Beck, Oster, Canaris, von Hammerstein, von Witzleben, Tresckow and other military men, it is almost equally so. Even if sabotage by means of explosives had been regarded as helpful, and it was not, these were not the resisters to use it.

But a different order of sabotage, materially nondestructive, was the central activity of the conspiracy. It took several forms. One was the sabotage of military orders and of Hitler's war policy by passing military secrets to other nations. (Oster's warnings to the neutral countries that so impressed Bonhoeffer as a "deed of free responsibility" is an example cited earlier.) Another was the sabotage of Hitler's foreign policy plans by passing secrets abroad. Too, there was "humanitarian" sabotage by altering or sidetracking orders that spelled imprisonment or death for those affected, or otherwise arranging for the safety of these people. (Bonhoeffer was involved in smuggling Jews to Switzerland by securing visas and other necessary papers through *Abwehr* channels.) Finally, there were endless instances of camouflaging or destroying evidence incriminating to the resistance. This bureaucratic brand of sabotage is the

[57] *Ibid.*

kind most easily and most effectively practiced by men in high offices. It requires the influence and skills they possess. The resisters practiced it incessantly and with amazing effectiveness. It can be said that if a regime such as Hitler's could have been toppled by ingenious administrative coups, these men might well have succeeded. But it could not, and they did not. It can also be said that this form of sabotage corresponded most closely to the moral posture of the conspirators.

The Nobility of Motives

Virtually every major account of the German resistance describes the revolt as an insurrection of conscience.[58] Those accounts by German historians by

[58] Special mention must be made of the following. Constantine FitzGibbon, *20 July;* Mother Mary Alice Gallin, *Ethical and Religious Factors in the German Resistance* (Washington, D.C.: Catholic University of America Press, 1955). These are two non-German accounts rather sympathetic in evaluating the resistance a success because of the nobility of motives and the courage exhibited. Dieter Ehlers, *Technik und Moral einer Verschwoerung;* Hans Bernd Gisevius, *To the Bitter End* (Boston: Houghton Mifflin, 1947); Rudolf Pechel, *Deutscher Widerstand;* Rudolf Pechel, *Freedom in Struggle* (Toronto: The Ryerson Press, 1957); Gerhard Ritter, *The German Resistance;* Hans Rothfels, *The German Opposition to Hitler: An Appraisal,* trans. Lawrence Wilson (Chicago: Regnery, 1962); Guenther Weisenborn, *Der lautlose Aufstand* (Hamburg: Rowohlt Verlag, 1953); Fabian von Schlabrendorff, *The Secret War Against Hitler,* trans. Hilda Simon (New York: Pitman Publishing Co., 1965); Eberhard Zeller, *Geist der Freiheit* (Munich: Gotthold Mueller Verlag, 1965). Most of these men were members of the resistance and make considerable of the silent revolt of conscience. A recent German account by one not involved in the resistance is: Karl Balzar, *Der 20. Juli und der Landesverrat* (Göttingen: Verlag K. W. Schuetz, 1967). Balzar's point is that the men of the conspiracy stand condemned because their deeds were treasonous. Once he has proven treason he feels that the judgment upon the resistance is unequivocal. How much Third Reich thinking still pervades this account by an Army officer is clear when he says that the *Austrian* resisters also committed treason! Some non-German accounts that play down or reject moral indignation as the driving force, or that judge the resistance harshly because there was little more than this, are the following: Hannah Arendt, *Eichmann in Jerusalem* (New York: The Viking Press, 1963); George Romoser, *The Crisis of Political Direction in the German Resistance to Nazism—its Nature, Origins, and Effects* (University of Chicago: unpublished Ph.D. Dissertation, Department of Political Science, 1958); William Shirer, *The Rise and Fall of the Third Reich* (New York: Simon and Schuster, 1959); John W. Wheeler-Bennett, *The Nemesis of Power: The German Army in Politics, 1918-45* (New York: St. Martin's Press, 1954). In my judgment, the profoundest analysis of the morality of millions of Germans in the Third Reich is Hannah Arendt's. But she, most atypically, is poorly informed about the conspiracy itself. Her judgments must therefore be strongly contested. To be sure, this is far from the central concern and contribution of her book, but since she makes the point, it should not go unnoticed. She writes: "No doubt these men who opposed Hitler, however belatedly, paid with their lives and suffered a most terrible death; the courage of many of them was admirable, but it was not inspired by moral indignation or by what they knew other people had been made to suffer; they were motivated almost exclusively by their conviction of the coming defeat and ruin of Germany" (p. 100). There were indeed few who, like Bonhoeffer, actually prayed for the defeat of Germany. But Miss Arendt's rejection of moral indignation cannot account for the continuing conspiracy when Hitler's victories did *not* lead to the "conviction of the coming defeat and ruin of Germany." Rather, the opposite is much more the case; the hard core resisted because they feared the triumph of Nazism. In the long run, that may

and large tend to regard the resistance a success because it was a moral success, i.e. a revolt driven by moral indignation. Most non-German accounts, however, term the resistance a failure because in the final analysis it elicited little *more* than moral outrage; that is, they regard political achievement as the chief gauge by which to evaluate the movement as a whole. Nevertheless, it is safe to say that for both German and non-German accounts a rough consensus does understand the conspiracy as a genuine insurrection of conscience. (This is not to imply that the revolt was not driven by other factors as well. It is to say that this is seen as a prime one.)

There are good reasons for the attention to moral outrage. Arguments asserting opportunism or personal ambition as the driving force of resistance shatter on one rock-hard fact: the core of the conspiracy continued working when Hitler's success was paramount and when German prognoses found Hitler in a position to consolidate his phenomenal war-won gains. The core continued its work when Hitler's bandwagon was rolling. In fact, it was Hitler's success that caused these men to plan ever more radical measures.[59] With the *height* of Hitler's power came the resolution to begin the revolt with the assassination of the *"Verfuehrer."* [60] It is true there were men who withdrew from the resistance when it appeared Hitler might well conquer Europe, just as there were men like Rommel who joined the movement in the late war years when Hitler and Germany were clearly doomed. The resistance was not without its opportunists; it knew the push for personal survival and the pull for personal advantage.[61] Too, there were those who joined because they were incensed over some personal maltreatment by the Nazis—the loss of a profitable post, for example. Yet neither the disgruntled, the dropouts, nor the late joiners constituted the core of the conspiracy. They were not the veterans in the protracted silent war against the regime.

The premise is justified that these men bore a genuine willingness to sacrifice themselves. Opportunism in their ranks was conspicuously rare. Bonhoeffer rightly spoke editorially when he said:

. . . Fundamentally we feel that we really belong to death already, and that every

---

also have meant the defeat and ruin of Germany, to be sure, but it was outrage at the present and foreseeable future which was overwhelmingly the deciding factor behind the subversive actions.

[59] Bonhoeffer writes in the resistance account: "As long as goodness is successful, we can afford the luxury of regarding it as having no ethical significance; it is when success is achieved by evil means that the problem arises." ("After Ten Years," *LPP*, p. 6.)

[60] *Biography*, pp. 655-56. *"Verfuehrer"* is an allusion to Bonhoeffer's 1933 radio address in which he warned the *"Fuehrer"* (leader) could become the *"Verfuehrer"* (deceiver). (See "Der Fuehrer und der einzelne in der jungen Generation," *GS* II, 35.)

[61] One of the more uncertain figures in the resistance was Hjalmer Schacht, President of the Reich Bank in the early 1930s and Hitler's chief economic adviser at that time. Bonhoeffer described Schacht to Bishop Bell as "an ambiguous supporter, a seismograph of contemporary events." ("The Church and the Resistance Movement," *GS* I, 404.)

new day is a miracle. It would probably not be true to say that we welcome death (although we all know that weariness which we ought to avoid like the plague). . . . We still love life, but I do not think that death can take us by surprise now.[62]

. . . Thinking and acting for the sake of the coming generation, but being ready to go any day without fear or anxiety—that, in practice, is the spirit in which we are forced to live. It is not easy to be brave and keep that spirit alive, but it is imperative.[63]

The nobility of motives comes clear in the willing acceptance of guilt and the deep sense of responsibility present in this group. First to prevent war, then to end it, indeed constituted the chief goal. But these men did not consider parenthetical such mass felonies as the Jewish exterminations, nor did they regard them merely as excesses of an otherwise redeemable system. In the much-disputed postwar question of "collective guilt" the men of the conspiracy would have been among those most emphatic about the reality of this phenomenon. Just as "The Structure of Responsible Life" in *Ethics* is bound to the resistance experience, so "Acceptance of Guilt" represents Bonhoeffer's identification with the moral posture which is characteristic of the conspiracy at large. The deep consciousness of guilt, resistance as an act of repentance and a revolt of conscience, responsibility as care for the coming generation at the likely sacrifice of the present one, the gradual learning of the deeds of free responsibility—all these Bonhoeffer found at work in the conspiracy. They made contact with themes in his own theology and gave them flesh.[64] From the perspective of the driving forces in resistance, Bonhoeffer's profile is again that of the others and the others' his. Even when his formulations are intensely christological and those of other resisters' broadly humanist, the moral silhouettes match surprisingly well.

The common pose was struck by General von Tresckow upon learning that the July 20 attempt had failed. Some hours later he committed suicide.

Now everyone will turn upon us and cover us with abuse. But my conviction remains unshaken—we have done the right thing. Hitler is not only the archenemy of Germany, he is the archenemy of the whole world. In a few hours' time I shall be before God, answering for my actions and my omissions, and I shall uphold with a clear conscience all that I have done in the fight against Hitler. God promised Abraham to spare Sodom should there be found ten just men in the city. He will, I trust, spare Germany for our sake, and not destroy her. Whoever joined the Resistance Movement had to realize that his life was doomed. A man's moral value begins only when he is prepared to sacrifice his life for his convictions.[65]

[62] "After Ten Years," *LPP*, pp. 16-17.

[63] *Ibid.*, p. 15.   [64] See pp. 32-73 above.

[65] Quoted from Fabian von Schlabrendorff, *They Almost Killed Hitler*, trans. Gero v. S. Gaenervitz (New York: Macmillan, 1947), p. 120.

An undoubtedly fruitful study would be a comparison of the German resistance with that

The willingness to remain "in the city" permits an aside on means—and brings to a conclusion this section on the nobility of motives.

On the surface, emigration does not appear a means of resistance. Most often it is not, even when it registers the strongest disapproval of the leader's rule. But a common phenomenon of war is also the establishment of an exile government and its efforts to bring down the homeland regime from head-quarters abroad, or at least to represent and rule in some sense. When emigration is a part of the plan to do this, it becomes a means for resistance.

Emigration is another of the means conspicuous by its absence among the conspirators. In one respect, this is most surprising. Like Bonhoeffer, a very large number of the German resisters had the opportunity to travel—the generals, diplomats and professors, for example. But not one did leave. Even as the plot failed only Goerdeler attempted to flee.[66] As the words of Bonhoeffer above indicate, these men were prepared for death.

---

of other underground movements against Nazism. Unless one were a "true believer" in a con-flicting ideology (such as Communism) the moral burden for the German resister would be considerably greater than that of resisters in the overrun nations. For, in their own country, the Germans had to decide how far they were to go in working for the defeat of the nation and to what extent they should aid the Allies in this defeat. More than that, the acts of the resisters would never be understood as acts of patriotism or heroism, as were the acts of resisters in the occupied zones, but as deeds of treason pure and simple. There was not only a lack of popular support and the absence of the knowledge that one was doing what the community wanted to be done; there was the added danger and difficulty inherent in the fact that one's own people was also, in a sense, "the enemy." "The figure of Judas, which we used to find so difficult to understand, is now fairly familiar to us," Bonhoeffer writes in the resistance account. ("After Ten Years," *LPP*, p. 11.) Public support and protection, as well as innumerable resources for resistance, were absent in Germany and present elsewhere. In the occupied countries, resistance was essentially a police-and-spy affair with terrible moral dilemmas first arising when the lives of one's own countrymen became part of the risk of resistance (perhaps in acts of sabotage and Nazi retribution for such acts). But in Germany, resistance was to a much greater degree a continuing moral dilemma because one's own people and nation, in the midst of war, were being risked. When acts of patriotism and acts of treason converge within the same action, as they did for the German resisters, extreme moral turbulence becomes inevitable. The German setting was a refining fire.

[66] Bonhoeffer did arrange escape plans through a trusted guard in Tegel Prison. This guard, a Mr. Knobloch, was the same one who smuggled out the prison letters and who now, after the July debacle, arranged with the Bonhoeffer family and others for Dietrich's escape. But Bonhoeffer changed his mind in the last days before the agreed date because family members, as well as other resistance contacts, had just been arrested or were being watched. He felt his escape at this time would endanger their welfare. (*Biography*, pp. 730-31.) The intense, autobiographical poem, "Jonah," was written just after this change of plans. Included are the lines:

". . . And Jonah said, 'Behold, I sinned before the Lord
of hosts. My life is forfeit.
Cast me away! My guilt must bear the wrath of God;
the righteous shall not perish with the sinner!'
They trembled. But with hands that knew no weakness
they cast the offender from their midst. The sea was there." (*LPP*, pp. 214-15.)

The resisters were convinced nothing effective could be done by Germans abroad unless these Germans had continual information from high offices in the homeland, the very offices resisters held. If Hitler were to be brought down by Germans, it must be done from within.

Beyond tactical considerations, a deep sense of responsibility and a strong patriotism moved these men. Like Bonhoeffer, many were tempted to go abroad and remain there. But if they did go they always returned. As Adam von Trott zu Solz, there were even strong cosmopolitan tendencies among some of these men, and yet of those foreseen as officers in the post-Putsch regime, not a single one lived outside Germany. Bonhoeffer's rejection of emigration was fully shared. Exile was too foreign to their particular understanding of responsibility, and to their conception of love of their country. In brief, exile was not in accord with their undeniably noble motives.

The Confluence of Values

A false impression may have been created by the foregoing discussions. While it is true the conspirators sought a politics and a morality opposed to that of Hitler, it is nonetheless also true that they had to overcome much of their own ethical and religious or philosophical education in the process. The heritage the resisters drew upon was not so unambiguously opposed to National Socialism as the foregoing may have led the reader to conclude. The conspirators had to work arduously through that inheritance, weighing at every point its strengths and its weaknesses. The time lost in doing so produced a resistance that offered much too little much too late.

The conspirators therefore had to become rebels in a double sense: against the Nazi ideology and against much of German ethical, religious, and philosophical thought. The all but total lack of an articulated right to resistance in German theological ethics is well known and need only be mentioned. The unqualified obedience to authority was taught as an unquestioned virtue in the religious instruction in the nineteenth and twentieth centuries, and this religious instruction was a part of all public school curricula. Much less could a right of resistance have been an article of faith for the German Armed Forces![67] Typical, rather, is the stand of the Chairman of the General Staff

[67] Postwar German historians cite the supposed exception of General Yorck von Wartenburg's disobedience of his Commander-in-Chief, and make of this an expression of the proud independence of the Prussian Army tradition. This in turn is taken a step further to explain why Hitler had difficulties with the Prussian staff members of his armed forces. A deep sense of military professionalism and an articulated code of morality for soldiers and officers were certainly resources for opposition to Hitler's demands. But active resistance is hardly synonymous with dissent and opposition. And here even the one exception does not hold. Von Wartenburg's army was a Prussian contingent in the imperial army, the Commander-in-Chief of which was

who himself became an acknowledged leader in the conspiracy, General Ludwig Beck. In 1938, when he strongly opposed Hitler's Sudetenland scheme, he stated: "Revolution and mutiny are words which do not exist in the lexicon of a soldier."[68] In short, among the conspirators there was considerable resistance against resistance.

Yet the omissions in the heritage constituted but half the problem—and not the more potent half. "The great masquerade of evil" that "has played havoc with all our ethical concepts"[69] is the more potent half. "For evil to appear as light, charity, historical necessity, or social justice is quite bewildering to anyone brought up on our traditional ethical concepts."[70] Some of "our traditional ethical concepts" are then criticized by Bonhoeffer.[71] The inadequacy of "our traditional ethical concepts" was also presented with noticeable pain and full clarity in Bonhoeffer's essay on "Civil Courage."[72] The matter now is to ask further about those traditional ethical concepts which proved inadequate and thereby impeded resistance.

The salient point can be made at the outset: there was a *confluence* of certain Nazi values and widely accepted, tenaciously held, traditional German values. This confluence created "havoc with all our ethical concepts." The havoc did not exempt even those dissenters who became conspirators. The confluence thus blunted moral vigor. It dulled the drive to confident action because the conspirators had first to sort through the confusion of their ethical concepts. For men given to seeking strong philosophical or theological footings for their actions, and for men whose resistance was rooted in moral sensitivities, this painful process took a long while. Thus much time, "the most valuable thing that we have, because . . . the most irrevocable,"[73] was lost in the procedure. The final outcome was the belatedness of strong action against Hitler.

Examples are legion of the flowing together of Prussian and other German sanctities with the Nazi ones. This confluence[74] is what churns up the moral

---

Napoleon! During the Third Reich, events such as the Roehm revolt and Fritsch crisis are clear proof of the nonexistence of a working doctrine of resistance in the military tradition.

[68] Quoted from Peter Bor, *Gespraeche mit Halder*, p. 113. Beck said other things as well, and they serve to explain why he became a leader in the resistance. During the war he wrote General Brauchitsch the following in an effort to recruit him for the strike against the state. "History will charge the highest officers of the German Armed Forces with guilt for the shedding of blood if they do not act in accord with their professional and political knowledge and conscience. Their obedience as soldiers has a limit at the point where their knowledge, conscience and responsibility forbid the carrying out of an order." (Quoted from *Vollmacht des Gewissens*, I, symposia sponsored by Europaichen Publikation e.V. [Frankfurt am Main: Alfred Metzner Verlag, 1965], p. 54.)

[69] "After Ten Years," *LPP*, p. 2.   [70] *Ibid.*   [71] See pp. 63-68 above.

[72] "After Ten Years," *LPP*, pp. 4-5.   [73] *Ibid.*, p. 1.

[74] The term "confluence" is chosen with a good deal of care. Much of the literature about these years in Germany fails to see the actual relationship between Nazi morality and resistance morality. Basically two verdicts are rendered, both of which are faulty. One verdict, typified by William Shirer, is that Nazi values were the cultural barbarization of Prussian values. There

turbulence and produces the ethical pathos. Many of these sanctities occupied a central place in the Third Reich: the obligations understood in the sacred German notion of "calling" (*Beruf*), which glorified a job well done, whatever its nature; freedom regarded as submissiveness and self-sacrifice; altruism as the willful abandonment of egoistic goals for the sake of realizing the goals of the national community; the prized place of duty and its execution with devotion and unrelenting thoroughness.[75]

The list can easily be lengthened—endurance, industriousness, the all-important respect for and obedience to the higher authorities, strength, pride, preparedness, honor, fidelity to the Fatherland, and so on. Whatever the grand perversions and the gross misdirections, these were Nazi values too. Thus the vast majority of a people, as they looked back in 1945, stood aghast at the route they had marched and were totally bewildered. For they knew they could not have done the immoral; had they not acted in accord with the traditionally cherished values?

Certainly there were Nazi values antithetical to Prussian ones. Schlabrendorff is correct in maintaining that the former repulsed the dissenters and contributed to the numerical growth of the conspiracy.[76] The Nazi affirmation of violence is one such value rejected, and discussed at some length above. Nor can the appeal to bestiality and to irrationality, and the behavior commended by these, find any counterpart whatsoever in the Prussian creed. Nevertheless it remains an equally consequential fact that there was indeed a very real confluence of a great many of the most cherished and widely held values. This resulted not only in a theoretical confusion in the ethical reflection of numerous resisters, but carried with it the negative and practical consequence of impeding

---

is a direct line from Prussian militarism to Third Reich militarism, to choose one of Shirer's favorite examples. (William Shirer, *The Rise and Fall of the Third Reich.*) The other verdict, typified by Fabian von Schlabrendorff, holds that precisely the Prussian values were the ones that became the source for dissent and resistance. Thus they show themselves to be deeply antithetical to Nazi values. (Fabian von Schlabrendorff, *The Secret War Against Hitler.*) For Schlabrendorff, a Prussian and a resister, Nazi morality is the outcome of abandoning Prussian values in their true sense and filling the vacuum with the mores of barbarians. But Schlabrendorff is not an adequate refutation of Shirer. Nor is Shirer correct. And neither is helpful for explaining what Bonhoeffer reports as true for the resisters—the havoc played with the traditional ethical concepts. Both Shirer and Schlabrendorff miss the confluence of cherished values. Shirer cannot adequately explain the degree to which the resisters drew upon their heritage for the moral strength to combat Nazism, and Schlabrendorff cannot adequately explain the moral turbulence to which Bonhoeffer witnesses. The phenomenon was more complicated than either of the two verdicts represented by Shirer and Schlabrendorff, a complexity I have tried to capture with the term "confluence." Understanding this complexity is essential to understanding the relationship between Nazi morality and resistance morality, and to understanding the belatedness of strong resistance action.

[75] The formalism and functionalism in this notion of duty provided National Socialism with a tremendous moral resource. Bonhoeffer saw this clearly: "The man of duty will in the end have to do his duty by the devil too." ("After Ten Years," *LPP*, p. 3.)

[76] Schlabrendorff's argument is discussed in note 74, p. 20, and the source is cited there.

the strength and activity of the resistance movement itself. This moral confusion, together with the contemplative nature of the conspirators, constitutes a source of the inaction that plagued the plot on Hitler's life. An agonizing awareness of this inaction lies behind a stanza of Bonhoeffer's poem written the day after the plot miscarried. In a very real sense, he is still reporting on the lessons of resistance.

> "Action"
> Daring to do what is right, not what
>   fancy may tell you,
> valiantly grasping occasions, not cravenly doubting—
> freedom comes only through deeds, not through thoughts taking
>   wing.
> Faint not nor fear, but go out to the storm and the action,
> trusting in God whose commandment you
>   faithfully follow;
> freedom, exultant, will welcome your
>   spirit with joy.[77]

In his understanding of the consequences to which the confluence of values would lead, Bonhoeffer was a step ahead of most of the conspirators. Thus his moral profile here anticipated, rather than coincided with theirs. He and his family saw more clearly and earlier than most that the moral wines were being poisoned. The rhetoric of Nazi evangelists and the applause of the populace never dissuaded the Bonhoeffers from the judgment that Hitler meant utter disaster for Germany. And they were among pitifully few who perceived from the earliest days that the practitioners of cherished and not ignoble values were unwittingly standing in the service of an unsurpassed criminality.

The confluence of values shows its most agonizing side in the means selected to begin the Putsch in many of the revolt strategies—a strike by the generals.

The civilian conspirators were long convinced that an end to Nazi rule could only come with the help of the Army. Bonhoeffer communicated the common conviction to England in 1941:

... The only group which can take action against the regime is the army (revolutionary action from other quarters would be suppressed by the SS). Now the opposition groups in the army are not likely to act unless they have reason to believe that there is a prospect of a more or less tolerable peace.[78]

The last sentence points to one of the reasons why the generals' strike was still-born. The oppositional generals wanted to end the war *but not lose it.*

---

[77] "Stations on the Way to Freedom," *LPP*, pp. 194-95.
[78] Bonhoeffer and Visser 't Hooft, "The Church and the new order [sic] in Europe," *GS* I, 364.

To be sure, they were not supporters of Hitler's peace by victory, because they did not wish the triumph of Nazism; on the other hand, they could not accept the "unconditional surrender" policy of the Allies (or the earlier, less drastic policies based upon capitulation). They sought a negotiated settlement that would not repeat the humiliation of Versailles and that would perhaps retain such areas as Austria, the Sudetenland, and the Polish Corridor. The dilemma for the generals' strike then was how to achieve revolt within, yet not effect capitulation without, i.e., how to end the war without losing it. (One reason Bonhoeffer and others had the task of making contact with the Allies was to secure a "wait and see" attitude from them at the time of the Putsch.) In short, the generals' support for a strike was dampened by a genuine fear of repeating Versailles; thus they sought support and guarantees from the Allies, but neither was forthcoming.

This was not the sole reason for the omission of the generals' strike; perhaps it was not even the decisive one. The diplomat and conspirator von Hassel noted in his diary: "The generals . . . concede all that is said . . . but cannot muster the courage for the deed." [79]

The non-action that plagued the generals' part in the *coup d'etat* was rooted in the havoc played with all their traditional ethical concepts. Von Hassel noted another time: ". . . enough generals prepared to move quickly and vigorously . . . if the command comes from above. . . . Here lies the problem." [80]

The predicament was almost farcical. The generals conceded that Hitler must be dislodged. But they could not strike against him without the command from their Commander-in-Chief. Thus someone other than Hitler must attain the post. Yet the prognostication for a successful revolt read that no one could—*unless* the generals moved. The reluctance to break from this vicious circle is the reason innumerable hours were spent prodding to action the very generals who agreed about what should be done.

The strike by the generals shattered when the values in their heritage and calling joined with many of Hitler's own. Von Hassel's phrase, "if the command comes from above," is but one of the indices of the moral irony generated by this confluence. To use Bonhoeffer's language, the men of duty in the end did their duty by the devil too,[81] even *after* they saw the demonic in their *"Fuehrer."*

The Lack of Political Vision

The final point begins with George Romoser's contribution to the discussion on the resistance. His thesis is that a crisis of political direction, indeed political

---

[79] Von Hassel, *Vom anderen Deutschland: Tagebuecher 1938-1944*, p. 303.
[80] *Ibid.*, p. 96. [81] "After Ten Years," *LPP*, p. 3.

bankruptcy, existed in the German resistance and that this inhibited from within the overthrow of the Nazi regime. While the military and civilian elites were passionate planners not without administrative talents, they were nevertheless most uncertain about the structure of the coming political order. They needed an order that would be a proper alternative to the Nazi system but that at the same time would not repeat the Weimar disaster.

"The central tragedy of the German resistance revolves around the problem of the narrowed range of political alternatives in the modern age."[82] The "narrowed range" was the outcome of the conspirators' rejection of party democracy as they understood this (Weimar) and their tendency instead toward some form of elitist parliamentary structure; yet even this consideration was blunted through their awareness that "the modern age" demanded some place in the political architecture for the participation of the masses. This place was not found, and, in this vital matter, a common mind was not reached. (It hardly need be mentioned that the thought of a dictatorship in any form was fully repugnant.)

Thus a clear conception of an alternative political structure remained unformed, thereby reinforcing an already strong inhibition to action by very alternative-conscious men. Such is Romoser's argument.

There was in fact some preparatory spadework being done in anticipation of the postwar order, and some political structures were taking shape on the underground drawing boards, as van Roon shows in a work that is a partial refutation of some of Romoser's contentions.[83]

Lack of discussion and concern about the political future was certainly not the problem. Examples are numerous, a few of which follow. Meetings were held in the Bonhoeffer residence for consideration of a constitutional monarchy or, minimally, for the service of the resister Prince Louis Ferdinand of the House of Hohenzollern as the commanding figure in a transitional phase.[84] Karl Goerdeler argued for a constitutional monarchy to the very end, as documented in his last lines, "Thoughts of One Sentenced to Death."[85] The Kreisau

---

[82] Romoser, *The Crisis of Political Direction in the German Resistance*, p. 116. See also his chapter, "The Politics of Uncertainty: the German Resistance Movement," in Hans-Adolf Jacobsen, ed., *July 20, 1944: the German Opposition to Hitler as Viewed by Foreign Historians* (Bonn: Press and Information Office of the Federal Government, 1969), pp. 61-77.

[83] Ger van Roon, *Neuordnung im Widerstand* (Munich: R. Oldenbourg, 1967), passim. This is surely the most careful and scholarly piece of historical writing on the German resistance and so deserves special mention. Yet the value is limited for our concerns because von Roon's subject is exclusively the Kreisau circle within the resistance movement. Historical accounts of the other major resistance cells await the high level of scholarship attained by van Roon.

[84] *Biography*, p. 678.

[85] Bundeszentrale fuer Heimatdienst, "Gedanken eines zum Tode Verurteilten," *20. Juli 1944: Dokumente und Berichte*, p. 35. "To me the best form of the State for our people appears to be the hereditary monarchy. Our non-political people, as changeable as the weather, need ballast in the Ship of State. The monarch should not rule. Rather, he should be the guard of the Constitution and the representative of the State." (*Ibid.*)

Circle envisioned a federation of provinces, each with a rather strong measure of autonomy and possessing a socialist cast.[86] The Communists had their organizational plans as well. So there *was* the absence of consensus and the common vision that Romoser asserts, as well as "the narrowed range" of alternatives within which the conspiracy elite did its searching. But there was also more ground tilled and more agreement reached on some matters than Romoser credits these men. Too, the rather extensive plans for a *transitional* government of the elite, together with the political possibilities that might have emerged from this provisional structure, seem to have escaped Romoser. Nevertheless, his basic contention that a major impediment to action stemmed from the lack of a common vision by plan-conscious men is both valid and important. He does not make another supporting point that he might have; namely, that many of the plans for the transitional government were propelled, not by a clear conception of a political structure, but by the *horror vacui* that could conceivably ride on the heels of a falling regime. (They were also propelled by the insistence that *some* form of *just* state replace the Nazi deformation, as we have seen.)

While not denying its importance, I wish to go beyond Romoser's point to make another and then draw a conclusion applicable to both.

There was not only a crisis of political direction because of the paucity of inherited political models; there was also a crisis because of the "nonpolitical" nature of much of the conspiracy's membership.

The term "nonpolitical" must be clarified, since we have labeled the resistance a "military/*political*" conspiracy. What is meant is that most of the members of the resistance represented interest groups that prided themselves in maintaining a certain distance from the tasks and methods of professional politicians.

From the side of the Church came the conscious sense of a boundary between ecclesiastical politics and state politics. Thousands of Confessing Church members conceived of their opposition to Nazism as something of a holding action designed to preserve this boundary between Church and State. Most often they did not join battles fought over other boundaries. It thus comes as the least of all surprises that even those churchmen who did participate in the military/political conspiracy, such as Bonhoeffer, should not be the bearers of a political blueprint for the future.

From the side of the military also came a conscious detachment from political involvement. A strong sense of professionalism reigned among the older Prussian officers especially, as well as the conviction that the army should

---

[86] "Organization of the Reich," Kreisau Documents, Appendix 1, in FitzGibbon, *20 July*, pp. 259-63.

stand on a base independent of changing regimes, even while in service to them. Too, they detested Hitler's grandiose and not unsuccessful formation of the "political soldier." This professionalism and independence dampened any drive among the military elite to set about the task of establishing a political structure for the coming generation. It must quickly be added that they were not unwilling to *assist* in planning; they were not irresponsible. But their whole bearing and background made them hesitant and inexperienced.

A third group, the members in the State Administration together with the civilian-trained men in the military apparatus, might appear the logical builders of the future political order. Here were the lawyers, jurists, administrators, foreign service officers, etc. They were not only employed by the State; they belonged to the politically informed and alert. Yet perhaps more than in most countries the civil service cultivated a certain detachment from political vacillations (the chaos of Weimar was in the very near past) and sought instead the security and perfection of the more enduring functions in the civil order. For this reason, as well as the numbing shock of watching their own State crumble, even these politically responsible and interested men were novices and searchers when the challenge to blueprint a new political order was pressed their way.

The high men of labor should not be overlooked. They were not numerous, but they had often been participants in groups with political visions—the Social Democrats and Communists, for example. Yet, as we have seen, not only was the left badly splintered before Hitler came to power, but he smashed the organizational power base that could give such political visions their needed support. Nevertheless, the labor leaders in the resistance were among the stronger contributors to the future-planning that was done.[87]

In brief, there existed all the makings of a crisis of political direction, whether seen from the standpoint of the German political heritage in the twentieth century or from the standpoint of the particular interest groups in the resistance. This crisis plagued such reflective and careful planners as these men were, men who bore a strong sense of responsibility for acting on behalf of the next generation.

Our prime concern, however, is the connection between this political stumbling and the moral profile. The tie was not new in German life and thought. At a time it could be least afforded, an old discrepancy surfaced again. It was the discrepancy between the high morality and even inner freedom of talented, reflective men, on the one hand, and the practical political vision and expression of such a morality and freedom, on the other. It was the discrepancy between right disposition and any embodiment of it in political models.

[87] See Ger van Roon, *Neuordnung im Widerstand,* for several examples.

Summary

The military/political conspiracy, to accept the judgment of German historians for the moment, was a moral success and a technical failure. It was both because most of its members shared certain characteristics with Dietrich Bonhoeffer and he with them.

The following is a summary of the reasons for both the success and the failure. Any generalization will invariably do injustice to the nuances in the resistance, to the rich variety and creativity present amid this remarkable assemblage. Yet the argument here is that, *whatever* the nuances and variety, it is the *shared* characteristics that in the final analysis account for both the strengths and weaknesses of the resistance. It is the moral profile of the *whole* which emerges that explains the power and the powerlessness of this group. For almost all the crucial determinants, Bonhoeffer himself is a moral profile of the conspiracy. However, I will not always name Bonhoeffer in the following critique of the conspirators' common profile and actions. But unless otherwise indicated, statements of judgment include Bonhoeffer.

The conspiratorial resisters comprised an intellectual, contemplative, elitist group. They were talented analysts, planners, and administrators who respected one another's talents and who consulted at length with one another in most every major endeavor. They were not technicians, they did not command "troops," and they failed to recruit the men who could have made a technical success of the Putsch. They constituted a democratic conspiracy in a totalitarian state, and they missed opportunities for success because they could not, via their "parliamentary" deliberations, reach crucial decisions quickly enough. They lacked, paradoxically, a dynamic, charismatic *"Fuehrer,"* or from another angle there were too many leaders of equal caliber. They were all leaders.

Their contemplative character had a double consequence. They constantly questioned the grounds for their activity, and they continually planned, down to minutiae, for revolt and reform. They were "philosophers" who were not activists, Putschers who were above all planners, conspirators whose chief deeds were conversational and written. They accomplished much by memoranda and "bureaucratic" sabotage, yet it appears that conspiratorial reflection often served as an ersatz for conspiratorial action and that powerlessness was compensated for by an increase of intellectual activity rather than action. This reflection on fundamentals and the passionate insistence on planning were shared by Bonhoeffer. His prodding to action puts him with the like-minded minority of (younger) men such as Stauffenberg, however.

The lack of physical engagement and, as in the case of Bonhoeffer, the failure to appreciate the technical aspects and the failure to recruit the skilled, are certain causes of the ruin of the resistance.

These men, including Bonhoeffer, were neither born nor educated for resistance, much less for conspiracy and the use of assassination. There were no professional revolutionaries among them, no conspirators in the grand manner. They were sensitive, deeply humanistic men who were roused to resistance by revulsion against Nazi ideology, methods, and certain Nazi values, particularly the affirmation of violence. The resistance core, because of their understandable rejection of Nazi means, was insistent upon exhausting all nonviolent and legal methods of resistance before turning to more radical measures. The means considered and those actually used are symptomatic of the moral posture of these men, although they are also very closely tied to the possibilities allowed by the situations in which these men found themselves: a strike by the generals; memoranda and "bureaucratic," "humanitarian" sabotage; attempts to influence Hitler, then to arrest and try him (all coverable at least quasi-legally); and, finally, the assassination effort. The paucity of violent means is striking—no destructive sabotage, no plans for more than one bomb, no gunfire, and so forth. Even when assassination was decided upon by some, it was rejected by many others for moral and other reasons. It must be added, even strongly emphasized, that resources for a right to active resistance were virtually nonexistent in the heritage of these men. An articulated right of resistance and an articulated theory of tyrannicide probably would have been helpful. The absence of such articulations is true for Bonhoeffer, too. Furthermore, and here Bonhoeffer again echoes the general tone, when the scales of legal to illegal and nonviolent to violent are employed as guages of the moral legitimacy of means and ends, the weight falls heavily upon the legal and nonviolent in matters of domestic politics.

A vicious circle, formed by both theological and historical factors, built itself in such a way that it probably secured the failure of the resistance movement. The resisters became just that because of a rejection of Nazi morality. This, together with various factors in their background, made them extremely undesirous of duplicating Hitler's means. Yet a domestic conspiracy rather emphatic about using legal and nonviolent means cannot storm and secure a fortress such as Hitler's. Such a resistance movement must either effectively resist with its own preferred methods *before* the State turns totalitarian, or it must take up the methods of its oppressors *after* the State has regimented all areas of life. The German Resistance did not do the former; and it turned to the latter too seldom and too late. With this assembly of reflective, compassionate, morally erect, hesitant men often bound by scruples, this is not a surprise. But it is certainly a tragedy. The children of darkness in their usual perverse sort of way were wiser in their own generation than the children of light. Bonhoeffer sought to overcome the blockage to the necessary means with his conception of "the deed of free responsibility." He and others did overcome many scruples. But the belatedness proved fatal.

The moral posture of these men is most impressive. Among conspiracies, this characterization must be virtually unique. With Bonhoeffer (indeed, he learned from the others here), there was a sober, unpretentious willingness to bear the guilt of their landsmen, to be deputies, to be men-for-others, to put their lives on the line for the future generation, to engage in resistance as an act of repentance for the crimes of their nation, within and without. A deeply impressive sense of responsibility and a "world-come-of-age" stature punctuate the annals of the resistance. These men and women were not enthusiastic about conspiracy, but they "knew" they "must" wear the shirt of Nessus. Although emigration was often available as a means of escape, it was never used. It was rejected chiefly because it would not serve to halt the triumph of Nazism. Here again, Bonhoeffer's profile was cut of the same material as his co-conspirers'.

A further word about the moral makeup must be added, however. The conspirators did find themselves caught in the ethical maelstrom that resulted from their growing awareness that the traditional, widely accepted and tenaciously held values had actually passed into the same stream with many Nazi values. The time needed to still the moral turbulence, and to sort through the ethical concepts whose value had once been merely assumed, resulted in lost opportunities. This confluence generated serious impediments, especially for the generals, that finally proved fatal. Bonhoeffer saw more clearly than most at this point in his realization that duty, industriousness, self-sacrifice, calling must always be subject to scrutiny from more ultimate perspectives.

For responsible, plan-conscious men, the absence of a political vision provided a further hindrance. Both the political inheritance and the interest groups preponderant in the resistance explain the lack of a clear, commonly held, political vision. This deficiency constituted another of the plagues that resulted in so little assertive, confident action by the gentle "revolutionaries." The political probing by this particular group of men indicates a rather wide discrepancy between their noble moral stance and practical political expression of it. On this point, Bonhoeffer's posture is the match of the others.

In short, a judgment that I believe holds for all of Bonhoeffer's ethics can be transferred to the resistance as a whole. The strength of the conspiracy was in its *right disposition* to action. Its weakness was in the lack of the disposition to *right action*. Both right disposition and right action were indeed present in some measure or another, at some time or another. But how the weight is distributed often matters immensely. It did matter immensely.

In the end the question is whether the moral is not inextricably bound to the technical and the technical to the moral. The failure of the revolt was not, strictly speaking, *because of* men like Bonhoeffer. On the contrary, without them there would not even have been beginnings. The failure was because there were *only* or nearly only such men. The ethics of "the structure of responsible life" should have led to the recruiting of those men who could also have made a *technical* success of the revolt. In that rare and grotesque setting of *necessità,* the Christian or humanist conspirator should have, *out of responsibility,* recruited the gangster, if the Christian or humanist himself could not be one. This indeed "plays havoc" with "all our traditional ethical concepts" but it is the shuddering lesson of Bonhoeffer and the German resistance if one grants the justifiability of the *coup d'etat* and of the tyrannicide attempt. The military/political conspiracy failed because nice fellows do not make good revolutionaries, unless they are able to work well in that precarious zone called "free responsibility" and unless they understand the inextricability of the moral and the technical. Then either they themselves will do what must be done or they will secure the proper personnel to carry out revolutionary tasks that know no innocence.

So Bonhoeffer was wrong at only one point in his account of the lessons learned in resistance. But the mistake was deadly. "What we shall need is not geniuses, or cynics, or misanthropes, or clever tacticians, but plain, honest, straightforward men." [88]

---

[88] "After Ten Years," *LPP,* p. 17.

APPENDIX A
Bonhoeffer, Gandhi, and Resistance

Bonhoeffer's favorite prophet is the early 1930s was Mahatma Gandhi. He actively sought and eventually secured an invitation to join Gandhi's ashram. But it had to be put aside when the call to direct Finkenwalde reordered the priorities.

The invitation from Gandhi was for a trip planned for 1935. In preparation Bonhoeffer read widely and undertook a study project. Yet this was not the beginning of his fascination with India. The interest was a long-standing one, and different reasons are given on different occasions. At times a simple search for knowledge and wisdom is expressed, as he sought to find a way amidst the turmoil of 1932.[1] Other times Bonhoeffer was seeking the gospel in other words and deeds in the face of his conviction that Western Christendom was on its deathbed.[2] Still other times his curiosity was directed toward finding a means of resistance legitimate for Christians. Such a time came in 1934 when Bonhoeffer concerned himself "very intensely with the questions of India,"[3] drew up the study project, and obtained the invitation from Gandhi. He corresponded about these matters with Reinhold Niebuhr, among others. Niebuhr discarded the letters about the study project, but he has recollections that merit recording. He told Bonhoeffer he felt it unwise that Bonhoeffer study with Gandhi for the following reasons: Gandhi was an ethical liberal with philosophical footings at great distance from the *Weltanschauung* of a sophisticated German Lutheran; furthermore, Nazi Germany was no place for attempting the practice of nonviolent resistance. Bonhoeffer had written Niebuhr about learning Gandhi's techniques for possible use in Germany, and Niebuhr now replied that Gandhi's success depended upon British political liberalism. Hitler's creed and deeds bore no resemblance to British ways and means. The Nazis would suffer none of the pains of conscience about using violence which the British did, and organized passive resistance would end in utter failure.[4]

Yet Bonhoeffer was not dissuaded, and he proceeded with plans for the excursion in the Orient. While they never materialized, the question of their meaning edges into reflection on Bonhoeffer's resistance. For the complex of his Christian pacifism and political resistance, what was the reason for the gaze East?

A hint egresses in an unpublished letter from Bonhoeffer to Niebuhr. The date is July, 1934, shortly before the ecumenical meeting in Fanø and thus shortly before Bonhoeffer's strongest statement on pacifism.

[1] *GS* I, 32.   [2] *Ibid.*, p. 61.   [3] *GS* II, 182.
[4] Interview with Reinhold Niebuhr, New York City, March 7, 1968.

After communicating his dissatisfaction with the far too compromising tack of the opposition churches in the *Kirchenkampf*, Bonhoeffer writes:

... The dividing line lies elsewhere, namely with the Sermon on the Mount. And now the time has come when the Sermon on the Mount must be brought to mind again on the basis of a partially restored Reformation theology—although, to be sure, with a different understanding of the Sermon than the Reformation's. And precisely at this point the present opposition will divide again. Before we reach that juncture, everything is only preparation. The new church which must come about in Germany will look very different from the present opposition church.

Incidentally I plan to go to India very soon to see what Gandhi knows about these things and to see what is to be learned there. I am awaiting a letter and invitation from him any day now. Do you perhaps know important people there to whom you could recommend me?

I am presently busy with a manuscript which concerns itself with the Sermon on the Mount, etc. [*The Cost of Discipleship*]. I have read the first half of your *Moral Man*, etc. with the greatest of interest and want to finish it during vacation.[5]

This letter, the contents of which are also substantiated in a letter to Erwin Sutz,[6] makes a crucial line clear, even if almost in passing: the Sermon on the Mount is Bonhoeffer's scriptural resource for churchly resistance (in other words, *The Cost of Discipleship* is a tract for the times), and Gandhi is linked with the Sermon and churchly opposition as a possible instructor. What "Gandhi knows about these things" is the reason for wanting to set out for India at this time.

Next a confession about the change in his life in the early thirties must be noted; the letter is from Bonhoeffer to a girlfriend.

... The revival of the Church and of the ministry became my supreme concern. ...
I suddenly saw as self-evident the Christian pacifism that I had recently passionately opposed. ...
My calling is quite clear to me. What God will make of it I do not know.[7]

The renewal of the Church and, inseparable from that in the 1930s, the churchly opposition to Nazism within its ranks and without—here is the cause of the thirst for Gandhi's wisdom and ways.

The question then is: why Gandhi?

It is doubtful Bonhoeffer was convinced by Niebuhr's emphasis upon the gap between Gandhi's philosophy and Bonhoeffer's theology. In the 1932 address on self-assertion, Bonhoeffer in effect summarizes *both* Gandhi's law of life and that of the *theologia crucis* as: "Through love and suffering we enter the All and overcome it." [8] Jesus Christ is the supreme revelation of this law of life but the Indian Messiah has given it powerful expression in our time.[9] Bonhoeffer, always in quest of "who

---

[5] Dietrich Bonhoeffer, "Letter to Reinhold Niebuhr, July 13, 1934." The full letter and one of February 6, 1933, are included as Appendix B. Used with the permission of Dr. Eberhard Bethge.

[6] *GS* I, 39-41.   [7] Quoted from the *Biography*, p. 155.

[8] "Das Recht auf Selbstbehauptung," *GS* III, 262.   [9] *Ibid*.

Christ is for us today," caught a vision that perhaps here in Gandhi and his India was the gospel in other words and deeds. Even though Bonhoeffer's Christology was intensely ecclesiological during these years, Gandhi cut a figure that Bonhoeffer could only align with his own Jesus of suffering *agape*. In the face of Bonhoeffer's conviction that Western Christendom was tossing about in the throes of its own death, the search for the form of Jesus Christ among men today happened upon especial illumination from the East. Still the episode remained a search, the flight of a vivid theological imagination, and not an embrace, whatever the drawing power of Gandhi's "theology" and trek.

This tableau of Gandhi as Bonhoeffer's Christology possibly incarnated "for us today" locates the contact point of the deep attraction to Gandhi. But it does not yet clarify the tie to resistance alluded to in the letter to Niebuhr and discussed in other correspondence between them. So the question persists: why Gandhi?

Bonhoeffer's intense study and meditation on the Sermon on the Mount had revealed "Christian pacifism . . . to be a matter of course." For Bonhoeffer this meant a radical obedience to the commanding Christ of the Sermon, a Christ whose commands must be concrete within the matrix of unrelenting work for church renewal and uncompromising opposition to Hitler. With such convictions and goals in such a matrix, the quest for genuine *"Christsein"* included the quest for *the political shape of the Sermon on the Mount* or, stated somewhat differently, *the politically credible articulation of the gospel*. As Herbert Jehle, who shared Bonhoeffer's India plans at this time, put it: "His interest in India was to see how the Sermon could be translated into our political action" (meaning that of the *Kirchenkampf* participants).[10] And as *The Cost of Discipleship* makes clear, for the self-proclaimed Christian pacifist of the cross the credible articulation of the gospel for political life meant nonviolence as the only legitimate political course for the disciple. Thus Bonhoeffer's attraction to Gandhi now included the desire to learn the techniques of passive resistance. The base line here is from the passion for peace so visible in Bonhoeffer's ecumenical work and the discovery of the Sermon on the Mount to Christian pacifism and a new interest in the methods of a long-intriguing figure.

As the letter to his girlfriend, the one to Niebuhr, and the conversations with Jehle indicate, Bonhoeffer's obsession with a politically credible articulation of the gospel was focused almost wholly on the *Church's* action. That is, the envisioned employment of Gandhi's techniques was not for the solution of German social problems in general, by recruiting followers from varying ranks of society through some nationwide appeal, but for arming the Confessing Church for her battles with the State and the State-backed *Deutschen Christen* and for her efforts to speak "for the dumb," the innocent victims of Nazi criminality. The intended appropriation of Gandhi was thus above all for ecclesiastical purposes and only very secondarily for broader civil ones.

In this connection it is not out of place to call to mind Bethge's comment: "In clearly distinguishing between the political struggle and the church struggle, Bonhoeffer differed little at this time [London, 1933-1935] from his theological friends in Berlin. Active responsibility for the production of a political alternative

---

[10] Interview with Dr. Herbert Jehle, Charlottesville, Va., March 1, 1968.

to the Nazi State, or at least for vigilant observance of the democratic constitution, he saw as being incumbent on those who were eligible by reason of their calling and position in the state machine." [11]

Bonhoeffer's thought in this period was two-sphere, although it did not bother him that churchly opposition contained a political dimension. But the political *Gestalt* of the Church must truly be Christian, and for Bonhoeffer at this time that included the nonviolence of the Jesus of the Sermon on the Mount. Nonviolence was one of the marks of the disciple's way of life—and of death.

Bonhoeffer did not expect that the way of passive resistance would bypass suffering. On the contrary he anticipated encountering physical punishment and, as a letter to Sutz indicates, even felt battles short of that were preliminary skirmishes only preparatory for necessarily bloodier days. [12] "And I believe all Christendom should pray with us that it will be a 'resistance unto death', and that people will be found to suffer it. Simply suffering—that's what it will be about." [13] In other words Bonhoeffer was not convinced by Niebuhr's argument that Germany was no place for nonviolent resistance because he expected no different treatment from the Nazis than Niebuhr did! Suffering would indeed come. But only by suffering would evil be overcome. [14] Bonhoeffer's pacifism of the *theologia crucis* was, in any case, not one easily affected by political, pragmatic considerations for consequences and strategies even when this pacifism sought a viable political form for discipleship. In fact, as the Fanø address states clearly, the question of consequences is the Serpent's; it is not the disciple's, who endures all in vicarious, believing suffering. [15] So Gandhi and not Niebuhr offered the more probable political articulation of the gospel for the pacifist of the *Kirchenkampf;* passive resistance seemed the political *Gestalt* that "today" conformed to Christ's form in the world.

We can summarize. In their correspondence Niebuhr advised Bonhoeffer against studying with Gandhi because of Gandhi's philosophical and ethical liberalism and because Germany under Hitler showed no prospects whatsoever for politically successful passive resistance. Yet Bonhoeffer was not dissuaded even though he held Niebuhr in highest esteem as a Christian ethicist. In asking why Bonhoeffer continued with his plans, we noted that as early as a 1932 address Bonhoeffer draws strong parallels between the Messiah of suffering love and loving suffering, and the Indian Messiah. Bonhoeffer's constant search for the form of Christ among men came upon this intriguing figure in the East just at the time Bonhoeffer was more and more convinced that Christendom in the West, Christ's traditional form here, was on its deathbed. The christological contact point was so strong that Bonhoeffer was not convinced by Niebuhr that Gandhi's "theology" and trek were at a great distance from the Jesus of the Sermon on the Mount and the *theologia crucis.* But this christologically rooted fascination with Gandhi was not the end of Bonhoeffer's interest. The self-proclaimed Christian pacifist, grounded scripturally in the Sermon and seeking church renewal, entered the *Kirchendampf* with all his energies. Now he saw in Gandhi the instructor, not only for the techniques of meditation and the

[11] *Biography,* p. 256.   [12] *GS* I, 40.   [13] *Ibid.*
[14] *CD*, pp. 157-58.   [15] *GS* I, 216-17.

communal life of disciples, but for the legitimate political methods of disciples in the struggles of the *Kirchenkampf*. Niebuhr's argument about the impracticality of passive resistance in the Nazi State was simply not on the same plane and asking the same questions as Bonhoeffer's theology of believing suffering. Bonhoeffer sought the political shape of the Sermon on the Mount in a way that would include the nonviolence demanded of disciples. And so Gandhi again fascinated Bonhoeffer. The two never met—except to die at the hands of the violence they abhorred.

APPENDIX B

Two letters from Dietrich Bonhoeffer to Reinhold Niebuhr, typed, with handwritten signature. The originals are located in the Reinhold Niebuhr Papers, Department of Manuscripts, Library of Congress Annex, Washington, D.C.

Instructor Dietrich Bonhoeffer
Berlin-Grunewald Wangenheimstr. 14
Berlin, Feb. 6, 1933

Professor Reinhold Niebuhr
New York, 600 W. 122nd St.
Union Theological Seminary

Dear Professor,

After such a long while, when we've heard nothing from one another and so many decisive events have occurred I'd enjoy discussing with you, I'd like to write you again today. But unfortunately it won't be a decent letter this time either. Instead, it's essentially the following request. My cousin, Pastor Hans Christoph von Hase, has applied for a scholarship to Union Seminary for next Fall; and even though he's my cousin, I would like to say a few favorable things about him. First this in general, that in light of my acquaintance with both parties concerned, the Seminary would be well advised if it recruited this man. He's an unusually well-informed person, he's alert, open, sociable, affable, possesses independent judgment and would certainly benefit a great deal from a year at Union. He would also be one of those young people who would later be in a position to properly represent here in Germany the training gained abroad. That's it; I can't say anymore in good conscience but I think this suffices. If you chose to put in a good word for him I would be grateful.

To include just a word about the conditions here in Germany would be rash. That neither economic nor political nor social matters will change drastically is rather unlikely; but a horrible cultural barbarization threatens even more, so that we'll also have to open a Civil Liberties Union here very soon. As you yourself can imagine, the specter of Communism cannot be exorcized with national incantations and casting of spells (rearmament, etc.). People are incredibly naive here. The course of the Church is as obscure as seldom before. But there doubtlessly have been a great many important changes in your quarters, too, since I left. All in all, without a doubt we, especially we in Europe, live in a tremendously interesting time, one we really wouldn't care to trade for another.

It would be a great joy if I should hear from you once again. But you are undoubtedly terribly busy—so it is with me as well. It's too bad that ties of friendship must suffer as a consequence.

Please pass along hearty greetings to my friends from that time, particularly Jim Dobrowski (whom I ask to return my essay on Negro literature that he must still have).

Please give my kind regards to your mother and your wife; I send my respects to you.

In friendship
yours truly,

Dietrich Bonhoeffer

Pastor Dietrich Bonhoeffer
23 Manor Mount   S. E. 23
13 July 1934

Dear esteemed Professor,

It'll surprise you to hear from me again after such a long interval. It's really too bad I haven't written, for I've often had in mind this last year getting your opinion on things. Just a short while ago my cousin came by and told me much about you. A kind invitation from your mother-in-law arrived, too, but unfortunately I could not follow up on it. So recently all sorts of lines lead to you. Nevertheless I'm writing you today for a particular reason. I need your advice and help in a few matters involving emigrants. It's only natural I've come to have a great deal to do with these things since my stay in London. What I'd like to find out now is whether and what kind of arrangements exist there for students (Jewish students, or those expelled from the university for political reasons) which might make possible either a continuation of their studies or retraining for another job. Just a short time ago a committee was formed especially for helping university trained people but the means available are almost nonexistent. Here in London I'm particularly concerned about a man, 23 years old, formerly president of the Republican Student Society, a lawyer who is in a bad way and whom I can't place anywhere. I doubt he has any special talents but he simply must be helped. Now what I should like to know is whether the possibility might exist in the States for him to continue his studies or begin something new—perhaps with a scholarship or something similar. That's the one case. The other is the author Arnim T. Wegner—Tillich will surely know of him—very left politically, suffered a terrible period in a concentration camp and is a total wreck. He's been unable to find anything here and is despondent over it. Pardon me for bothering you with these matters, but it's only a small slice of what we see daily and which finally leaves one simply standing there, unable to help any further. My congregations are very understanding in supporting my work. That's a substantial help.

219

The most recent events in Germany have now shown beyond a doubt where we are headed. I am only astonished that no Protestant pastors were among those shot on the 30th of June. In our circles it's becoming increasingly clear, particularly after the recent muzzling of Frick, that the time of the *Kulturkampf* has arrived. It's curious seeing how long it takes before a Protestant clergyman even considers that possible. Also, they wish to know far less about these things in Westphalia than, for example, we in Berlin. The danger of an orthodox, so-called "intact" Church is very great in the western part of Germany and I consider it very possible that one day the State will actually find its best ally in this form of church. An "orthodox" Church is certainly a more secure guarantee for the Nazi State than Mueller's church. With all the pressure for an orthodoxy of this sort we'll have to guard against this danger in particular. Many among us are very shortsighted here. A man such as Mueller would not shy from subscribing to our entire orthodoxy and perhaps even more or less honestly, measured subjectively. The dividing line lies elsewhere, namely with the Sermon on the Mount. And now the time has come when the Sermon on the Mount must be brought to mind again on the basis of a partially restored Reformation theology—although, to be sure, with a different understanding of the Sermon than the Reformation's. And precisely at this point the present opposition will divide again. Before we reach that juncture, everything is only preparation. The new church which must come about in Germany will look very different from the present opposition church.

Incidentally I plan to go to India very soon to see what Gandhi knows about these things and to see what is to be learned there. I am awaiting a letter and invitation from him any day now. Do you perhaps know important people there to whom you could recommend me?

I am presently busy with a manuscript which concerns itself with the Sermon on the Mount, etc. I have read the first half of your *Moral Man,* etc., with the greatest of interest and want to finish it during vacation.

With most sincere regards in gratitude for the many pleasant hours with you in New York and with the cordial request that you relay my respects to your wife—

Sincerely yours,

Dietrich Bonhoeffer

INDEX OF NAMES